Alcohol and the Negro:

EXPLOSIVE ISSUES

ALSO BY JOHN R. LARKINS

*The Negro Population of North Carolina,
Social and Economic*

*The Employment of Negroes in Public Welfare
in Eleven Southern States*

*Patterns of Leadership Among Negroes
in North Carolina*

A Study of Negro Parolees

Alcohol and the Negro:

EXPLOSIVE ISSUES

BY

JOHN R. LARKINS

Published by

RECORD PUBLISHING COMPANY

ZEBULON, NORTH CAROLINA

1965

To
Catherine and Sandra

Preface

The manufacture, sale, and use of alcoholic beverages and the social, economic, and political status of the Negro have been major issues in America since its earliest history. There have been other issues, but these two have been among the most persistent. At times, they have been separate and at other times they have coalesced; but they have always been present. These issues have had and continue to have a profound influence upon most of our major institutions. This book is concerned with the impact of alcohol and the Negro upon religion; the economy, politics, and social control. The history and patterns of use are also included. It is hoped that the findings of this book will shed some light on two of the most controversial and emotion-packed issues to confront the American people.

It has been necessary to include considerable elementary historical material. This may not be of any value or help to historians or scholars in related areas. However, it is hoped that this material will be of help to the general public in understanding the origin and development of these issues. There is an awareness that there is a need for more research and investigation relative to the influence of these issues on the lives of the American people. Since this book is dealing with events or conditions of the past that have had only limited investigation and research, and events of the present that have emerged too rapidly and recently to have been fully understood, it is inevitable that there will be questions raised about some of the findings and analyses. The times demand whatever light there is available to be shed upon the urgent, stubborn, and perplexing issues of race and alcohol. The far-reaching influence that these two issues have exerted and continue to exert upon the lives of so many people, justify this effort. This book is an attempt to call attention to and point out these issues. It is hoped that it will stimulate more objective, detailed and comprehensive research.

In the writing of this book, the author has attempted to trace the development of these issues and their impact upon specific institutions from the early history of the country until the 1960's. Each chapter is intended to be complete within itself. This approach has resulted in some repetition of materials in the various chapters.

September 1965   J. R. L.

Contents

Contents

Illustrations

Courtesy The Pittsburgh Courier

INTRODUCTION

Alcohol and race are two of America's indigenous problems.

It is true that there are abstemious societies, some of the Moslem Arab nations, but abstention is part and parcel of the religious and cultural complex.

America was a frontier society which propounded for itself the problem of race by importing slaves and it was a drinking society which also propounded for itself the problem of Prohibition.

Drinking habits throughout America reveal the frustration and the anxiety of our national life. Many Americans consume certain brands of alcohol and consume it in a certain way to lend themselves status and prestige. Negroes do not escape this either. There are indeed Negro drinking patterns and a close study of these patterns will show how the problem of race affects an entire marginal society of some twenty million Americans.

The Negro, only now edging into the open society, has less chance of escaping these problems than anyone else. He drinks, too, and he drinks in the way the white society drinks but with more intensity and perhaps with more reason. Mr. Larkins sets out here to tell us what these reasons are.

It would be an injustice to think of this Larkins' study solely in terms of its timeliness. Timely indeed it is and the association of the use of alcohol with the current Negro civil rights movement is not only inescapable but proper. This book will continue on as required study of one of the great dilemmas of mid-twentieth century America.

The facts and the conclusions in this work parallel those published sometime ago by the Alcoholic Institute at Yale, but it should be noted that Mr. Larkins presents us with a much narrower and therefore a much brighter focus.

What this book is really all about is the compulsions which result from pressures which lead to certain social patterns, and alas, certain personal habits. These are conditions we had better understand if we are ever going to change and better them.

Charlotte, North Carolina   Harry Golden
August 25, 1965

1

BOOTSIE

By OLLIE HARRINGTON

Courtesy The Pittsburgh Courier

"Aw, Bootsie, whyn't'choo go on home? Man, if I let you have another'n you'd be the first cullud man to go into orbit!"

CHAPTER ONE

HISTORY—ALCOHOL AND THE NEGRO

THE EARLY SETTLERS: COLONIAL DAYS

THE INTRODUCTION OF ALCOHOL

THE American liquor problem is as old as the white man's knowledge of the American continent. The traditions of practically all American Indian tribes include references to ancient customs and rites having to do with the indulgence of the aborigines in native intoxicants. The age-old liquor habits and customs of Europe were introduced to this continent at a very early date. They came with the first explorers. The earliest settlers appear to have given particular attention to the kinds and quantities of intoxicating liquors which accompanied them on their voyage across the Atlantic Ocean to their new homes amid the forests of the Western world. In 1609, when Henry Hudson, the British navigator, sailed into New York Bay and found some Delaware Indians on the island, he made friends with them by giving them intoxicating liquor. One of the chiefs drank a cup of liquor and became so drunk that his companions thought he was dead. When he was aroused, he confessed he had been pleased with the sensation, and all of the Indians followed his example.[1] The ship that brought Governor Winthrop to Massachusetts Bay in 1630 had included in its supplies 42 tons of beer, 14 tons of water, one hogshead of vinegar, two hogsheads of cider, and four pumps for water and beer.[2]

Various alcoholic drinks were universally regarded as wholesome by the early settlers. Puritan clergymen, Dutch merchants and Virginia planters agreed that the use of alcoholic beverages was not only beneficial, but necessary; although they were quick to rebuke individual excesses. The Puritans were a strict group. They did permit drinking in the Massachusetts Bay Colony; drunkenness, however, was punished. Not long after the early settlement of the country, local taverns appeared among the villages of the scattered colonies. The social status of the tavern-keeper was considerably higher in those days than it is for his modern-day counterpart. He was the keeper of the villages' morals; it was his responsibility to see that his patrons remained sober. Only a man of the best character could operate a tavern.[3]

With the cessation of the Indian wars, the western frontier became safe for settlers and many of them poured through the Appalachian Mountains into the great Northwest Territory. These settlers did not have room to pack along their beer, but they learned a new trick—the distillation of corn pressings into hard liquor. The widespread use of distillation among the pioneers introduced a new drink into American society which resulted in a great increase in drunkenness. Prior to this time, many of the people had not been able to afford to buy enough ale or beer to produce drunkenness, but with this new method of producing alcohol, a man was able to drink himself unconscious at little expense.[4]

The use of intoxicating liquors as beverages thus began at an early date in the New World, and increased by leaps and bounds. There was no condemnation of intoxicating liquors, per se, not even on the part of moral and religious forces, except in the matter of drunkenness. The extensive use of alcoholic beverages was characteristic of the entire Colonial period. The colonists used alcoholic beverages in connection with all of their activities. "Worn out by the endless work on their little farms; discouraged by poor harvests; fearful of famine, plague or Indian attacks, they had to have some release for pent-up emotions, some way to forget the world."[5]

In all of the colonies, many found release in drinking. Alcoholic beverages were an integral part of Colonial economy and prosperity, and were consumed by everyone of both sexes and all ages. In New England, funerals were considered social events, and the family of the deceased always provided a table of liquor. After viewing the corpse, the mourners would pass on to the table loaded with decanters and pitchers and drink.[6] Nor were the laity the only ones involved; a convocation of the clergy, both in the North and South, called for the best liquors that the local hostelry could supply. In Boston, a man was requested to keep a tavern near a church so that thirsty sinners who attended might secure drinks. "The vestries of certain Episcopalian churches met at the tavern, where the chief business transacted was the consumption of good rum at the expense of

4

the congregation."[7] Drinking accompanied the business of the government also. The town selectmen and the justices attended to their affairs of office in a tavern. "There, over a bowl of toddy or a mug of flip matters of local and Colonial concern were decided, and civil and criminal cases heard."[8] Drinking was also associated with some useful activities such as sheep shearing. In Virginia, the planter class drank in the pattern of the English back home. The yeoman farmers drank their ale and beer.[9]

The drinking of alcoholic beverages was a form of social intercourse. It sparked discourse and was regarded as a vehicle for communication among equals. In America, because it was denied that whites and Negroes could be equals, it was also denied that alcohol could be an admissable vehicle in their intercourse. This resulted in the development of two patterns in the social use of alcohol. Thus, the problem of alcohol and the Negro dated from the very beginning of the colonies.

THE INTRODUCTION OF THE NEGRO

Negroes were introduced into the Virginia Colony in 1619. The same year, Virginia found it necessary to take cognizance of the excessive use of alcohol by enacting a law against it.[10] The earliest Negroes in Virginia were considered servants and not slaves; "they fell into various servant categories long familiar to the common law of England, none of which in a practical sense included perpetual and inherited chattel bondage."[11] During this period, the majority of laborers coming into the colonies were white servants whose terms, as time went on, were to become fixed by indenture, and the Negroes, so far as the law was concerned, were also regarded as servants. Nor were there any laws in the colonies to prevent their becoming free, after a term of service, and entering society as artisans and holders of property. Their status was not fixed by law until the 1660's.

Virginia was responsible for the initial legislation affecting the conditions of Indians and Negroes and slavery was recognized by law in Virginia in 1661. As the Negro population increased in the Virginia Colony, the fear of uprisings resulted in the enactment of laws keeping the Negroes under control. Virginia's precedent was followed by the neighboring colonies.[12]

A Maryland law of 1663 stated: "All Negroes or other slaves to be hereafter imported into the province shall serve 'durante vita', and all children born of any Negro or slave, shall be slaves as their fathers were for the term of their lives."[13] This was the first legal step where any black skin would itself ultimately be equated with slavery. In actual practice, the type of economy which developed in the New World required a constant labor force. This was first provided by white servitude, the historic base upon which Negro slavery was constructed. In significant numbers, the Africans who were latecomers fitted into a system already developed. The reason for the origin and development of slavery was economic, not racial. "Slavery had nothing to do with the color of the laborer, but the cheapness of labor."[14] Thus, could a constant labor force be always at hand. "It appeared to be the only solution to the problem of labor, and these colonists were not inclined to shrink from the enslavement of a people, if such a procedure was to have a salutary effect on the economic life of the colony."[15]

TRIANGULAR SLAVE TRADE

During the eighteenth century, the New England colonies became the greatest slave-trading section of America. The "demand for Negroes in the sugar islands of the British and foreign West Indies, together with the growing employment of blacks in the tobacco and rice growing colonies of the South, furthered the growth of the New England trade."[16] There came into being in this period, the famous triangular slave trade between New England, Africa, and the West Indies. In triangular trade, ships sailed from America with a cargo of manufactured goods; these goods were exchanged for Negroes on the Coast of Africa; they were also traded for sugar and molasses in the West Indies; and for rum in New England. The rum was sold for a money profit.[17] Vital to triangular trade were rum, slaves and molasses. Rum was used as money; it was the principal article of barter in the slave trade. At this time a muscular young Negro could be bought for 20 gallons.[18]

THE NEGRO, ALCOHOL, AND THE COLONIES

As the number of Negroes increased and spread throughout the colonies, the whites became concerned about their behavior, especially in their use of spirituous liquors. Southern whites were convinced that Negroes and Indians were too irresponsible to

6

be entrusted with the use of alcohol.[19] This situation was to be taken care of by license systems.

Maryland

In 1660, a Maryland innkeeper gave bond in the amount of a thousand pounds of tobacco that he would, for five years, keep good order at his house. He agreed not to allow servants and apprentices to get liquors or to remain tippling there without their master's knowledge.[20] Also in Maryland, after a petition to the governor and council and several complaints by the Society of Friends about the drinking near their meeting houses, a law was passed in 1725. This law forbade the sale of liquors within specified distances of Friend's meeting houses, with the exception of inns.

The Friends were also troubled by the racing of horses and the "great crowds of idle whites and blacks, they said, drank and behaved riotously there."[21] In 1747, Maryland passed another law which forbade horse racing and ordered the constables of the neighborhood to disperse all slaves at the time of the yearly meetings, if necessary by whipping and the assistance of a posse. This act also prohibited the sale of liquors to servants, Negroes and other slaves within three miles of any Quaker meeting in either Talbot or Anne Arundel counties. The provisions of this act applied also to free Negroes. During the nineteenth century, the free Negro population of Maryland increased. The law of 1747, "as applied to free Negroes (sic) had in view two objectives: (1) to protect the interest of property holders, and (2) to prevent disorders on the part of Negroes under the influence of rum." In order to counteract the influence of rum upon the Negroes, expedients were devised to prevent or discourage their efforts to buy alcoholic beverages.[22]

The Carolinas

The Proprietors in the Carolinas sought early to encourage the importation of Negro slaves into the colony. "In 1663, they offered to the original settlers 20 acres for every Negro man slave and ten acres for every Negro woman slave brought into the Carolina Colony in the first years."[23] From the entry of the Negro into the Carolina Colony, there was concern about his behavior and how to control him. With the increase in the num-

7

ber of Negroes many of the whites in the Carolinas became apprehensive. In 1686, the Colonial legislature passed laws to insure the domination of white masters over their slaves. The initial law forbade Negroes to engage in any kind of trade.

By the beginning of the eighteenth century the northern part of the Carolina Colony had developed a history that was in some respects separate and distinct from that of the southern portion. As a result, the Carolina Colony divided into North and South in 1729. Up to separation, North Carolina and South Carolina shared the same slave code.

In a sense, South Carolina was the daughter of the Barbados and in frequent communication with that West Indies Island. By 1712, the South Carolina assembly had copied virtually verbatim the preamble and some of the ensuing clauses of the Barbadian Act of 1688. In order to prevent slaves from drinking alcoholic beverages, the 1734 provincial assembly authorized the organization of several patrols. These patrols were directed to visit each plantation at least once per month (chastising any slave found absent without a pass) and to enter any tippling house or any other house, where anyone might have seen a slave enter.[24] In the area of North Carolina, there was a practice of restricting the purchase of liquor to certain classes. At first, slaves were allowed to purchase without the consent of their masters; by 1758, indentured servants and slaves could not buy liquor without such consent. Free Negroes were permitted to purchase whiskey until 1852; after that, it was illegal to sell liquor to them.[25]

Georgia

The establishment of Georgia, the thirteenth English colony on the Atlantic seaboard, was interesting and unique. In its founding the trustees placed three restrictions on the settlers: there were to be no free land titles, no alcoholic beverages, and no Negroes. The trustees were determined to keep slavery out of the colony. From the outset, these prohibitions were destined to make trouble. There resulted a decade of quarreling and bickering which almost led to the complete failure of the enterprise. Traders from South Carolina supplied the white inhabitants and Indians with spirits and restrictions on the use of alcohol were violated so often and became so widespread that their enforcement failed, and the act was repealed in 1742.[26] As for the unpopular restriction against the importation of Negroes, it was repealed in 1750. In conformity with the practices of the other colonies in the status and treatment of the Negro, Georgia adopted a slave code.[27] Influenced by the fear of insurrection, it was designed to keep the Negroes under complete control. After slaves were admitted to the colony, laws were enacted which prohibited them from the purchase of articles without the permission of their masters. Included in the laws were conditions regulating the sale of spirituous liquors.[28]

New Jersey

Although originally established (1664) as a Proprietary Colony, New Jersey was a Crown Colony from 1602 until it achieved independence in 1776. During the Proprietary period, a person selling rum or giving liquor to Indians or Negroes, except for the relief of physical illness or distress, was liable under a law of 1685 to a penalty of five pounds. The regulations against bartering, trading with, or selling rum to slaves were re-enacted during the periods of the Royal Governors and in the state legislature.[29]

New York

The exact date of the introduction of Negroes into New Netherland, later New York, is not as definitely recorded as their first appearance in Jamestown, Virginia. Slavery became firmly established, however, under the rule of the Dutch. Because of their preoccupation with commercial affairs there were few laws to circumscribe the movements of the slaves. They did not bother to institute a rigid system of slavery with a harsh slave code.[30] The situation changed, though, after the English captured New Netherland from the Dutch in 1664. From the beginning of the English rule slavery became one of the most important economic institutions of the colony. The English introduced regulations regarding Negroes similar to those which prevailed in other colonies. Fear of insurrection was widespread among the New Yorkers and did not diminish; this resulted, as time went on, in the changing and strengthening of their slave code.[31]

9

Pennsylvania

Before William Penn received his grant of land from King Charles II, in 1682, Negroes were living in the area that was later to be named Pennsylvania. When Penn settled his colony there were already Negroes in the Philadelphia area. During the early years of the history of the Pennsylvania Colony, regulations over the activities of the slaves rested principally in the hands of the owners. A Pennsylvania law of 1725-1726 was enacted to stop their assembling and placed other restrictions on them. Negroes were not permitted to go farther than ten miles from home without written leave from their masters under penalty of ten lashes. After nine o'clock at night, they were prohibited from visiting tippling houses. The laws regarding tippling houses, carrying arms and assembling applied to free Negroes as well as slaves, but were enforced so loosely that the application was more theoretical than real.[32]

Delaware

Delaware was a part of Pennsylvania until 1703 and the Pennsylvania laws applied to Delaware prior to this date. As a result, Delaware's history is inextricably interwoven with that of Pennsylvania's. Slavery existed in Delaware as early as 1636. The early laws of Pennsylvania applied to Delaware until 1721, at which time the first separate laws were enacted. The Pennsylvania laws prohibited the use of alcoholic beverages by Negroes prior to 1721.[33]

The New England Colonies

Negro slavery was introduced into New England sometime between 1624 and 1638 with the weight of evidence leaning toward the latter.[34] At first slavery existed only by custom and laws were needed to make it a legal institution. "Massachusetts was the first colony to take this step . . . The Bay Colony legalized perpetual servitude. In 1641, 20 years before any similar pronouncement by a Continental English colony, Massachusetts had ordained the legal enslavement of Indians, whites and Negroes."[35]

The fear of Negro and Indian uprisings inspired the people of Massachusetts to enact legislation to control both races. These acts preceded the actual slave codes which began in

1680 and continued to develop almost until the end of the Colonial period. The slave statutes attempted to deal with running away, drunkenness, theft, destruction of private property, prevention of riots and insurrections, curtailment of the slaves' freedom. In the New England colonies stringent laws were enacted to keep liquor from the Negro slaves, Indians, and white indentured servants. Again Massachusetts set the example and "in 1693 forbade any licensed innholder, taverner, common victualler, or retailer to allow any apprentice, servant or Negro, except by special permission of their owners, to drink in their houses."[36] There was little, if any variation in the treatment of Negroes, slaves and freedmen, in the New England colonies— Massachusetts, Maine, New Hampshire, Vermont, Rhode Island, and Connecticut. Practically all of them patterned their laws after Massachusetts. The Negroes in New England were not subjected to the harsh codes or severe treatment which Negroes— free and slave—were accorded in the southern colonies. During the Colonial period, the New England masters held a firm grip on the institution of slavery and refused to listen to those advocating freedom for the slaves, until the Revolutionary period.

Even though the northern colonies permitted slavery in the eighteenth century, these colonies soon were getting rid of slavery as quickly as possible. Sentiment and interest in the North were against slavery. In the South, the entire social system was built upon slavery.[37] The demand for labor to cultivate the farms made slavery profitable in the southern colonies and a considerable portion of the wealth of this section was invested in slaves. The economic system of the North did not lend itself to slavery. There was no demand for slaves to clear land, plant and harvest crops in the colonies of the North and so slavery was not profitable. Slavery ended earlier in the New England colonies than the rest of the country. On the eve of the War of Independence, American Negro slavery knew no sectional boundaries. Every colony recognized it and sharply defined the legal position of the free and enslaved black.[38] On the verge of the colonists' thrust for independence, they found themselves confronted with the excessive use of alcoholic beverages and the enslavement of Negroes and Indians.

When the War of Independence had been fought and won by the colonies, the Declaration of Independence boldly asserted

11

the national rights of man but made no mention of slavery; the Constitution subsequently sanctioned and protected slavery as an institution without naming it. Following the Revolution there were some important developments and changes in the position of the Negro. "Human bondage, it seemed certain, would hence-forth assume a sectional character, for the North had sentenced it to a slow death. In 1800, some slaves still remained in the North; most of them in New York and New Jersey, but most of the northern states had either abolished slavery outright or provided for its gradual extinction."[39] With the ending of the War of Independence, it was reasonable to expect some changes in the legal status of the Negro.

After the war manumission and anti-slavery societies became widespread. The first such society was organized in Philadelphia in 1775. During the next decade, Rhode Island and Pennsylvania passed acts looking toward the abolition of slavery. In 1785, the New York Society for Promoting the Manumission of Slaves was organized and in 1788 a similar society was created in Delaware. By 1792, there were anti-slavery societies in every state from Massachusetts to Virginia. The objectives of all of these societies were not the same. Some sought to prevent the slave trade and others were concerned with the deportation of Negroes from the state. Most of the societies, however, en-visioned the complete abolition of slavery.[40]

WHISKEY AND TAXES

Early in the eighteenth century, a change took place in Colo-nial drinking customs. When the settlers came to the New World they were accustomed to wines and malt liquors as their principal alcoholic beverages and they sought by domestic production to supply these needs. The scarcity of grapes and high quality malts, as well as skilled brewers and malters made it necessary to use such substitutes as apple cider, wine from white grapes, and peach brandy. But even with all of the imported alcoholic beverages, the domestic production of wines and beers, and the various substitutes, the demand for alcoholic drinks was not ade-quately met and the colonists turned to distilled liquor. It was this change to the use of spirituous liquors which brought about the transformation of Colonial drinking customs.[41]

The popularity of distilled spirits among all classes increased during the latter half of the eighteenth century. Originally distilled from grain by the western farmers for home consumption, whiskey soon became a favorite beverage having high commercial value. Bulky grain was marketed with difficulty over bad roads, but whiskey representing concentrated value was readily salable. It even passed in some districts as an acceptable substitute for money.

The transition from colonies to states which marked the period of the American Revolution, did not alter the fundamental Colonial legislation. Insofar as they were applicable, the liquor laws were re-enacted by the new state governments, and with minor variations remained in force until early in the nineteenth century. The first serious and effective efforts against the use of distilled liquors as beverages began about the same time as the movement for American independence. Prior to that time, the principal agitation along temperance lines had been against drunkenness.[42]

The taxation of the liquor traffic for revenue purposes began early in the history of the country. Several of the colonies enacted laws imposing a duty on imported liquors and an excise tax on those manufactured within their borders. When the Constitutional Convention met in Philadelphia in 1787, "the delegates were practically unanimous in the belief that the central government should be strengthened by giving it power to lay and collect taxes, regulate commerce, control the issue of currency, assume the financial obligations of the confederation and prevent the impairment of contracts."[43]

In July 1789, the members of the First Congress of the United States approved an excise tax on imported distilled spirits.[44] Two years later, in 1791, Congress passed a measure increasing the duty on all imported liquors manufactured in the United States. Congress amended the excise tax law in 1792 changing the amounts of import duty on distilled liquor; it also provided for the licensing of distillers. Again in 1794, the excise tax law was amended by Congress to lighten the burden on country distillers. The tax on distilled spirits provoked opposition and resistance. The backwoodsmen of Pennsylvania, whose grain had to be reduced to whiskey if it was to be profitably transported to the market, rose in rebellion in the summer of 1794. The President issued a proclamation calling out the militia of four states and ended the Whiskey Rebellion. This furnished an opportunity to demonstrate the authority of the new government.[45]

This was the first conflict over the question of where the rights of state government on taxation ended and those of the federal government began.

The year of the Whiskey Rebellion, 1794, witnessed the Third Congress enacting important legislation relative to the slave trade. "No vessel was to be fitted out or sail from any place in the United States to engage in the traffic of slaves. The penalty for the violation of this law was the forfeiture of ships. The legislation also provided that anyone engaged in the slave trade was subject to a fine of $2,000. One-half of this fine would go to the United States and the other half to the person who would sue and prosecute the claim."[46]

SLAVERY AND ALCOHOL IN THE NEW STATES

At the beginning of the nineteenth century anti-slavery groups were continuing their drive to secure stringent federal legislation prohibiting the slave trade. Their efforts were rewarded when the Ninth Congress enacted legislation which forbade the importation of slaves into the United States after January 1, 1808. Anyone convicted of violating the act was to be fined and imprisoned. This act, however, did not stop the importation of slaves into the United States. It was necessary, in 1820, for Congress to enact additional legislation. Under the new provisions, crew members of any vessel (foreign or United States) engaged in the slave trade, who seized Negroes with the intent to make them slaves, were to be considered pirates. The penalty for anyone found guilty or aiding and abetting was death.[47]

When the importation of slaves from Africa ceased in 1808, slaves became more valuable and the domestic trade more profitable. Powerful social and economic forces made slavery the cheapest and most productive form of labor in the South. By 1815, about the time of the great movement of the population to the cotton kingdom, domestic trading of slaves had become a major economic activity.

After 1800, the westward movement began in this country. The newly settled frontier lands influenced the evolution of the institution of slavery and the history of the Negro in America. The acquisition of these territories, and then later their admission to the Union as slaveholding or non-slaveholding states determined the treatment accorded Negroes. Slavery became an explosive political issue.

The Constitutional Convention meeting in Philadelphia, in 1787, operating under the articles of Confederation enacted the Northwest Ordinance. The Ordinance prohibited slavery and involuntary servitude in the Northwest Territory now comprising the states of Ohio, Indiana, Illinois, Wisconsin, and most of Michigan. This Ordinance played a significant role in the settlement of the territories northwest of the Ohio River, and was also an important milestone in the progress of America toward freedom and individual liberty. Between 1777 and 1787, when slavery was prohibited in the Northwest Territory, six northeastern states were abolishing slavery: Vermont, 1777; New York, 1779; Pennsylvania, 1780; New Hampshire, 1783; Connecticut and Rhode Island, 1784. By 1830, whether by legislative, judicial or constitutional action, Negro slavery had been virtually abolished in the North. By the time the new nation was established, slavery in New England was dying rapidly.[48]

THE SOUTHERN STATES

Kentucky became a state in 1792. Among the early inhabitants were Negro slaves who had been taken by settlers from Slave States. Slavery was legally recognized and permitted in this state. A measure was enacted in 1846 prohibiting Negroes from manufacturing and selling whiskey. Ten years later, 1856, the state had passed laws regulating the use and sale of liquor to Negroes—free and slave.[49]

From 1777 to 1789, Tennessee was part of the region included in the North Carolina territory. After ratifying the constitution in 1789, North Carolina ceded the Tennessee country to the United States. The act of cession as finally accepted by Congress, April 1790, stipulated that "no regulation made or to be made by Congress shall tend to emancipate slaves."[50] Thus the newly created federal government was not to interfere with an

15

institution which the toppling Confederation had prohibited in the Northwest Territory. Slaves in Tennessee were forbidden to engage in trade or traffic of any kind without written permission from their owners. The regulations related to general trading with slaves were not too stringent. Provisions carrying the harshest penalties for trading with slaves were those relative to the prohibition of the sale of intoxicating liquors. "No merchant, tavernkeeper, distiller, nor any person could sell liquor to a slave who did not have a permit. The master who knowingly permitted his slave to sell intoxicating liquors, without a written permit was forced to pay to the person who sued for this violation not less than $50 for each offense."[51] State laws aimed at the use of alcohol by Negroes were frequently enacted by city or local ordinances, throughout the South. Both Nashville and Memphis supplemented state legislation in this area. Memphis, in 1859, enacted an ordinance imposing a fine for selling or giving liquor to minors or Negroes, slave or free. A Nashville ordinance of 1852 made any person who gave liquor to slaves subject to a five dollar fine for the first offense and fines for subsequent violations at the discretion of the court. The person who sold liquor to slaves was made punishable at the discretion of the court.[52]

Legal slavery was rejected in the constitutions of the states formed from the Northwest and Indian territories: Ohio, Indiana, Illinois, Michigan, Iowa, Wisconsin, California, Minnesota, Oregon, and Kansas.[53]

Louisiana was admitted to the Union in 1812. In 1806, the first session of the Louisiana Territorial legislature adopted a Black Code against the sale of spirituous liquors to Indians and Negroes. The Code required that intoxicating liquors be forbidden to slaves under penalty of a fine.[54] Despite legislative efforts to prevent it, many Louisiana slaves drank alcoholic beverages in their idle moments. There were always grog shops where Negroes could obtain an illegal dram. One newspaper editor lamented the fact that "food and clothing meant little to the Negro if he could not get whiskey."[55] Another newspaper carried an editorial that stated: "It is no uncommon sight to see staggering drunken Negroes in our streets at nine or ten o'clock at night, and hear them cursing like madmen."[56] Negroes were able to obtain whiskey, and from all indications, it was not too difficult for them to do so. The arrests and penalties for selling liquor to Negroes were not enough. But in the minds of the slaveholders and non-slave owning neighbors, there was constantly the fear of rebellion. They believed that under the influence of drink, the Negro might forget the subordination which the whites considered his duty.

When Mississippi attained statehood in 1817, slavery was a well-established southern institution. It was approved and supported by informal custom as well as formal law. The attempts to control and regulate Negroes were probably harsher and more severe in Mississippi than in any other Slave State, possibly because Negroes outnumbered whites in several counties. The use of alcoholic beverages by Negroes created considerable concern and fear among the whites in many local communities. The state laws prohibited the use of whiskey by Negroes, but they were permitted to use it under special conditions or circumstances: "particularly as a preventive of chills, to slaves who had worked in the rain, or who had been performing heavy tasks."[57] In 1832, a citizen who objected to the amount of freedom enjoyed by slaves published a letter in a newspaper. "He disliked the custom of allowing slaves to wander about the country at Christmas, many of them more or less drunk." Another observer presented an entirely different point of view; he stated that "slaves were seldom drunk except at Christmas, when the sober ones were more easily counted than the drunk."[58]

Slaves were first introduced into the region which is now Alabama in 1716, when that territory was part of France's Louisiana Colony. Later, this territory was acquired by England. At the close of the Revolutionary War, in 1783, England surrendered the territory east of the Mississippi River, and north of 31° to the United States. Congress designated a part of it in 1798—the Mississippi Territory. While Alabama was part of the Mississippi Territory, the foundation for its future slave code was laid. During this period, 1798 to 1817, legislation was enacted to govern slaves and free persons of color. The provincial laws governing the slaves were in many instances strict, but they may not have all been strictly enforced. The laws prohibited any tavern or retail liquor dealer from selling or delivering strong drink to any slave without the consent of his master.[59] After Alabama became a state in 1819, laws were passed to cover practically every other aspect of Negro

17

life. Although the laws prohibited Negroes from buying or selling whiskey, they violated these laws. There were white men who constantly violated the law by buying liquor from slaves and selling it to them. Efforts to enforce the law were made continuously. In 1859, a white man was convicted in the Municipal Court of Mobile of selling liquor to slaves, fined $50, and sentenced to 30 days in jail. Another white man was convicted of a similar offense in a circuit county court; he was fined $500 and the cost of court.[60]

Free Negroes in Alabama, as in the other Slave States, occupied a peculiar position in society and were confronted by numerous restrictions. They were separated from white people by color and social position and from slaves by their freedom. Many of the laws related to slave activities were applied to free Negroes. Legal limitation of the activities of free Negroes began shortly after statehood was achieved. An act by the 1822 general assembly forbade them to keep taverns or retail liquors. The penalties for violation of this act were for the first and second offense—ten and 20 dollars, respectively.[61]

Missouri was part of the Louisiana Territory purchased from France in 1603. In June 1812, an Act of Congress created the Territory of Missouri. Here, as in other areas, the question of slavery was closely connected with the liquor issue. Slavery was retained and laws were passed in an attempt to prevent Negroes and liquor from getting together. In 1818, both Maine and Missouri applied for admission to the Union. A deadlock developed between northern and southern forces relative to Missouri's admission. Should it be admitted as a slave or non-slave state? Under the Missouri Compromise of 1820, both were to be admitted to the Union without reference to the slave issue. It was stipulated that in the remainder of the Louisiana Territory lying north of Missouri's southern boundary, slavery and involuntary servitude were to be forever prohibited.[62]

The Missouri Grocer Regulation Act of 1833, made any person selling whiskey to Negroes liable to a fine of 15 to 50 dollars, cost of court, and loss of license. An act passed in 1835 regulating inns and taverns provided that keepers be fined ten to 50 dollars for bartering liquor with slaves, free Negroes, and apprentices without their master's consent in writing. This law also placed a fine of $300 upon the masters who allowed their slaves to sell or deliver liquors or wines to any place without the consent of the owner. In spite of the law, both blacks and whites engaged in illicit liquor dealings. The Missouri laws as they involved whiskey and Negroes were relatively severe. Insurrections in other states may have influenced the making of these laws. In 1845, the act of 1835 was revised to increase the punishment of a slave for selling liquor to 39 lashes and required the owners to pay all costs. If a person operating a store sold liquor to a slave without the consent of the master and the Negro was made drunk and died, the vendor of the liquor was liable for legal damages. This was the law, even though a clerk sold the liquor without the proprietor's knowledge.[63]

In 1803, the region that eventually became Arkansas was bought as part of the Louisiana Purchase. On the admission of Louisiana as a state in 1812, the Arkansas district became Arkansas County of the Territory of Missouri. From admission as a state in 1836, slavery was legal in Arkansas. The treatment of Negroes—slave and free—was patterned after Missouri. Through custom and law, Negroes were prohibited from using liquor. By 1853, laws had been passed in Arkansas making the sale of liquor to slaves illegal, and the sale of liquor by slaves and free Negroes.[64] This did not prevent Negroes from drinking alcohol whenever they were able to secure it.

Originally settled by the Spanish in the sixteenth century, Florida was the first portion of the United States occupied by Europeans.[65] England won Florida from the Spanish and governed it from 1763 to 1783 and then was forced to surrender it back to Spain at the end of the American Revolution. In 1819, Spain ceded Florida to the United States, in payment for war debts between these two countries. Florida became a state; its constitution made provisions for the enslavement of Indians and Negroes. The Spanish, English, and American governments of Florida recognized and accepted the institution of slavery.

The exact date of the entry of the first slaves into Florida is unknown. A small number were introduced into the territory late in the sixteenth century. About "one hundred years later, the privilege of introducing slaves was accorded to one De Aila as a reward for meritorious services, and his arrival in 1687, with Negroes seems to have occasioned much rejoicing in the colony."[66] The Negro population was increased by many of them escaping from other territories and states into the Spanish Territory of Florida. By 1815, "there were in Florida, many runaway slaves, who escaped from their Georgia owners. They adopted the manner and life of the redskins."[67]

During the early nineteenth century, there was concern about the drinking among Indians and Negroes in Florida. There was a close relationship between the Indians and Negroes in all aspects of life, and especially in drinking and fighting the whites. The use of alcohol was prevalent among the general population over the years and the gaining of statehood did not appear to reduce the amount of liquor consumed. Negroes patterned their behavior after the whites and drank whiskey, as in the other states. The laws and customs of Florida aimed at controlling Negroes and preventing them from using alcoholic beverages were patterned after neighboring states. Slaves were prohibited from buying and selling without the consent of their masters; this prohibition included spirituous liquors. Free Negroes were compelled to have white guardians for travel; if one was caught without a certificate, he was presumed to be a slave.[68]

As early as 1492, the Coast of Texas had been explored by the Spanish. The first black man set foot on Texas soil in 1528. He was not a slave, but an African Moor. The region out of which Texas evolved was under Spanish control until the nineteenth century. In 1820, Moses Austin rode into Texas and marked the advent of Anglo-American civilization and the real beginning of the history of modern Texas.[69] The early colonists were given permission to import slaves and by 1835, slaves were estimated to be 12 percent of the immigrant population. From all indications the majority of the Texans approved the institution of slavery.[70] The Republic of Texas, born in 1836 in the bloodletting ordeal of revolution, maintained a virile independence for almost ten years before it joined the American Union as the twenty-eighth state.[71] The rugged colonizers who settled and later generations that maintained Texas, drank heavily and frequently; enormous quantities of intoxicants were imbibed. Grogshops were among the first business houses in Houston and Galveston, and their number multiplied with the rapid growth of the towns. All over Texas, whiskey flowed from barrels at the order of men from all walks of life. Holidays, election days, and campaign rallies were times for unrestrained license in drinking.

Negro slaves were considered valuable property and had to be protected; therefore, drinking was controlled in order to keep them from harm, but they were permitted to drink on special occasions and holidays. The use of liquor by free Negroes was watched carefully; this was done because of fear of insurrection by this group.[72]

TENSIONS MOUNT

The fear of insurrection was responsible for the enactment of more stringent laws to control the activities and movements of Negroes in the early nineteenth century. The Denmark Vesey Uprising in South Carolina and the Nat Turner Insurrection in Virginia inspired the enactment of many repressive measures throughout the South, and especially the laws relative to the use of alcoholic beverages.

For a number of years, the anti-slavery and liquor forces worked together. During the 1840's and 1850's, temperance and abolition became part of other major movements of reform. A supporter of legislation encouraging prohibition of alcoholic beverages was also likely to be a supporter of the anti-slavery movement. The temperance movement was completely stifled in the South because of its identification with anti-slavery. "Although Temperance agitation had developed in southern states during the 1820's, by the late 1830's Temperance was unable to gain any strength in the South."[73]

Between 1850 and 1860, the decade leading up to the Civil War, the people of the United States witnessed many tense and crucial episodes. The majority of these were closely related to slavery. Among the major problems confronting the people was the controversy over slavery in the newly acquired territory in the southwest. The disposition of the territories had become a central issue. As a result, two sets of extremists had arisen: northerners who demanded no new slave territories under any circumstances and southerners who demanded free entry of slavery into all territories. Some leaders believed that the new territory should be divided into slave and free sections as in the Missouri Compromise. Many of those from the North, especially the abolitionists, wanted total exclusion of slavery from the territories. There were others of the opinion that the question should be decided by the people themselves in the new territories. Finally, there were those who insisted that slavery could not be legally excluded anywhere. The question of the fugitive slave was another problem.[74]

As tension mounted, there were many events which created conflict and hostility between the North and South. Two which may have helped to hasten the bitter war were the raid of John Brown, and the Republican victory at the polls in 1860. On Sunday, October 16, 1859, with a small band of men, Brown seized the federal arsenal at Harper's Ferry, Virginia. He planned to secure ammunition to fight the Virginia slaveholders. As a result of an immediate general alarm, federal and state troops were dispatched to this area. Brown and his men were overwhelmed, captured and on December 2, 1859, John Brown was hanged. His words and deeds after the trial electrified and stirred many of the people of this country; the raid had a stunning impact on the South. Slaveholders became alarmed and they believed that the abolitionists would go to any lengths to eliminate slavery. In 1860, the Republican party adopted a platform taking a position against the further extension of slavery into western territories. The party also adopted a policy of non-interference with the institution of slavery in the states. When it became clear that the Republican candidate would stand on an anti-slavery platform, the South began once more to utter threats of secession.

At the same time, on the eve of the Civil War, prohibition had not been forgotten by the American people. The campaign against alcohol in the decade preceding the war was intensive. The use of alcohol had become a burning question everywhere and a much debated subject of conversation.[75] The measures taken to prohibit the use of alcoholic beverages by Negroes became more repressive as a result of the John Brown raid.

THE CIVIL WAR

With the triumph of Abraham Lincoln in the Presidential election of 1860, the reaction of the slaveholding states was swift. This election was to be the most fateful in the history of the country. In December 1860, South Carolina dissolved its union with the other states and seceded from the Union. By February 1861, six other states had followed South Carolina's action and withdrawn from the Union—Mississippi, Florida, Alabama, Georgia, Louisiana, and Texas. In his Inaugural address in March 1861, Lincoln indicated that he did not plan to interfere with slavery where it existed. One month later, however, the sectional differences had erupted into the Civil War.[76]

The Confederates began the bombardment of Fort Sumter, South Carolina, April 12, 1861. The war so long dreaded had begun at last. The South had fired the first shot and captured a federal Fort by force. There could be no more ignoring the stark fact of rebellion by the Confederate states. After the war had started, Virginia, North Carolina, Tennessee and Arkansas withdrew from the Union, thus increasing the states of the Confederacy from seven to 11. There was considerable dissension among the states on the question of secession. North Carolina voted against secession, but was forced to reverse its decision in May 1861, when Virginia joined the Confederacy. North Carolina was subsequently the last state to secede from the Union.[77]

An accurate and objective appraisal of the behavior of Negroes during the struggles which involved their freedom is difficult because of the conflicting nature of much of the evidence. Many of them joined the Union army and left their masters; others remained on the plantations and continued the same pattern of living as before the war.

There was considerable drinking during the Civil War among the civilian and army populations, both North and South. "When the northern volunteers started out for camp in 1861, some turned to their Bibles and meditated upon the ends of man. But the others were in a more festive mood . . . Army life brought many soldiers into contact with spirituous liquors for the first time and their experience during the four years undoubtedly widened the demand for hard liquor in the years that followed."[78] The northern armies drank more liquor per capita than those of the South. This was not due to a greater capacity, but more reliable sources of supply. The federal troops had more money, hence more whiskey. They spent more time in travel and they were more often stationed in the large cities. Sometimes whiskey was manufactured in the Union army. The soldiers of the South, on the other hand, got their whiskey in the streets and back alleys of towns from sutlers and from bootleggers who employed other soldiers as agents. Peddlers circulated discreetly using canteens to transport the whiskey and tin thimbles to measure it out.[79]

Early in the war the supply of whiskey flowing into the Confederacy was reduced because it was cut off by the enemy. Manufacture was controlled because the Confederacy needed alcohol for chemical, mechanical and industrial purposes, and as a solvent in medicines. Although whiskey was a regular component of the Confederate navy ration, it was under strict rationing and allowed in the army only under circumstances of protracted fatigue. The shortage of whiskey induced the southern states to take action to alleviate this situation. State by state, by executive order or legislative enactment, the southern states ordered strict prohibition of whiskey for the civilian population. This action was not taken as a social measure, but as a necessity for food conservation. The issue was regarded as bread versus liquor.[80]

Even though the whites in the South were against the use of alcohol by Negroes, the war effort prevented their doing much about the behavior of Negroes. "Between 1861-1865, the white people of the South were too absorbed in the conduct of the war and struggle for existence to devote much energy and thought to the control of the Negro, when it was just possible to leave him alone."[81]

RECONSTRUCTION

With the end of the war in 1865 the legal status of slaves had changed and they could no longer be considered as property; approximately four million former slaves were informed that they were free. There were some southern whites who believed that the slaves had been generally content with their lot. "Their escape from the overseer's rule attracted them now as a holiday does children . . . The first step many took in their new life was to wander away from their old homes. They left the plantations and flocked to the military posts or to the city streets."[82] Negroes had been enslaved for over 200 years. They had not been permitted to leave the homes of their masters without a pass; to trade with anyone without permission of their owners; and their behavior and activities had been controlled from birth to death. It was to be expected that the slaves would leave the plantations and the influence of their former masters. After securing their freedom, numberless Negroes fled toward Union lines. "Others of the four million were merely moving about to test their freedom . . ."[83]

There was no abatement in alcohol consumption during the Reconstruction period; there may have been an increase. In their army life, many young soldiers had been introduced to the use of alcohol and they found little incentive to stop when the war ended. Grogshops were opened in many country settlements and at crossroads and dotted the larger cities. The excessive use of alcohol by the total population was considered a problem both North and South; the presence, however, of large numbers of free Negroes in the South created additional problems of control. "Since they had been denied whiskey while in slavery, they gave full reign to their appetites in freedom. With little experience in self-control, they would spend their last piece of money for a drink of whiskey, and they would steal this article . . . Many Negroes spent half their earnings for liquor."[84]

During the Reconstruction period in Mississippi, a native white observer, in describing conditions in Woodville declared, "It was not uncommon to see 1,000 Negroes on foot and on horseback, marching around the public square and yelling like madmen. Most of the Negroes would be drunk. Large numbers of rural Negroes went to the nearest village on Saturday and sought recreation or diversion. They engaged in public drunkenness, disorderly conduct . . . which led the way to the mayor's court and city jail."[85]

In North Carolina, as in other states, the Negro took advantage of freedom after the Civil War. It was believed by some whites that the Negro often drank to an excess and public drunkenness was not uncommon. "Liquor gave to the Negro a feeling of being equal or superior to the white man, an atttiude intolerable in the South."[86]

The extent of the use of alcoholic beverages by the newly freed slaves was largely a matter of speculation. Many of the ex-slaves had patterned their lives after their masters; some of them continued to practice moderation in their alcohol consumption after they were free. Charles Stearns, a northern teacher, planter, missionary, and eyewitness, in Columbus, Georgia, commenting on the use of alcohol by Negroes stated: "Drunkenness is not a prominent vice among the Negroes; during my six years residence on our plantation, I do not recollect witnessing more than two or three cases of intoxication, and one of them was on the part of non-resident, and this among a total population of over two hundred persons. But neither is total abstinence one of their virtues. Nearly all Negroes will drink when it is given to them, but they do not like to spend their money for it, when they need other things so much."[87]

During Reconstruction, a number of Negroes expressed concern with the behavior of members of their group. They resented the fighting, cursing and excessive use of alcoholic beverages all over the country. Among those who spoke out against these conditions was a minister in Tennessee. In April 1872, Reverend A. E. Baldwin, pastor of the Union Street Congregaional church of Memphis, painted a dismal picture of vice and crime in that city. He pointed out that there were 200 licensed dram shops selling liquor by the glass over the counter and countless numbers of grocers selling liquor.[88]

The period of Reconstruction was one of great and rapid change in the total society of the South. The people were insecure, confused, and under emotional strain. The conflicts and problems confronting the people were not oriented to any racial group; they involved the total population of the region. These problems were largely related to adjustment to a different way of life for all. Many of the incidents of violence were the work of bad men. "Whiskey was a potent cause in making a malicious man more malicious, or of transforming for a time an ordinary citizen into a dangerous man."[89]

Reconstruction was neither a sectional nor a racial problem, it was essentially a national problem. After the war, in most places in the North, Negroes continued to face political, social, and economic proscription; they also encountered petty persecution and discrimination. The mass exodus of Negroes from the South to the North increased the fear that the newly liberated slaves would bring about competition for work, would depress wages, and create unemployment. This aroused hostility among the white workers. Out of these conditions there arose discriminatory practices in the social and political policies adopted by many northerners in the twentieth century. Although the Negro was theoretically and legally free to participate in the total life of the North, in actuality he was prevented from doing so through social custom and tradition. He was unable, for example, to secure accommodations and services in hotels, saloons and eating places.

During the Reconstruction period, the problem of controlling the Negro was of great concern to southerners. The southern state legislatures, in 1865 and 1866 enacted a series of laws, varying in harshness, to define the status and rights of Negroes. These laws bore a close resemblance to the ante-bellum Black Codes; they could not be recognized as measures which respected the rights of Negroes as free men: "Negroes were to possess no firearms or alcoholic beverages . . . The effect of these was to consign the Negro to a position of legal inferiority."[90]

The Thirteenth Amendment to the Constitution of the United States abolished slavery; the Fourteenth Amendment conferred citizenship upon Negroes. It prohibited any state from abridging the privileges or immunities of any citizen. Negroes were not supposed to be deprived of life, liberty, or property without due process of law. The Fifteenth Amendment enfranchised the Negro and attempted to protect his political rights.[91] The postwar decade witnessed the violation of the legal guarantees of the Constitutional rights of Negroes by the uncompromising former masters who refused to recognize in the Negro any semblance of equality. In order to protect Negroes in the South, it was necessary for Congress, in 1875, to enact the most far-reaching civil rights legislation it had ever considered. This legislation provided that "all persons within the United States, regardless of race, color or previous condition of servitude were subject only to restrictions established by law and applying to all citizens alike; they should be entitled to the full and equal accommodations and facilities of inns, public conveyances on land and water, theatres and other places of public amusement."[92] Violation of the act was punishable by a fine or imprisonment and a heavy penalty to be recovered by the person who was the victim. The federal courts were given exclusive jurisdiction of offenses arising under this statute.[93]

27

In the South, segregation on the basis of race continued to be the custom in public places where alcoholic beverages were served. Usually Negroes frequented and patronized their own establishments in purchasing and consuming liquor. Between the beginning of the Civil War, and the November 1876 election, the social and political status of Negroes underwent revolutionary changes. Following the war, the southern legislatures enacted laws which restricted the freedom and activities of Negroes who were free in name only. The civil rights of the Negro were disregarded and violated, in spite of federal laws and efforts to maintain them.

When Rutherford B. Hayes was elected twenty-third President of the United States in 1876, a dispute arose regarding the election returns in three southern states—Florida, South Carolina, and Louisiana. In all three, there was evidence of fraud and intimidation. Hayes' election marked the end of the Republican rule in the South and the beginning of second-class citizenship for the Negro. In his Inaugural address, Hayes made it evident that he was determined to withdraw all national protection from the colored people of the South, and to put the whites squarely on their honor in their treatment of the Negroes.[94] This new phase of Reconstruction witnessed the withdrawal of federal troops from the South; the abandonment of the Negro as a ward of the nation; the end of any attempts to guarantee the free man civil and political equality; and the acquiescence of the rest of the country to the South's demand that the whole problem be left to the disposition of the white people.

From 1877 to 1900, the Negro was systematically deprived of his rights and the practice of *Jim Crow* became the accepted method of dealing with Negroes in the areas of public accommodation throughout practically the entire United States. *Jim Crow* maintained a separation between whites and Negroes in the use of certain public facilities. In some places, this separation was the result of practice, but in the South, it was brought about largely through legislation. The segregation or *Jim Crow* statutes were the public symbols and constant reminders to the Negro of his inferior position. The segregation laws were comparable to the Black Codes of the old regime.[95] During the same period some of the border states enacted legislation concerning service to Negroes in hotels, restaurants and saloons. A Delaware law

28

gave the proprietor of any inn, hotel or tavern the authority to decline to serve or accommodate persons who were offensive to the major portion of his clientele. The owner or operator had the power to determine who was offensive. Some states— New York, Pennsylvania, Massachusetts, and Wisconsin—specifically mentioned saloons in their public accommodation laws. In Pennsylvania, the renewal of a liquor license depended on racial non-discrimination. Barkeepers who refused to serve Negroes in Massachusetts were denied a license to operate a place of business.[96]

THE TWENTIETH CENTURY

THE PROGRESSIVE ERA

At the beginning of the twentieth century; among the issues confronting the people of the United States were the social, economic, and political status of the Negro, and the use of alcohol. The twentieth century also witnessed the advent of the Progressive Movement.[97] This Movement attempted to use the government as a positive instrument of reform. Prohibition was one of the reforms that the Progressive Movement had as its goal; this was to be accomplished through political action. During the Progressive era—1900 to 1920—there was a marked upsurge in the century-old crusade against the manufacture and use of alcoholic beverages.[98] In the attack on alcohol a crusade developed against the place (saloon) rather than the drinker. The saloon was one of the primary outlets for the retail sale of alcohol. Although the saloon was located and operated in rural areas and small towns, "the saloon was considered pre-eminently an urban institution. For the smalltown American Protestant, it epitomized the social habits of the immigrant population . . . The saloon was a source of the corruption which he saw as a bane in political life." [99]

RIOTS

Negroes lived in high hopes that the twentieth century would bring a new and more civilized approach to the solution of racial differences. Their hopes for better treatment were shattered as violence and hostility increased in the North as well as in the South. Between 1900 and 1920, an epidemic of

29

race riots swept the country causing anxiety and concern. In August 1904, two Negroes were accused of the brutal murder of a white farmer, his wife and three children, in Statesboro, Georgia. They were tried, convicted and sentenced to be hanged. The white citizens worked themselves into such a frenzy of race hatred that Negroes were whipped, killed and many of their homes wrecked. A mob of whites overpowered a company of militia and other authorities and the Negroes who committed the murders were taken from them, dragged away, and burned alive.[100]

The South's most sensational riot occurred in Atlanta, Georgia, in 1906. For months the city had been lashed into a fury of race hatred by loose talk and a movement to disfranchise Negroes. The main issue of the gubernatorial campaign of 1906 was the disfranchisement of the Negro; as a result there was much racial antagonism stirred up against the Negro. Prior to the 1906 election in which the Negroes were disfranchised and white supremacy emerged triumphant, a number of crimes were committed by Negroes against white women. The riot which broke out September 22, 1906 was cited by flaming headlines in the newspapers reporting four assaults on white women by Negroes. The *Atlanta News* printed four extras, which were carried through the streets by newsboys crying out each successive assault. A later investigation revealed that two of the cases reported might have been attempted assault, but two were undoubtedly cases of fright on the part of the Negroes as well as the white women because of the tense situation.[101]

The South did not have a monopoly on riots and harsh and abusive treatment of the Negro. In the North, the treatment was as vicious and hostile as elsewhere in the country. Negroes were publicly attacked in New York, Philadelphia and other northern cities.

The northern riot that shook the entire country occurred in Springfield, Illinois, in August 1908. A white woman claimed that she had been dragged from her bed and raped by a person whom she identified as a Negro who had been working in the neighborhood. Before a special grand jury, the woman admitted that the Negro had had no connection with the incident. She admitted that she had been severely beaten by a white man whose identity she refused to reveal. The woman's acknowledgment that the Negro was not involved did not satisfy the whites. A mob formed which destroyed Negro business establishments and drove Negroes from their homes. Fire was set to a barbershop, and the barber lynched. It was necessary for the governor to call out the militia. Before order was restored two Negroes had been lynched, four white men had been killed, and more than 70 persons had been injured.[102]

PROHIBITION ACTIVITY

Between 1900 and 1910, there was increased activity by the forces of prohibition. During the same decade that witnessed the riots in different sections of the country, the prohibitionists increased their attempts to eliminate the sale of alcoholic beverages. They were remarkably successful. By 1906, approximately 35 million people in the United States were living in prohibition territory and the saloon had been banished by law from territory aggregating more than two million square miles. The records of the prohibitionists every year from 1895 to 1906, showed an increase in dry territory and dry population. County option laws placed more than 1,500 counties in all parts of the nation under prohibition legislation.[103]

The presence of the Negro continued to influence the liquor question and the prohibition movement. White southerners had special reasons for advocating prohibition. "It offered them a moral refuge from their guilty fear of the Negro, as well as a method of controlling one of his means of self-assertion. Liquor sometimes gave the Negro strength to repudiate his inferior status. The Negro should be prevented from drinking alcohol."[104] Whether justified or unjustified, a large number of southerners feared that liquor was the cause of race conflict. The danger spot, they believed, was the saloon. In the saloon, the worst elements of both races met and drank, although at separate bars. "In any southern community with a barroom, a race war is a perilously possible occurrence. The danger is not in the upper class, but in the lower levels of both races. Two-thirds of the mob lynchings and burnings at stake are the result of whiskey drunk by black men and bad white men."[105]

The immigrants were to the rest of the country what the Negroes and lower-class whites were to the South. The population of the 11 states of the old Confederacy, although practically

31

untouched by immigration, contained several million poor whites and Negroes. Unlike the foreign stock in the North, these southern lower-class whites were primarily rural and posed much the same challenge to middle-class southerners as that posed by foreign stock elsewhere in the nation. Because of this situation, the use of alcoholic beverages continued to be a major problem in the South.

By 1910, "Negroes were politically handicapped by poll taxes and other devices in every southern state. They could still be bought corruptly by paying their poll taxes, giving them a few drinks and a little ready money, and voting them in droves at the polls. By this means, the liquor interests were believed to have defeated dry campaigns in Florida, Texas, and Arkansas." [106] "Some writers have interpreted the rise of the state prohibition campaigns in the South after 1906 as an effort to control the Negro. Our interpretation is quite different. After 1900 whatever political power the Negro had was broken by effective legal disfranchisement . . . It was the disfranchisement of the Negro which made the political movement for prohibition feasible in the South." [107]

The drive for national Prohibition began in 1913 and was achieved in 1920. The period from 1906 to 1913 was one in which the accomplishments of the prohibition forces had a most important bearing on the entire prohibition movement throughout the nation. It was demonstrated that the same methods which worked so successfully in local communities were the best to use in the state fight against liquor. It had repeatedly demonstrated that organized moral forces, operating through legitimate and proper political channels could win in uneven contests against the most strongly organized liquor interests working corruptly. The backbone of the liquor traffic had been broken when Congress committed the federal government to a policy of supporting legislative efforts for suppression of the traffic. [108]

WORLD WAR I AND PROHIBITION

When the United States entered World War I in April 1917, many states had their own prohibition laws. More than 60 percent of the people and 80 percent of the United States were under prohibition. In May 1917, Congress forbade the sale of liquor to soldiers in the army. The Food Control Bill (September 1917) went further, banning the manufacture and importation of distilled liquor for beverage purposes. It also gave President Woodrow Wilson discretionary power to reduce the alcoholic content of beer and wine or prohibit their manufacture altogether. Wartime prohibition was included in the imperative 1918 Agricultural Bill. This belated conservation measure became the law on November 21, 1918—ten days after the Armistice had been signed. Its prohibitary effective dates—after May 1, 1919, for the manufacture of beer and wine; after June 30, 1919, for the sale of all liquors, were projected even further into the peaceful future.[109] To secure the enactment of prohibition legislation by Congress, the dry campaigners used the arguments that sober soldiers and factory hands performed their duties better than those using alcoholic beverages. Of added appeal to the general public and the members of Congress was the argument that in this time of conservation, grain was more necessary for bread than for whiskey. The law was passed and went into effect January 16, 1920. And so it became a violation of the law to manufacture, sell, transport, import, or export intoxicating liquors. "The National Prohibition Act, better known as the Volstead Act, spelled out the practicalities of enforcement and undertook the challenging semantic task of defining intoxicating liquors."[110]

With the enactment of the Eighteenth Amendment, a large segment of the American people believed that the issues concerning the manufacture, transportation, and use of alcoholic beverages had been settled. A few months after the dry era began, near Austin, Texas, a moonshine still was found neatly hidden in a thicket on the farm of Senator Morris Sheppard, author of the Eighteenth Amendment. The still was producing 130 gallons of alcohol a day.[111] This was an indication of the future resistance that would be encountered by law officials in the enforcement of the Prohibition laws. When the Volstead Act became law, it changed not only the drinking habits of the American people, but their way of life. Prohibition was the product of the age-old conflict of country against city, of the God-fearing, solid, dry Yankee farmer against the corrupt urban rich, and the immigrants with their foreign religions and customs and their imported beer and rum. Prohibition represented the last attempt of rural America to stem the tide of history that was transforming the country from an agricultural into an industrial nation.

THE NEGRO AND WORLD WAR I

The outbreak of the First World War stopped the flow of European immigrants at the same time that war industries throughout the nation were expanding and the need for manpower was increasing. Prior to the advent of the war, there had been little employment opportunity to encourage Negroes to move to the city. During the war period, the demand for laborers in northern industry provided an opportunity for Negroes to leave the rural South and turn to the urban centers of the North. Recruiting agents from numerous industries located in or near northern cities went South and persuaded a large number of Negroes to leave. The migration of Negroes from the South to the North was not a new phenomenon. They had migrated from place to place from the time they had been introduced into the country as slaves. During the pre-Civil War years these movements had not been voluntary but depended on the sale of slaves to plantation owners. Following Emancipation, Negroes had continued to move from section to section in the South and Southwest. It was only in these areas that agricultural workers were needed in large numbers and the Negroes at that time were predominantly farm laborers.[112]

The migration of Negroes to the urban areas of the North and Midwest created problems and conflict. Many of them arrived with the impression that they would be free to live and move about as they desired. They were not long in discovering that their living and other activites would be largely restricted to specific sections of the cities. In addition, there were hotels, stores, restaurants and saloons that preferred not to serve Negroes; in fact, many of them refused to do so. For a Negro to go into the majority of the hotels, saloons, nightclubs, and restaurants located in the downtown section of any northern or midwestern city, was unthinkable. This was also the case on the West Coast. And as the migration of Negroes to the other sections of the country increased, hostility toward them grew.

As the United States entered the war in 1917, there had not been any appreciable change in the social, economic, and political status of the Negro. Segregation, discrimination, exploitation, and all the other evils had continued to be the Negro's plight. After they enlisted or were drafted in the army, the treatment accorded them left much to be desired. The Negroes wanted to fight in the war and they were needed; about 400,000 Negro males were drafted. They were placed in segregated labor camps or as servants. They met discrimination everywhere and derogatory rumors about Negro soldiers were spread.[113] The training of Negroes in the army, plagued the government from the beginning of the war. There were many complaints to the War Department concerning the treatment of Negro soldiers in the army and outside of it. Commanding officers and many of the whites often insulted Negroes by calling them "coons, darkies, and niggers."[114] Frequently Negro soldiers were forced to work under unhealthy and undesirable conditions. There was considerable friction between Negro soldiers and the Military Police and as the war progressed this friction was intensified. The War Department issued orders calling for fair and impartial treatment of Negro soldiers—there was little discernible improvement. There were clashes between white and Negro soldiers until the end of the war.

The Negro soldiers stationed in the South caused the War Department its greatest concern. In September 1917, the men of the Twenty-fourth Infantry—all Negro—became involved in a riot with white civilians in Houston, Texas. These soldiers were goaded to desperation by repeated acts of hostility and because of the failure of the War Department and other branches of the federal government to protect them, they resisted with arms. In the riot which followed a number of both Negroes and whites were injured, and some whites were killed. With only a slight pretense of a trial 13 Negro soldiers were hanged for murder and mutiny, 41 were imprisoned for life, and 40 others were held pending investigation. The Brownsville incident wounded the pride of American Negroes and shook their faith in their government.[115] Another large riot in Spartanburg, South Carolina, was barely avoided. A Negro soldier had been beaten while buying a newspaper in a hotel. The next night a group of soldiers started marching from their camp to the city in order to "shoot it up" but were stopped by a white officer.[116]

World War I ended in 1918. A week after the Armistice, one might have observed a subtle but ominous change. What would be the attitude of the Negro troops when they returned from France? Rumors filled the air, and by the time the soldiers began to return, suspicion and fear had taken deep hold upon both races. Mob violence which had greatly declined during the war, burst out fresh. In city after city, race riots flamed up with casualities on both sides. The tension tightened everywhere and with dread suspense the nation awaited the outcome."[117]

POST WAR:

RACIAL CONFLICTS

Throughout America, the tensions of postwar readjustment flared into open violence. On the labor front and along the color line, there were deep-seated frustrations and latent suspicions. The South was particularly nervous about race relations and the place of the Negro. A large number of returning Negroes had elevated their aspirations and were determined to be treated as human beings. Their horizons had been widened through travel and they were not satisfied to occupy the same subordinate position in the total system of American life. Their thinking constituted a threat to the caste system of the South. In the North and South the attitude developed that Negroes must be kept in their place. And so interracial conflicts swept the country. The riots were not confined to any section of the country. They were northern and southern, eastern and western; wherever whites and Negroes lived together. The year of 1919 was one of almost unmitigated horror and tension. Violent and bloody race riots broke out in Washington, Chicago, Omaha, Philadelphia, Phillips County, Arkansas, and etc.

In the summer of 1919, the people of the United States witnessed the greatest racial strife that the nation had known. This most serious of the racial outbreaks occurred in Chicago on a hot day in late July; the result of an altercation at a bathing beach.

A young Negro swam across an imaginary line which was supposed to separate Negroes from whites. White swimmers commanded him to return to his part of the beach, and some threw stones at him. The Negro swimmer drowned and the Negroes declared that he had been murdered. When his body was recovered, it showed no marks of having been stoned. But it was too late to save the city from a riot that was already in progress. Distorted rumors were circulated among Negroes and whites concerning the incident and subsequent events at the beach. The fight which involved the police and white and colored crowds, set off six days of rioting.[118]

THE VOLSTEAD ACT AND
THE EIGHTEENTH AMENDMENT

The problems confronting the federal government in enforcing the Volstead Act were accentuated by the racial strife. The problems were serious enough without this added element. While the Volstead Act had been pending in Congress the dry leadership had committed two blunders which, together with congestion in the courts, eventually brought enforcement to the edge of disaster. It had permitted the lawmakers to set up the Prohibition Bureau in the Treasury Department, which did not want it, instead of the Department of Justice where it belonged; and to exempt the field agents of the bureau from the Civil Service. Supposedly, this left all appointments in the hands of the Commissioner of Internal Revenue; actually, they were handled through the Prohibition Commissioner and the state and city directors and administrators.[119]

When the Volstead Act became the law of the land in 1920, Congress had the power to pass an enforcement law. This law, the Eighteenth Amendment, prohibited the manufacture, transportation, and sale of intoxicating liquor and conferred upon Congress the power to enforce that prohibition by appropriate legislation. A large majority of the members of the Congress represented prohibition constituencies; it had the power, and it was its duty to take such action. Instead of using this opportunity to carry out the will of the people and bring the long struggle against the liquor traffic to a finish, Congress passed a weak and unenforceable law.[120]

Almost no one seemed to realize that the Amendment would be difficult to enforce. Certainly the first Prohibition Commissioner, John F. Kramer, displayed no doubts. "This law," he declared, "will be obeyed in cities large and small, and in villages, and where it is not obeyed it will be enforced . . . the law

37

says that liquor to be used as a beverage must not be manufactured. We shall see that it is not manufactured, nor sold, nor given away, nor hauled in anything on the surface of the earth or under the earth or in the air."[121]

THE CHAOS OF PROHIBITION

Efficient administration of the Prohibition law was just as essential as its enactment. The prophecies of Kramer and many other public figures were entirely wrong; the people immediately began to violate the law. Thousands of places in every major city began operating spots where alcoholic beverages could be purchased and the same situation existed in many rural areas. The illicit manufacture of alcoholic beverages sprang up all over the country.

The American people drank oceans of alcoholic beverages during the Prohibition era. This disregard and flaunting of the law was not confined to any social, economic, or racial group, but was widespread throughout the country. "The President, Attorney-General, cabinet members, senators, congressmen, and other government officials openly drank and served liquor that had reached them through smugglers, rum-runners, moonshiners, gangsters, and bootleggers. They associated with, and helped to enrich and make invincible the criminals of the underworld, whom it was their duty to put behind prison bars."[122] Rich and fashionable people summoned the criminal bootleggers to their homes, purchased their contraband liquor, and served it openly. They poured their millions into the hands of the smugglers, moonshiners, gangsters, and racketeers. They helped elect to office men who would protect these criminals and share their profits. The less affluent and ordinary citizens also had their sources of supply. Some of them had bootleggers of probity and some standing in the community who looked after the health of their clients as a matter of conscience and good business. "The poor man's cheerful, well-lit saloon had been shut down, and in its place was a dirty, murky speakeasy. The rich man still drank comfortably and unmolested in his club. The employee had to make do on rotgut and abide the consequences."[123]

There have been and continue to be many theories and conjectures relative to the causes responsible for the failure of the Volstead Act. The attempt to administer the Volstead Act with an enforcement agency composed largely of political appointees, and containing a large number of actual or potential criminals, resulted in corruption on a scale unparalleled in American history. Stories of dry agents escorting liquor trucks, protecting smugglers, and even helping them unload their cargoes, accepting bribes for information about raids, and in general conniving with illicit booze traffic, appeared in the newspapers day after day. At federal, state, and local levels alike, Prohibition became so soiled with graft and dirty politics that hyberbole becomes an understatement in attempting to describe it. "The failure of the enforcement of the Volstead Act was due to administrative stupidity, political graft, the federal structure of the United States, an antiquated legal system, and the flaws in the act itself."[124]

The moral collapse which followed in the wake of the Eighteenth Amendment and the First World War caused the almost complete breakdown of law enforcement throughout the United States. Criminals were able to take over the importation, manufacture, distribution and sale of illegal alcohol. The criminals and gangs, already organized for other purposes, required only a comparatively short time to perfect the setup of their new liquor departments, to establish sources of supply, and to secure their operations against undue interference. By the middle of the 1920's, by force of arms and through the payment of huge sums to politicians and officials, the gang chieftans had become virtually all-powerful. The corruption high and low, the favoritism, the bumbling, were not the worst aspects of Prohibition. What really upset the people was murder. "The guns of the law, it seemed, roared almost as loud as the 'gangland' backfire and fired more recklessly. Hundreds of men, even women and children, were killed, and the Prohibition Bureau did its best to minimize or suppress the evidence."[125]

No large city escaped the ravages of the gangs, but nowhere else did they attain such power as in Chicago. All the levels of Prohibition came to a head in the Illinois metropolis, and were symbolized by Al Capone. On January 17, 1920, the day after the passage of the Act, the impossible enforcement of Prohibition by competent men in this country was demonstrated in Chicago. Half a dozen masked men overpowered eight trainmen at a railroad switchyard and hijacked $100,000 worth of medicinal liquor from two freight cars. John H. Lyle, a man who lived through the long Chicago horror stated, "They were the pioneers, the advance guard of an army of scoundrels, chiselers, and killers, who were to murder, maim, corrupt and prosper as criminals have never prospered—throughout Prohibition's fourteen bloody and scandalous years."[126] There have always been lawbreakers in American life and probably always will be. Since the founding of this country, corruption of some government officials—city, county, state, and federal has been possible. "It is ironically true that the outburst of corruption and crime in Chicago in the nineteen-twenties was immediately occasioned by the attempts to banish the temptation of liquor from the American home."[127]

By the middle of the 1920's, discussion of Prohibition had become almost a national obsession; it overshadowed all other problems. The people talked of little else. By 1928, the argument over Prohibition had reached such intensity that it could no longer be kept out of presidential politics. Governor Alfred E. Smith of New York was accepted as the Democratic party nominee, despite his well-known wetness. He campaigned lustily for two modifications: first, an amendment to the Volstead Act, giving a scientific definition as to the content of intoxicating beverages; and second, an amendment to the Eighteenth Amendment. The latter proposal was to give to each individual state, only after approval by popular referendum, the right wholly within its borders to import, manufacture, and sell alcoholic beverages. The sales were to be made only by the state itself and not for consumption in any public place. The Republican candidate, Herbert Hoover, in reply, called "Prohibition, a great social and economic experiment, noble in motive and far-reaching in purpose."[128] Hoover did not claim nobility in its results. As he was elected over Governor Smith by an overwhelming vote, the advocates of Prohibition gained confidence.

The Prohibition era witnessed the revival of the Ku Klux Klan in the South and the organization of cells in the New England states, New York, Indiana, Illinois, Michigan and other northern and midwestern cities. The Klan, by taking the law into its own hands, stimulated much of the lawlessness and violence that characterized the postwar period. The activities and violence of the Klan members were aimed largely at Negroes, Catholics and Jews. The gangsters and violators of the Prohibition laws also contributed heavily to the killings and disorders during the 1920's. The paradox of the activities of the Klan and gangsters was that the former attempted to *enforce* the laws "Keeping Negroes in their place," and the latter *violated* the laws. Both ended by dispensing violence, hatred and the wrecking of government.

Herbert Hoover had done more than endorse the motives of the prohibitionists. He had promised a study of the enforcement problem by a governmental commission. One of President Hoover's first acts after he entered the White House was to appoint a National Commission on Law Observance and Enforcement, which had been authorized by Congress in the first deficiency appropriation of March 1929. The Commission was composed of 11 outstanding citizens representing several areas of interest. George W. Wickersham, former Attorney-General of the United States, was named Chairman.[129]

The body, known as the Wickersham Committee, after studying the problems of Prohibition enforcement for almost two years, made a final report to the President in January 1931. "The report of the Commission was a thorough and well-documented exposition of what was going on in the country . . . it was a great disappointment. The Wets insisted that it did not go far enough, and the Drys said it went entirely too far; the few neutral observers complained that it was so loaded with 'ifs, ands, and buts,' that it made very little sense."[130] The main conclusions by the majority of the Commission were that they opposed: (1) repeal of the Eighteenth Amendment; (2) restoration in any manner of the legalized saloon; (3) the federal or state governments going into the liquor business. The Commission conceded that few things were more easily made than alcohol. The majority of the members of the Commission were of the opinion that there was as yet no adequate observation of enforcement. Newton D. Baker, former Secretary of War, was the only member of the Commission favoring "the immediate repeal of the Eighteenth Amendment and the return of the whole question of liquor control to the states."[131]

No individual or group has been able to determine the amount of money derived from the alcohol industry during the Prohibition era. It was estimated that when Al Capone took it over in the 1920's, it was a going concern doing a gross business

41

of more than 70 million dollars a year.[132] When the other major
cities and the rural areas of the country were added to Capone's
intake in Chicago this represented a fantastic amount of money
involved in the business. The number of people who became
rich or wealthy during the absence of legal alcoholic beverages
is unknown; it is estimated, however, that the number was large.
Prohibition helped to provide funds for those engaged in the illicit manufacture, transportation and sale of alcoholic beverages
and for others to establish legitimate businesses.

THE NEGRO AND ILLICIT ALCOHOL

From all indications, the Negro's relationship to the illicit
liquor traffic was largely that of consumer, small manufacturer,
and seller. Because of the marginal position occupied by the
Negro in the economic system, he was unable to engage in the
alcoholic beverage business on as elaborate a scale as other
groups. The big profits in bootlegging did not come from a still
in the cellar or in the woods turning out a few gallons. If individuals or groups were to operate on a large scale, the following
were mandatory: access to considerable capital; a strong and
well-organized group with influential political connections—
federal, state, and local—to operate with protection; and knowledge of big business operation. The Negro was unable to meet
any of these requirements. In the North where the syndicate and
gangsters controlled liquor and other rackets, Negroes were left
out except for small quantities for retail purposes. In practically
all of the urban areas of the country, organized crime was largely
controlled by groups of Italians, Sicilians, Irish and Jews. In the
South, Negroes were sometimes employed by whites to manufacture or distill whiskey on a large scale. Usually these whites
had political connections and could protect the Negroes. Occasionally Negroes and whites joined in partnership to make
whiskey.[133]

In a rural community in eastern North Carolina, almost
wholly inhabited by Negroes, "rather than attempt to earn a
living by farming the poor land, practically the entire Negro population, years ago, turned to the manufacture of liquor as an accepted source of livelihood . . . The chief considerations in bootlegging are not matters of conscience, but the economics of ob-
taining adequate materials and sales."[134] Women, to supplement

42

the family income, quite frequently engaged in selling "nips or shots," of white or corn whiskey at 25¢ to $1.00. As a rule, the profits derived were meager. Often the amount of money spent by Negroes to purchase whiskey for consumption exceeded the amount earned from the sale or transportation of it.

Profitable employment opportunities were made available to Negro musicians and entertainers in some of the business establishments selling alcoholic beverages and engaging in prostitution. Although this situation existed in many cities, it was especially widespread in Chicago. A number of Negro entertainers and musicians earned large salaries and many of them, later, became nationally and internationally famous in their fields. The Chicago musicians largely played "jazz," a type of music indigenous to New Orleans. Jazz was brought to Chicago in 1918 with the arrival of King Joe Oliver, the renowned cornet player from New Orleans. The end of Prohibition was responsible for a decrease in employment opportunities in places of entertainment; and especially in the case of Negro musicians and entertainers. As the Depression worsened, there was an exodus of jazz-playing musicians from Chicago to New York and Hollywood.[135]

THE DEPRESSION

Then came Tuesday, October 29, 1929, and the Stock Market crash which resulted in the total collapse of the economic machinery and institutions of the United States. The impact of what was to be our severest and largest economic Depression upon daily life could be observed everywhere. The panic had written finis to a chapter of American economic history.[136] As the Depression wore on and unemployment increased, the people became desperate. They began to realize "the days had passed when men who lost their jobs could take their working tools elsewhere and contrive an independent living, or cultivate a garden patch . . . or go West and begin again on the frontier."[137] When they lost their jobs they were helpless. Desperately, they turned for aid to the only agency responsible to them for correcting the wrongs done to them by a blindly operating economic society. They turned to the government.

The Depression had a far-reaching impact on Prohibition and was perhaps the straw which broke the camel's back. The

43

Wets exploited this national disaster to the utmost. The Prohibition laws were being flaunted more generally and openly than ever before; even in what had formerly been comparatively sober puritanical communities. With the Depression there seemed to be a collapse of public morals. There was much drunkenness and an increase in women's drinking. In the fall of 1930, in Washington, D. C., a bootlegger was discovered selling his wares in the austere precincts of the Senate Office Building. The open sale of whiskey in New York provided an example of the total disregard of the enforcement of the Prohibition laws. In this city, by 1931, "enforcement had become such a mockery that the choice of those who wanted a drink was no longer simply going to a speakeasy or calling up a bootlegger; there were cordial and beverage shops, doing an open retail business; their only concession to appearance was that bottles were not ordinarily displayed."[138]

In the summer of 1932 the two major political parties held their conventions in Chicago. The Republicans nominated incumbent President Herbert Hoover. For their standard-bearer the Democrats selected Franklin D. Roosevelt, former Governor of the State of New York. Among the major issues confronting the people of the country at this time was Prohibition. The Republicans adopted a moist plank, which asked for resubmission of the Eighteenth Amendment to the states. The Democratic plank demanded outright repeal of Prohibition. Roosevelt won a landslide victory over Hoover.

THE NEW DEAL

President Roosevelt took the axe to Prohibition as soon as he entered the White House. Nine days after his Inauguration the President requested Congress to permit the manufacture and sale of beer with an alcoholic content of not more than 3.2 percent. Congress immediately did so, and the law became effective on April 7, 1933. A resolution was introduced into Congress to submit the Twenty-first Amendment (repealing the Eighteenth) to state conventions. The resolution passed the Senate on February 17, 1933; the House concurred three days later, on February 20th. "At thirty-three and a half minutes past three (Mountain Time) in the afternoon of the 5th of December, 1933, Utah became the 36th State to ratify the Twenty-first Amendment to

the Constitution, repealing the Prohibition Amendment."[139]   The
President declared Prohibition at an end after a reign of 14 years.

REPEAL

Many reasons have been given for the repeal of Prohibition.
In recent years there have been studies projecting the point of
view that Prohibition was related to cultural conflicts, a struggle
for status between white Anglo-Saxon Protestants and other ethnic
and religious groups.   An increasing number of social scientists
hold that "the Depression had enormously strengthened the demand for increased employment and tax revenues which a re-
opened beer and liquor industry would bring and it made issues
of status secondary to economics and class issues."[140]

Some of the states recovered a lucrative source of revenue
with the repeal of national Prohibition.   After a few years, high
taxes were imposed on alcoholic beverages by federal and state
authorities avid for funds.   These practices so raised the price
of the legal article that a considerable illicit traffic still persisted.
Some states outlawed bars and saloons in favor of bottle sales by
special shops, drugstores, or grocery stores.   "The public serving
of liquor became the role of cocktail lounges, beer gardens, nightclubs and restaurants, where sitting rather than standing, eating
as well as imbibing, and the presence of both sexes brought at
least overt changes in American drinking habits.[141]

THE NEGRO

Although there had been some slight improvement in the
social and economic status of the Negro prior to the Depression,
the situation of the masses continued to be precarious or disadvantaged.   When the Depression arrived, many Negroes lost
their jobs.   "The Depression hit the North worse than the South,
nevertheless, Negroes continued to go North to such an extent
that the relative increase in the Negro urban population was
even greater in the North than in the South. . . Negroes continued
to go North whether or not there were any employment openings
for them there."[142]   The general social conditions in the North
were better.   Negroes found less segregation, greater legal security, superior educational and hospital facilities, and higher earnings if any jobs were to be found.   "The North also offered much

45

more in public relief to Negroes in economic distress than the South. This fact was undoubtedly behind much of the Negro migration to the North during the thirties."[143]

Negroes were struck harder by the great Depression than the whites. They lost their jobs in greater numbers in the cities. Many of those who retained employment, especially in agriculture, were driven down to starvation wages.

Between 1930 and 1933, there was utter distress and pessimism among Negroes throughout the country. By the late 1930's, conditions were better. There had been no race riots for several years; lynchings had reached a new low. But there had been little or no significant improvement in the social and economic positions of the Negro on any front. In the South, the Negro's opportunity to vote was still greatly restricted; he was not able to use public facilities available to whites; he was refused equal economic opportunities, and he was constantly made to feel inferior. If he migrated to the North, more often than not he ended up in an urban ghetto. In the North, he could vote, ride on non-segregated buses and trains, and send his children to non-segregated schools. But he lived in a slum and could work only at the most menial tasks. He remained a social inferior, for he was forbidden access to most hotels, restaurants, cocktail lounges and bars except as a servant. He was, in effect, forbidden to expand his opportunities beyond the limits set for him by the white majority.[144]

The repeal of the Eighteenth Amendment did very little to improve the economic position of Negroes. They were still unable to "break through" to the higher levels of employment in the liquor industry. They continued to be employed in unskilled and low-paying jobs in the manufacture, distribution and sale of alcoholic beverages. Negroes did not own or control any distillries or breweries, nor hold franchises for the importing of whiskies, wines or malts. It was not until the 1950's and 1960's that there was any appreciable improvement in the Negro's employment status in the alcoholic beverage industry.

The New Deal, at the same time, however, marked a turning point in the history of the American Negro. Northern Negroes were permitted to participate on an equal basis in the various federal relief and work programs. They also acquired a new sense of their political power. Although there was considerable discrimination against Negroes in the local administration of New Deal measures in the South, the New Deal made a lasting improvement in southern racial practices. The philosophy of the New Deal was profoundly antagonistic to the racist assumptions of many people of this country.[145]

WORLD WAR II

The World War II years (1941-1945) provided Negroes with greater and more diverse economic opportunities than they had ever enjoyed in the past. In the armed forces, a few Negroes were permitted to obtain a measure of equality. The progress of the Negro in the postwar years occurred in a period of unprecedented prosperity. The need and scarcity of labor opened up new jobs for the Negro and increased his pay. He was brought into association with white society in a way that had been denied him in the past. The Negro's increased purchasing power provided him with an economic weapon that American business firms increasingly acknowledged and respected. White businessmen were forced, however reluctantly, to learn that it was good business to sell to, and to employ Negroes.

As in past wars, there was considerable drinking by members of the armed forces at home and abroad as well as by the civilian population. The supply of alcoholic beverages, especially whiskey, was greatly limited during World War II. The bulk of the malts and grains used for the manufacture of beverages was converted to the war effort and related purposes. In some states, North Carolina for example, whiskey was rationed in the same way as some other products in short supply such as meats, sugar, and tires.

THE KOREAN WAR

The intervention of the United States in the Korean War, June 27, 1950, served as a constant reminder to all Americans of their country's new role in world affairs. The fighting of the war was complicated by the injection of the color issue which Northern Koreans (Communists) exploited. Their propaganda pamphlets emphasized things like: "Today under the orders of a Southern President, United States planes are bombing and strafing colored people in Korea."[146] The Korean War was significant because a

47

large number of American Negroes sympathized with the people of Asian countries. Although discrimination against Negroes and other minority groups in America was decreasing, it was obvious that America could not win the Asiatic mind while discriminating against colored people at home. One result of the growing awareness of this fact was the deliberate shift to new regulations abroad and new customs at home. So it was that significant gains in the Negro's status in the army and on the homefront came about as a result of the Korean conflict.

Shortly before the election of 1948, President Truman issued an Executive Order, declaring it to be "the policy of the President that there shall be equality of treatment and opportunity for all persons in the armed services . . . This policy shall be put into effect as rapidly as possible, having due regard to the time required to effectuate any necessary changes without impairing efficiency or morale."[147] In January 1950, the Secretary of the Army, Gordon Gray, issued a supplementary policy statement, reiterating the President's general position. When the Korean War began, the Air Force was largely integrated, but segregation was the general pattern in the Army, Navy, and Marine Corps. On the homefront, treating whites and Negroes separately during the training period was enormously slowing down the war effort. The Commanding General at Fort Jackson, South Carolina, issued a verbal order that the next draftees to arrive were to be put in a platoon in the order of their arrival. This ended segregation at Fort Jackson.[148]

The Army had wielded the greatest of all powers—the power of example. It had shown that racial barriers could be removed without causing disruption and with a marked increase in the efficient use of human beings. Integration was speeded up in the Navy and Marine Corps as a result of the Army's move. This spilled over into many parts of American life. Integration in the armed forces affected non-military situations North and South. Many churches, USO clubs, cafes, and taxicabs began voluntarily to admit Negroes on an equal or near equal basis. Military pressure was also used to change local racial practices. In a northern Army Post, the Provost Marshall ended *Jim Crow* in a nearby tavern by informing the owner that his cafe would be declared off limits unless all soldiers were served.[149]

CIVIL RIGHTS

Between 1952 and 1960, during the two terms of President Dwight D. Eisenhower, the Korean War ended and substantial gains in civil rights were made by the American Negro. The efforts of the Administration on behalf of the Negro were overshadowed by a series of historic Supreme Court decisions on civil rights. On May 17, 1954, the Supreme Court, in an unanimous decision ruled that racial segregation in public schools was unconstitutional in that it denied citizens equal protection of the law.

The Supreme Court did more than any other branch of government to destroy the barriers erected by racial prejudice. Congress also contributed to greater equality for minority groups. In 1957, for the first time in 82 years, it enacted a measure designed to protect the voting rights of the Negro. This act established a Commission on Civil Rights. It was an important act in beginning to redress voting inequities. In 1960, Congress passed another Civil Rights Act which provided the authority for federal judges to appoint voting referees to hear the applications of persons claiming they had been denied the right to register and vote by state election officials.[150]

ALCOHOL STILL A THORNY PROBLEM

As the Negro's place in society continued to receive considerable public attention, the liquor issue also continued to be a thorny one. In May 1950, Congress appointed a Special Committee to Investigate Organized Crime in Inter-state Commerce. Senator Estes Kefauver of Tennessee was appointed Chairman of this Committee. The findings revealed that organized criminal groups operating in inter-state commerce were entrenched in our larger cities. They were engaged in the operation of gambling enterprises, the distribution of narcotics, and prostitution. Many of these racketeers were survivors of the Prohibition era. After the repeal of the Prohibition laws, these groups and syndicates had shifted their major criminal activities to other enterprises or operations. The Committee discovered that many of the nation's leading hoodlums had started as bootleggers during Prohibition. The transition from bootlegging to the legitimate liquor business had not been too difficult. Many of these hoodlums had penetrated the distribution end of the liquor business. In March 1951, the Committee held a hearing with revenue and liquor commissioners from the majority of the southern states. These liquor commissioners presented a sordid story of a huge bootlegging operation extending into the South out of Cairo, Illinois. With its highjacking trucks, camouflaging liquor shipments, counterfeiting, and corruption of public officials, this bootlegging operation reminded many of the 1920's.[151]

The sale and use of alcoholic beverages and the place of the Negro in American society continue as areas of controversy in the 1960's. The Director of the Institute of Scientific Studies for the Prevention of Alcoholism in the United States, addressing an audience at American University, August 1961, stated that "almost half of the population of the United States is affected by alcoholics and problem drinkers . . . An alcoholic is usually estimated to affect seven people, members of the family and immediate friends. With nine million alcoholics and problem drinkers in the nation, you have involved about half of the people of the United States."[152] In October 1963, in one of the largest cities in the country, it was pointed out that the underworld was draining millions of dollars in profits from the beer taps and liquor bottles of New York bars and nightclubs and from wholesale liquor trade across the nation.[153]

One of the most colorful and publicized events of 1963 was the Civil Rights Protest March on Washington. *The New York Times* reported in the headlines of its August 29, 1963 edition that, "200,000 Negroes Marched for Civil Rights in Orderly Washington Rally." This "march" did not come full-blown upon the scene, its seeds had been sown two decades earlier. These seeds were nurtured and refertilized by the continued segregation and discrimination of Negroes in all areas of public life. In 1941, Negro workers led by A. Phillip Randolph, threatened to march on Washington to protest discrimination in industries receiving government contracts. The "march" was cancelled when the President of the United States issued an Executive Order which forbade discrimination in industries with government contracts and which established a Fair Employment Practices Committee. The threatened "march" of 1941 was primarily concerned with the employment of Negroes. The major goals of the 1963 marchers were much more comprehensive and they had implications for nearly all people of this nation. One year after President Kennedy sent a comprehensive Civil Rights Bill to Congress, it passed the United States Senate. The Bill had passed the House of Representatives in March 1964. After the Amendments to the Bill had been accepted by both branches of Congress, it was sent to the White House for the President's signature. On Friday, July 2, 1964, President Lyndon Johnson signed the Civil Rights Act of 1964.

From 1619, when the first 20 Negroes landed at Jamestown, Virginia, to 1964, is a relatively short period of time in the history of civilization. Since the founding of this country, its people have witnessed and participated in many of the far-reaching and revolutionary events in the world's history. From the earliest settling of the country, they have been confronted with problems and issues of great magnitude and complexity. They have been forced to make decisions about some issues which continue to perplex present-day society.

Among the major issues confronting the people for over 300 years have been the control of alcoholic beverages and the legal status of the Negro. In 1619, it was necessary for Colonial Virginia to pass an act aimed at controlling the excessive use of alcoholic beverages. Although the Negro had been in Virginia since 1619, it was not until the 1660's that a decision determining his legal position was made. He was to be enslaved and denied the rights of other men. The decisions, laws, practices and policies made concerning these two issues had and continue to have a far-reaching influence and impact upon our social, economic, political, and religious institutions. From all indications, future generations will have to wrestle with both of these issues, and they will continue to create problems and conflicts. Over the years, the excessive use of alcoholic beverages has tended to decline as a major issue, but not as a problem. The race issue has increasingly created more conflicts and generated considerable violence. The people of this country have been reluctant, and at times have refused to come to grips with these issues. Many are hoping that the Civil Rights Act of 1964 will reduce the friction and hostility inherent in the issue. There are others who are aware of the grave danger of trying to introduce so sweeping a social change by the cold, hard force of law.

1 Ernest Cherrington, *The Evolution of Prohibition in the United States of America* (Westerville, Ohio: The American Press, 1920), pp. 9, 16.

2 *Ibid.*, p. 17.

3 Thomas Spitler, "The Use and Mis-Use of Alcohol," *Inventory*, 13 (July-August 1963) p. 14.

4 *Ibid.*, p. 15.

5 Foster Rhea Dulles, *America Learns to Play* (New York: Appelton-Century Co., 1940), p. 16.

6 Gerald Carson, *The Social History of Bourbon* (New York: Dodd, Mead, & Co., 1963), p. 4.

7 John Allen Krout, *The Origins of Prohibition* (New York: Alfred A. Knopf, 1925), p. 39.

8 *Ibid.*, p. 41.

9 Carson, *op. cit.*, p. 4.

10 Cherrington, *op. cit.*, pp. 10-11.

11 Stanley M. Elkins, *Slavery: A Problem in American Institutional and Intellectual Life* (Chicago: University of Chicago Press, 1959), p. 38.

12 John Codman Hurd, *The Law of Freedom and Bondage in the United States* (Boston: Little, Brown, & Co., 1862), Vol. 2, p. 18.

13 Quoted in Stanley M. Elkins, *op. cit.*, p. 40.

14 Eric Williams, *Capitalism and Slavery* (Chapel Hill: The University of North Carolina Press, 1961), p. 19.

15 John Hope Franklin, *From Slavery to Freedom* (New York: Alfred A. Knopf, 1947), p. 71.

16 Lorenzo Johnston Greene, *The Negro in Colonial New England* (New York: Columbia University Press, 1942), pp. 24-25.

17 Williams, *op. cit.*, pp. 51-52.

18 Kenneth Allsop, *The Bootleggers and Their Era* (New York: Doubleday & Co., 1961), p. 25.

19 Hurd, *op. cit.*, Vol. 2 , pp. 1-30.

20 Jeffrey Brackett, *The Negro in Maryland: A Study of the Institution of Slavery* (Baltimore: The Johns Hopkins Press, 1889), pp. 102-103.

21 *Ibid.*, p. 102.

22 *Ibid.*, p. 103; and James M. Wright, *The Free Negro in Maryland: 1634-1860* (New York: Columbia University Press, 1921), pp. 102-103.

23 Franklin, *From Slavery to Freedom*, p. 76.

24 Ulrich B. Phillips, *American Negro Slavery* (New York: D. Appelton & Co., 1936), pp. 492-493; and H. M. Henry, *The Police Control of the Slave in South Carolina* (Emory, Virginia: Emory and Henry College, 1914), pp. 32-33.

25 Daniel J. Whitener, *Prohibition in North Carolina, 1715-1945* (Chapel Hill: The University of North Carolina Press, 1945), pp. 7, 39.

26 Ralph Betts Flanders, *Plantation Slavery in Georgia* (Chapel Hill: The University of North Carolina Press, 1945), pp. 7, 39.

27 *Ibid.*, pp. 6-11.

28 *Ibid.*, pp. 24-25.

29 Henry Scofield Cooley, *A Study of Slavery in New Jersey* (Baltimore: The Johns Hopkins Press, 1896), p. 36.

30 Edwin Vernon Morgan, "Slavery in New York: The Status of the Slave Under the English Colonial Government," in *American Historical Association Papers* (New York, 1891), Vol. 5, Part 4, pp. 335-350.

31 *Ibid.*, pp. 335-350.

32 Edward Raymond Turner, *The Negro in Pennsylvania: 1639-1861* (Washington, D. C.: The American Historical Association, 1911), p. 32.

33 Franklin, *From Slavery to Freedom*, p. 97.

34 Greene, *op. cit.*, pp. 17-18.

35 *Ibid.*, p. 125.

36 *Ibid.*, p. 135, and Bernard C. Steiner, *A History of Slavery in Connecticut* (Baltimore: The Johns Hopkins Press, 1893), pp. 12, 78.

37 Eben Greenbough Scott, *Reconstruction During the Civil War in the United States* (New York: Columbia University Press, 1895), p. 15.

38 Leon F. Litwack, *North of Slavery: The Negro in the Free States, 1790-1860* (Chicago: University of Chicago Press, 1961) p. 3.
39 *Ibid.,* p. 3.
40 Harold Underwood Faulkner, *American Political and Social History* (7th ed.; New York: Appelton-Century-Crofts, 1957), p. 141, and Litwack, *op. cit.,* p. 3.
41 Clarence H. Patrick, *Alcohol, Culture, and Society* (Durham: Duke University Press, 1952), p. 35.
42 Cherrington, *op. cit.,* p. 3.
43 Faulkner, *op. cit.,* pp. 152-153.
44 Barnett Hollander, *Slavery in America* (New York: Barnes & Noble, 1963), p. 33.
45 *Ibid.,* p. 34; Carson, *op. cit.,* p. 16; and Faulkner, *op. cit.,* p. 167.
46 Hollander, *op. cit.,* p. 34.
47 *Ibid.,* p. 35.
48 *Freedom to the Free: 1863 Century of Emancipation 1963,* A report to the President of the United States Civil Rights Commission (Washington, D. C.: United States Government Printing Office, 1963), pp. 14-15; Hollander, *op. cit.,* pp. 16-17, and Litwack, *op. cit.,* p. 14.
49 Hurd, *op. cit.,* Vol. 2, pp. 18, 171, 173.
50 Chase C. Mooney, *Slavery in Tennessee* (Bloomington: Indiana University Press, 1957), pp. 7-8.
51 *Ibid.,* pp. 14-15.
52 *Ibid.,* p. 15.
53 Hurd, *op. cit.,* Vol. 2, pp. 116, 127, 132, 136, 196, 202.
54 E. Bonner, *History of Louisiana* (New York: Harper & Bros., 1843), pp. 185-186.
55 Joe Gray Taylor, *Negro Slavery in Louisiana* (Baton Rouge: Louisiana Historical Association, 1963), pp. 126-127, 205, 235.
56 *Ibid.*
57 Charles S. Sydnor, *Slavery in Mississippi* (New York: Appelton-Century Co. 1933), p. 50.
58 *Ibid.,* p. 80.
59 James Benson Sellers, *Slavery in Alabama* (Tusaloosa: University of Alabama Press, 1950), pp. 3, 11, 15, 24.
60 *Ibid.,* p. 363.
61 *Ibid.,* p. 234.
62 *Freedom to the Free, op. cit.,* pp. 14-16.
63 Harrison Anthony Trexler, *Slavery in Missouri* (Baltimore: The Johns Hopkins Press, 1904), pp. 66-68.
64 Hurd, *op. cit.,* Vol. 2, pp. 171-173.
65 George R. Fairbanks, *History of Florida* (Philadelphia: J. B. Lippincott Co., 1871), p. vii.
66 *Ibid.,* p. 166.
67 Hubert Brown Fuller, *The Purchase of Florida* (Cleveland, Ohio: Burrows Bros., & Co., 1906), pp. 41, 228.
68 Fairbanks, *op. cit.,* pp. 276-277.
69 Lewis J. Wortham, *A Story of Texas* (Fort Worth, Texas: Wortham-Molyneaux Co., 1924), pp. 1, 16.
70 William Ranson Hogan, *The Texas Republic* (Norman: University of Oklahoma Press, 1946), pp. 21-24.
71 *Ibid.,* pp. 23, 39, 40, 43.
72 *Ibid.,* pp. 39-40
73 Joseph R. Gusfield, *Symbolic Crusade* (Urbana: The University of Illinois Press, 1963), pp. 6, 52-54.
74 Franklin, *From Slavery to Freedom,* p. 261.
75 Cherrington, *op. cit.,* p. 140.
76 Faulkner, *op. cit.,* p. 407.
77 James Truslow Adams, *History of the U. S.* (New York: Charles Scribner's Sons, 1933), Vol. 3, p. 26.
78 Carson, *op. cit.,* p. 71.

79 *Ibid.*, pp. 74-76.
80 William M. Robinson, "Prohibition in the Confederacy," *The American Historical Review, 37 (1931-32)*, pp. 50-58.
81 Bell Irvin Wiley, *Southern Negroes: 1861-1865* (New Haven: Yale University Press, 1938), pp. 41-42.
82 Peter Joseph Hamilton, *The History of America: The Reconstruction Period* (Philadelphia: G. Barrier & Sons, 1905), Vol. 16, p. 35.
83 John Hope Franklin, *Reconstruction: After the Civil War* (Chicago: University of Chicago Press, 1961), p. 3.
84 E. Merton Coulter, *The South During Reconstruction, 1865-1877* (Baton Rouge: Louisiana State University Press, 1947), p. 336.
85 Vernon Lane Wharton, *The Negro in Mississippi, 1865-1890* (Chapel Hill: The University of North Carolina Press, 1947), pp. 128, 235.
86 Whitener, *op cit.*, p. 57.
87 Charles Stearns, *The Black Man of the South and the Rebels* (New York: The American News Co., Boston, 1872), p. 334.
88 Alrutheus Ambush Taylor, *The Negro in Tennessee, 1865-1880* (Washington, D. C.: The Associated Publishers, 1941), p. 40.
89 William Watson Davis, *The Civil War and Reconstruction in Florida* (New York: Columbia University Press, 1913), pp. 557, 601-602.
90 *Freedom to the Free, op. cit.*, pp. 465-467.
91 Faulkner, *op. cit.*, pp. 465-467.
92 Charles S. Mangum, Jr., *The Legal Status of the Negro* (Chapel Hill: The University of North Carolina Press, 1940), p. 28.
93 *Ibid.*, p. 28.
94 Ella Lonn, *Reconstruction in Louisiana After 1868* (New York: G. P. Putnam's Sons, 1918), pp. 518-519.
95 C. Vann Woodward, *The Strange Career of Jim Crow* (New York: Oxford University Press, 1955), pp. 6-8.
96 Mangum, *op. cit.*, pp. 54-55.
97 Elkins, *op. cit.*, p. 13.
98 Harry J. Carman, Harold C. Syrett, and Bernard W. Wishy, *A History of the American People Since 1862* (New York: Alfred A. Knopf, 1961), Vol. 2, p. 412.
99 Gusfield, *op. cit.*, p. 99.
100 Franklin, *From Slavery to Freedom*, p. 432.
101 E. Franklin Frazier, *The Negro in the United States* (New York: The Macmillan Co., 1949), pp. 163-164.
102 Franklin, *From Slavery to Freedom*, pp. 434-436. The status of lynching is the concern of Arthur Raper, *The Tragedy of Lynching* (Chapel Hill: The University of North Carolina Press, 1933).
103 Cherrington, *op. cit.*, p. 255-256.
104 Andrew Sinclair, *Prohibition: The Era of Excess* (Boston: Little, Brown, & Co., 1962), p. 29.
105 James H. Timberlake, *Prohibition and The Progressive Movement, 1900-1920* (Cambridge: Harvard University Press, 1963), p. 120.
106 *Ibid.*, p. 120.
107 Gusfield, *op. cit.*, p. 105.
108 Cherrington, *op. cit.*, p. 286.
109 Henry Lee, *How Dry We Were* (Englewood Cliffs, New Jersey: Prentice-Hall, 1963), pp. 2-3.
110 *Ibid.*, p. 3.
111 Herbert Asbury, *The Great Illusion* (New York: Doubleday & Co., 1950), p. 144.
112 Louise Venable Kennedy, *The Negro Peasant Turns Cityward* (New York: Columbia University Press, 1930), p. 9.
113 Gunnar Myrdal, *An American Dilemma* (New York: Harper & Row, 1944), p. 745.
114 Franklin, *From Slavery to Freedom*, p. 451.
115 Walter White, *A Man Called White* (New York: The Viking Press, 1948), pp. 102-103, and Franklin, *From Slavery to Freedom*, p. 452.

54

116 Myrdal, *op. cit.*, p. 1309.
117 "The Interracial Commission Comes of Age", leaflet printed by the Interracial Commission (Atlanta, Georgia: February 1942).
118 St. Clair Drake and Horace R. Cayton, *Black Metropolis* (New York: Harcourt, Brace & Co., 1945), pp. 65-67.
119 Asbury, *op. cit.*, p. 174.
120 Fletcher Dobyns, *The Amazing Story of Repeal* (Chicago and New York: Willet, Clark & Co., 1940), p. 265.
121 Frederick Lewis Allen, *Only Yesterday* (New York: Bantam Books, 1959), p. 174.
122 Dobyns, *op. cit.*, p. 330.
123 Lee, *op. cit.*, p. 91.
124 Sinclair, *op. cit.*, p. 182.
125 Lee, *op. cit.*, p. 167.
126 John H. Lyle, *The Dry and Lawless Years* (Englewood Cliffs, New Jersery: Prentice-Hall, 1960), p. 39.
127 Allen, *Only Yesterday*, p. 187.
128 *Ibid.*, p. 18.
129 *Ibid.*, p. 182; Asbury, *op. cit.*, p. 326; and Dobyns, *op. cit.*, pp. 351-353.
130 Asbury, *op. cit.*, p. 328.
131 *Ibid.*, p. 328; Sinclair, *op. cit.*, p. 184; and Dobyns, *op. cit.*, chap. 10.
132 Asbury, *op. cit.*, p. 293.
133 This information was received from the following sources: newspaper articles; interviews with a number of Negroes arrested for violating prohibition laws; and police records.
134 Sanford Winston and Mosette Butler, "Negro Bootleggers in Eastern North Carolina," *American Sociological Review* (December 1943), pp. 692-697.
135 Allsop, *op. cit.*, pp. 181-190.
136 Dixon Wecter, *The Age of the Great Depression* (New York: The Macmillan Co., 1948), p. 24.
137 Frederick Lewis Allen, *Since Yesterday* (New York: Bantam Books, 1961), p. 42.
138 *Ibid.*, p. 25.
139 Allen, *Since Yesterday*, p. 113.
140 Gusfield, *op. cit.*, p. 127.
141 Wecter, *op. cit.*, p. 94.
142 Myrdal, *op. cit.*, p. 295.
143 *Ibid.*, p. 295.
144 Carman, Syrett, and Wishy, *op. cit.*, p. 767.
145 Myrdal, *op. cit.*, p. 463, and Sinclair, *op. cit.*, p. 405.
146 Eric F. Goldman, *The Crucial Decade* (New York: Alfred A. Knopf, 1956), p. 176.
147 *Ibid.*, p. 183.
148 *Ibid.*, p. 183.
149 *Ibid.*, pp. 184-185.
150 Harry Golden, *Mr. Kennedy and the Negroes* (New York: The World Publishing Co., 1964), pp. 136-137.
151 *The Kefauver Committee Report on Organized Crime* (New York: ARCO Publishing Co., 1951), pp. 153-155, and *Senate Report 307, 82nd Congress, 1st Session* (Washington, D. C.: U. S. Government Printing Office).
152 From an account of a speech delivered by Dr. Winston H. Beaver, in the *Raleigh Times*, August 1, 1961.
153 *The New York Times*, Wednesday, October 23, 1963.

DARK LAUGHTER

By OLLIE HARRINGTON

Courtesy The Pittsburgh Courier

"It's real nice to see Brother Bootsie's smilin' face amongst us again ... BUT ... sisters, remember that old Satan's got all kinds of smooth ways to really mess up a congregation!"

RELIGION—ALCOHOL AND THE NEGRO

CHAPTER TWO

Religion—Alcohol
and the Negro

CHAPTER TWO

RELIGION—ALCOHOL AND THE NEGRO

THE colonists who came to these shores from the time of the founding of Jamestown, Virginia, in 1607, were largely of English and Scottish stock, augmented by a number of Dutch, Swedish, German, and Irish. They were predominately Protestant and gave a Protestant direction to American religious life from the very beginning. A group of English settlers, the Puritans, were dissatisfied with the newly established Church of England. The beginning of Protestantism and the colonization of America were contemporaneous events. The American colonies were settled at a turbulent period in the history of England; there was considerable unrest in every area of life. Revolutions in politics and religion were in progress at the very time American colonization was underway. The old political faith as well as the ecclesiastical establishments were under attack from every quarter. The parliamentary party opposed the *Divine Right of Kings* and contested also the *Divine Right of Bishops*[1] Many of the first American colonists were dissenters from the established Church of England.

The early settlers were first preoccupied with economic problems. Another major concern was the preservation of their wonted way of life; above all, the transplanting of their churches. Back home, the church had been for most of them, the meaningful center of life. As soon as they landed in the New World, they began to re-establish their churches.[2] Many of the colonists came to America as religious non-conformists. They were excluded from the orthodox or accepted religious bodies and persecuted in their homeland. Religious intolerance appeared early in the colonies. In New England, the Puritans sought to establish a national church in which membership was limited to the converted who could give satisfactory evidence of their conversion in terms of experimental religion. Those who dissented were persecuted and exiled.

There were conflicts in the colonies between religious denominations—Catholics, Protestants, and Jews. Catholics did not have an easy time in Colonial America. Their church was proscribed in most of the colonies and actively persecuted in some. Only in Maryland, Pennsylvania, New York, and Rhode Island were they tolerated. During the latter part of the eighteenth century there was some relaxation of hostile feeling toward them, but there was no real relief until the Revolution and the Constitution assured them a secure and equal status under the federal government. For nearly a century, there was a struggle between the Protestants and Catholics. The treatment accorded Jews, in the Colonial era, was similar to that of Catholics, and at times, more severe. From the very beginning, when American Jewry first established itself in this country as an ethnic immigrant group, they were treated with disdain and at times persecuted. This anti-Semitism has continued until the present in some sections of the country. After considerable hardship and struggle, Judaism achieved its status in the *American Way of Life* as one of the three major "religions of democracy."[3]

The history of the church and religious movements in the United States fall outside the purpose of this chapter. A brief discussion of their European background and early American history were presented to throw some light on the problems and issues confronted by the colonists as they attempted to transplant their churches and religious faiths to this country. Religion has played and continues to play an important part in American social and cultural development. The excessive use of alcohol and the status of the Negro, especially slaves, became the concern of all the major religious denominations. Although there were other issues, it is possible that these two issues have exerted as much influence and had as great an impact upon religion and the activities of the church as any others in the history of American society. As early as 1630, when John Winthrop arrived with 700 Puritan settlers, he recorded in his Journal concern about the excessive use of alcoholic beverages. The Puritans passed laws forbidding nearly everything that gave people pleasure except liquor. Many of the Puritans were hard drinkers, as well as the first distillers of rum in this country.[4] From the time the Negroes were enslaved some of the church members were concerned with their status. The first protest against slavery was made by the Quakers in 1688. Later, they were

59

joined by other religious denominations. The most important and far-reaching schisms in the American churches were caused by Negro slavery, and the effects of that bitter contest are still with us.

COLONIAL DAYS

In the early Colonial period, the clergymen and church members did not frown upon or discourage the moderate use of alcoholic beverages. At ordinations and other religious ceremonies alcoholic beverages were served. Large quantities of liquor were consumed at funerals. In 1678, at the funeral of a preacher's widow in Boston, the mourners drank 51 half-gallons of malaga wine. In Virginia, it took 4,000 pounds of tobacco to pay the liquor bill of a single funeral. The cost of liquid refreshments was paid by the family of the dead person but if the deceased was a pauper the town or village defrayed the expenses. The custom of drinking at funerals began to decline in the early part of the eighteenth century, and by 1750 it had virtually disappeared.[5]

The preacher in Colonial times found himself in an unusual position regarding the use of alcoholic beverages. He could scarcely have remained temperate and performed satisfactorily the duties of his office. The clergyman was a man of great importance in the community; to offer him a drink was to show respect and esteem. If he refused it, he was looked upon as a hypocrite, and the donor felt insulted, or at least slighted. If he consistently abstained, he was believed to hold unsound views about everything else, and he was lucky to retain his pastorate. If he could not hold his liquor, he was a weakling and not a true man of God. When the preacher entered a store or business office, he was called upon to respond to as many toasts as there were men present. Upon calling on a member of his church, the gratified householder met him at the door with a mug of an alcoholic beverage. He was served drinks almost continuously during his visit, and on departure he was expected to quaff a good-by cup. Irrespective of the number of calls he made during the day, the preacher went through or tried to go through the same procedure. In this period, many of the preachers were continually in a state of befuddlement.[6] Although clergymen were encouraged to drink, their excessive use of alcoholic bever-

60

ages was frowned upon. In order to discourage drunkenness among the preachers, a law was enacted in Virginia in 1676. Ministers who became drunk were fined one-half year's salary for the first and second offense, and stripped of every right for the third offense.[7] Not all the colonists accepted the excessive use of alcoholic beverages. The Puritan clergymen condemned this practice early in the history of the country. In fact "Puritanism had not been established fifty years on American soil, when its high priest took alarm at the serious inroads made by the prevalence of intemperance."[8]

The last half of the eighteenth century and the first half of the nineteenth century was considered the most intemperate era in American history. There were numerous social, economic, and political forces influencing both the use of alcoholic beverages and the treatment accorded the Negro. Rum became a major medium of exchange in the slave trade between America, Africa, and the West Indies. Along with this, the discovery and development of a way to distill alcohol reduced the price and encouraged an increase in its use. The first waves of European migration brought a large number of people who were not Anglo-Saxon and Protestant. They did not have any religious restrictions on the use of alcoholic beverages; as a result, the American drinking habits were influenced by their presence. During the first half of the nineteenth century some of the Protestants opposed to the use of alcohol joined forces with the denominations of the abolitionists. The attitudes toward these two issues were reflected in the activities of most of the Protestant denominations and church programs. In the first half of the nineteenth century the general attitude toward the taking of a dram was tolerant. Just when and how the use of alcoholic beverages and the Protestant churches came to a parting of the way is unknown. During this era of intemperance, few drank harder than the preachers. Many of them drank large quantities in the homes of their parishioners, at ordinations, and funerals. There were few preachers who did not drink at every opportunity and to excess, also there were quite a few engaged in the liquor business, owning interests in distilleries and taverns. By the middle 1700's, some of the dominant religious sects had begun to discipline members for drunkenness. It was, however, many years before any of them officially promulgated rules relating to abstinence, or to the manufacture and sale of ardent spirits. The first important sect to make even a roundabout approach to this problem was the Methodist.[9]

TEMPERANCE

OVERTURES

The first serious and effective efforts against the use of alcoholic beverages began with the movement for American independence. By the nineteenth century (1800) Protestant ministers and church members were manifesting unusual interest and activity in the liquor traffic. Prior to 1810, temperance attitudes of the Christian church were largely limited to the attitudes of outstanding ministers who preached against the traffic, and resolutions of advice and restrictions of church bodies couched in general terms intended to affect the conduct of individual members.[10] The most effective propagandist for temperance was usually the Protestant clergyman, who devoted a large proportion of his sermons to the denunciation of the liquor traffic, indicting intemperance as the great barrier in the way of the church. It is possible that the greatest force possessed by the early reformers of the liquor traffic was their explanation of the manner in which the use of ardent spirits frustrated the accomplishment of the church's mission. From many platforms and pulpits they expounded, "Since the Church of Christ had been established on earth for the purpose of saving souls, there could be no doubt that its purpose was thwarted by any influence which assigned human beings to perdition. Intemperance, plainly making its victim unfit for salvation, was the hideous enemy of organized religion."[11] During the last quarter of the nineteenth century, there developed a curious connection between preachers of the gospel and rum selling in the western expansion of the country. The West was dotted with saloons run by ex-clergymen from the East. "They had exchanged the minister's cloth for the bar rag."[12]

Temperance advocates were well aware of the value of an alliance with organized religion. They stressed the divine origin of their reform and the religious character of the propaganda. The formal movement of the church temperance lines began in 1810, and it marked the dawn of a new age in church activity.[13] This activity of necessity had to reach outside of the closed church community into the realm of the social life of the nation. This period of larger church activity, in cooperative effort for temperance, began at the time when the church throughout the United States was in the midst of one of the greatest religious revivals to sweep over the American continent.[14]

THE AMERICAN TEMPERANCE SOCIETY

The first national temperance association, the American Temperance Society, was founded in 1826 in Boston, Massachusetts. This movement was led by Congregationalists and non-Evangelical ministers. Prior to this time, numerous local societies and one or two state organizations had been created and played their part in the temperance movement. The American Temperance Society had an electrifying effect on the people throughout the country. Immediately state and local auxiliaries by the hundreds sprang into existence. They were bound together by a common purpose and program—religion and temperance.[15] In their campaign to commit Protestant sects to their proposition, the temperance forces directed their chief attacks against church members who received their livelihood from the liquor traffic. The American Temperance Society knew of no principle of the gospel that would justify a business which filled the poorhouses and fostered every manner of crime. From all over the country, reports indicated that the obstacle in the way of temperance was the example of church members who sold ardent spirits.[16]

Some church congregations made total abstinence a necessary qualification for membership. Protestant sects were far from unanimous in their adherence to the temperance movement. The Congregational Reformed church, in upstate New York, openly denounced the reform and forbade its members to participate in it. About the same time, Primitive Baptist churches in Tennessee actually ex-communicated members who were guilty of joining a temperance society.[17] Some of the Germanic background churches, especially the Evangelical and Reformed churches did not support the anti-alcohol movement. They went on serving beer at church affairs and bazaars to Prohibition day.

63

It was pointed out earlier in this chapter that both alcohol and the Negro became burning issues with the Protestant sects. Possibly nowhere else in the world Negro slavery exercised such an influence upon the Christian church as in the United States. All the great American churches grew up in more or less intimate contact with the institution of slavery and all were of necessity affected by it. When the first Africans were imported in the seventeenth century, some purchasers opposed converting them to Christianity for fear baptism would give them a claim to freedom. After the Colonial legislatures provided that conversion would not have this effect, the opposition diminished. Thereafter, most masters encouraged Christian proselytizing among their bondsmen and conversion proceeded rapidly.[18] Some students of Negro life believe that the church has meant more to the Negro than any other institution.

As a slave, the Negro had no control of his life. He was considered less than human and was bargained for and sold like any other property. He was considered incapable of mental discipline through formal training. Along with this, the Negro was denied the rights of citizenship which enabled one to own property and participate in the affairs of government. He had to worship and serve God under close supervision. In this strange and somewhat hostile environment, it became necessary for the Negro to work out for himself a technique of survival. Possibly the most significant technique of survival developed during the days of slavery might well be called a religious technique, which is represented by the Negro spirituals and by the early efforts to establish and develop the Negro church. The creation of the spirituals was not an accident in Negro life. It was an imperative creation in order that the slave might adjust himself to unfamiliar conditions in the New World. Early the church, and particularly the independent Negro church, furnished the one and only organized field in which the slave's suppressed emotions could be released, and the only opportunity for him to develop his own leadership.[19] Before the Civil War, Negro slaves, as they became Christians found themselves in the same churches as the whites. In the southern churches, the slaves and free Negroes were segregated from the whites. This was also the situation with most of the free Negroes in the

North. Both North and South, the majority of the Negroes holding church membership were to be found in the Methodist and Baptist churches.[20] But whatever the arrangements, whites admitted Negro members to all churches everywhere in the ante-bellum South.

The religion of the slave was strictly controlled by his master. Religion was aimed at controlling the behavior of slaves. Christianity offered the Negro an interpretation of his existence in an alien world; it did not undertake to change his earthly conditions. Slave owners developed various methods of providing religious training. The slaves were not only denied legal and civil rights, but this proscription was extended to the privileges of education and worship. Many of the slave owners and others in the South, thought that teaching slaves to read and write would create dissatisfaction in their minds and lead to insurrection. The same apprehension applied to instruction in religion. Every southern state with the exceptions of Maryland and Kentucky had stringent laws forbidding anyone to teach slaves reading and writing, and in some states the penalties applied to the educating of free Negroes and mulattoes as well. In North Carolina, it was a crime to distribute among them any pamphlet or book, including the Bible. The southern whites were not disposed to withhold the consolations of divine worship from their slaves. The conditions, however, were not to be laid down by the church as an institution, not even by the planters as laity, but by planters simply as masters.[21]

ANTI-SLAVERY AGITATION

During the first half of the eighteenth century, the first of the momentous revival movements in American Protestant history got underway. It was initiated in New England in 1734 and eventually spread to the other colonies. Denominational lines were crossed and large numbers of people were caught up in the movement. As a result, colleges and Indian missions were established and the public conscience was quickened, and the real beginning of anti-slavery agitation may be traced to this revival movement.[22] This movement was viewed with concern by many slaveholders. At this time in the eighteenth century, the southern Baptists and Methodists exhibited considerable anti-slavery sentiment. Many slaveholders were reluctant to have the preachers and missionaries of these denominations work among their slaves. When the southern wings of these churches changed their positions and southern clergymen became ardent defenders of slavery, the master class looked upon religion as an ally. Some of the churchmen expressed beliefs that the gospel, instead of creating trouble and strife, was the best instrument to preserve peace and good conduct among Negroes. This was a persuasive argument and it ultimately opened the way for the gospel on the larger plantations.[23]

During the latter part of the eighteenth century, there were forces at work among the English speaking people which were to exercise a great influence in affecting public opinion regarding the institution of slavery. The great humanitarian impulse grew largely out of the Evangelical revival and the diffusion of liberal ideas. The latter constituted the philosophy of the American Revolution and resulted in an increase in public opinion against the "peculiar institution." The people of this country and England, along with France, were becoming more sympathetic and humanitarian in their attitudes toward the unfortunate and downtrodden. It was under such influences that the first anti-slavery society was formed in America, the Philadelphia Society (1775). All of the states north of Delaware and Maryland provided for the immediate or gradual abolition of slavery. At the close of the War of Independence the leadership of the new nation was practically unified in its opposition to the institution of slavery.[24]

After the colonies became states, the masters continued to have control over the religious activities of their slaves. The conscientious master welcomed having the gospel preached to his slaves, provided they should *hear* it under the conditions he prescribed, but not *read* it. In Alabama, slaves were encouraged to attend Sunday services because of the good influence the masters thought it would have on them. It was believed by many slaveholders that, "A Christain slave might be expected to be a slave graced with meekness and the spirit of obedience. His value as a faithful servant was enhanced."[25]

In Mississippi, public opinion was not adverse to the religious training of Negroes. Secular education was denied the slaves, but religious training was not. The ever present fear of insurrection was responsible for the strict control of the religious

66

activities of Negroes. Also there were legal limitations on the religious life of the slaves designed to keep the forms of worship from being used as a cloak for conspiracy.[26] Some of the restrictions of the slave owners found their way into the laws of the states, e.g., one of the acts of South Carolina forbade religious meetings of slaves or free Negroes either before the rising, or after the setting of the sun. In Mississippi, if authorized by their masters, slaves were permitted to attend the preaching of a white minister.[27]

As long as proper precautions were being taken there was little opposition to religious activity among the slaves. Owners had reasons to be suspicious if the emphasis was on instruction or if there were Negro leaders. The chief restrictions in Mississippi were that "no free Negro could exercise the function of a minister of the gospel. A violation of this restriction carried with it a penalty of 30 lashes. A master could permit one of his own Negroes to preach on his plantation; no outside slaves could attend the meeting. In all convocations of slaves, at least two reputable white persons must be present."[28]

The Negroes of Charleston, South Carolina, were permitted to worship in their own church until 1822. When a plot of insurrection was discovered among the Negroes, the city government had the church building demolished. The majority of the Negro members returned to the white congregations where they soon overflowed the galleries and even the boxes which were assigned them at the rear on the main floors.[29]

NEGRO PREACHERS

Negro preachers were feared by the slave owners and attempts were made to control them. In most states, Negro preachers were outlawed between 1830 and 1835, and thereafter Negro religious services were presided over by some white person. More and more, however, Negroes were required to attend the churches of their masters.[30] The Nat Turner Insurrection of 1831, in Virginia, brought forth many new repressive measures against Negro preachers, and the attendance of church services. Turner was a preacher and considered fairly well educated for this period. There was considerable fear and dislike of Negro preachers among many slave owners in the South. The manager of a large Mississippi estate considered, "Negro preachers the worst characters on the place and believed that their preaching excited the Negroes too much and interfered with subordination and order."[31] The people of Mississippi reflected the general thinking about Negro preachers in the Deep South between 1830 and 1850. There was such a general dislike for Negro preachers that in the parts of the state where slaves were mostly to be found, preaching by Negroes became generally prohibited. In other sections, slaveholders seemed to have had no objection to Negro preachers.[32]

THE CHURCH'S FAILURES

The enslavement and treatment accorded the Negro were justified and supported by the churches and religious sects. Among the various Christian missionaries who undertook the conversion of the Negroes during most of the eighteenth century, only the Quakers who generally met with opposition among the planters, were in favor of the emancipation of slaves.[33] Christianity failed to offer the Negro hope of freedom in this world. The manner in which Christianity was taught or communicated to him tended to degrade him. The Negro was taught that his enslavement was due to the fact that he had been cursed by God. His color was a sign of the curse.[34] While such was being taught the slave, some of the leading ministers of the South were setting forth the same doctrine in books for the American people. They advocated theological justification of the enslavement of the Negro which gave religious support to the philosophical justification of slavery. A leading minister published a book in which he defended the doctrine that slavery is ordained of God to continue for the good of the slave, the good of the master, and the good of the whole American family, until another and better destiny can be unfolded. The most celebrated theological justification and religious endorsement of the enslavement of the Negro was that by a professor at William and Mary College in Virginia. In a book published in 1832, he justified the enslavement of the Negro on the grounds that the Negro possessed the strength and form of a man, but had the intellect of a child and was therefore unfit for freedom.[35]

SCHISMS

The Baptists

The slavery controversy affected the churches throughout the nation—North and South. This was particularly true of the Baptists, the Methodists and Presbyterians. The Congregationalists were generally anti-slavery, but they were largely confined to the northern states with practically no slaveholding members. The steps leading to the schisms in the Baptist and Methodist denominations over slavery were interesting and revealing. The oldest and most prominent Baptist organization in the United States, at the period of the slave controversy, was the General Convention of the Baptist Denomination in the United States for Foreign Missions. This had been formed in 1814 with headquarters in Boston but drew its support from Baptist churches throughout the country. In 1832, a Baptist Home Missionary Society was formed and was also supported by the churches—North and South. Both of these societies held joint meetings every three years; the meeting known as the Triennial Convention. When the Convention met in Baltimore in 1841, and in Philadelphia in 1844, slavery was a live issue. At the 1841 Convention some southern groups protested the anti-slavery activities of their northern counterparts. They accused the northern abolitionists of being meddlesome and informed the Convention of the impossibility of further cooperation, unless the abolitionists on the Board of Managers were dismissed. Through the efforts and cooperation of the northern moderates a schism was averted in this organization. The meeting ended without further disturbance, for the moderates of both sections were in control, and an understanding had been reached that slavery was a subject which should not be discussed by the Convention.

Between 1841 and 1844 there was increased anti-slavery agitation among northern Baptists; they were growing rapidly in number and influence. In May 1843, an American and Foreign Free Baptist Missionary Society was projected in Boston, and a pledge was signed by all friends of the movement, promising to separate themselves from all religions that were supported in common with slaveholders. Their threat to withdraw from the main body was based upon the action taken in the Triennial Convention in 1841.

When the Triennial Convention met in Philadelphia, in 1844, there were 456 delegates present. Of this number, 92 were from slaveholding states. The delegates discussed the slavery issue and the majority decided that slavery did not concern the Convention. The Home Missionary Society also met in Philadelphia at the same time. They, too, discussed slavery pro and con and came to the same conclusion as the General Convention.

The solution to the vexing, emotional, and complicated issue was again avoided and left to the Boards of the two societies to determine. A decision by these two bodies was not long in coming. The southern associations withdrew from the old Board of Home Missions and formed a Board of Domestic Missions supported by Baptists of the South. This decision came about as a result of the Georgia Baptist Convention, in April 1844, which recommended for appointment as a missionary a candidate who was a slaveholder. There was considerable discussion and opposition to this candidate by members from the North and West. When the Board of Home Missions reached a decision in October 1844, it declared that the application to appoint the candidate introduced the subject of slavery. This was in direct contravention of the letter and purpose of the constitution, and they therefore were not at liberty to entertain the application of the candidate.[36]

The decision of the Foreign Board of the Baptists regarding the question of the appointment of slaveholding missionaries was of far-reaching and greater importance. This came about as a result of a member of the Alabama Baptist Convention raising a question about the propriety of those in the South sending any more money to the members in the North for missionary and other benevolent purposes before slavery was understood by both parties. The Alabama Convention passed a series of resolutions. Among them was one demanding that the authorities in control of the bodies receiving funds from the Baptist churches state whether or not slaveholders were equally eligible with non-slaveholders to all the privileges and immunities of the several unions. On December 17, 1844, the Board declared that in 30 years no slaveholder had applied to be a missionary and since the Board did not send servants, it could not send out slaves. The Board also stated: "If anyone should offer himself as a missionary having slaves and should insist on retaining them as property, we could not appoint him. One thing is certain, we can never be a party to any arrangement which would imply approbation of slavery."[37] This decision led to the withdrawal of the southern Baptists from participating

70

with their northern counterparts in the cause of missions. Steps toward separation were soon taken. The Virginia Baptist Foreign Missions took the initiative and withdrew from further connection with the Boston Board. Along with the Virginians, they recommended a southern Convention, and southern churches and associations generally passed resolutions favoring this move. The Convention met at Augusta, Georgia, May 1845 with 377 delegates present representing eight slaveholding states. A constitution was presented for the southern Baptist Convention to promote foreign and domestic missions. In this way, the great Baptist denomination divided over the slavery issue.

The Methodists

As among the Baptists, slavery became an acute issue in the Methodist Episcopal church. The bishops, as they travelled from conference to conference, tried to discourage the discussion of slavery. In 1835, two bishops sent a pastoral letter to New England Methodists pointing out the evils which had already resulted from slavery discussion and warning them of even greater disasters if the discussions were continued. Between 1836 and 1844, the slavery issue continued to rage unabated among the Methodists. After considerable conflict and discussion, the crisis in the slavery controversy was reached in the General Conference of 1844. The Conference met in New York in May, and 180 delegates represented 33 Conferences. From the beginning of the month's session slavery was the burning issue. An appeal of a slaveholding minister who had been suspended from the Baltimore Conference for refusing to free his slaves brought the question to the center of the stage. After long debate, in which the whole slave issue was reviewed, the Conference voted overwhelmingly to uphold the decision of the Baltimore Conference. The Methodists were confronted by a very important decision at this time concerning the issue of slavery. They had to decide what to do with a bishop from Georgia who, by a second marriage, had become the possessor of a few household slaves and the first Methodist slaveholding bishop. For 11 days, the delegates debated what to do with the bishop. Those from the South defended his ownership of slaves on the basis that he had violated no rule of the church. The anti-slavery brethren wanted the bishop to get rid of his slaves or resign. Compromises were proposed and delay for another four years was suggested, all to no avail. When the vote was taken on the resolution that the bishop be asked to cease his Episcopal labors until he should rid himself of his slaves, it was carried by a large majority.

The decision revealed the anti-slavery temper of the majority of the Conference and presaged the separation of the Methodist church on the issue of slavery. The closing days of the 1844 Conference witnessed considerable activity drawing up a *plan of separation*. The day after the General Conference adjourned, the southern delegates met and determined to call a Convention of the southern churches to meet in Louisville, Kentucky, May 1, 1845. At this Convention, the delegates voted by an overwhelming majority to separate from the northern church body. During this period, opinion in the North was fast crystallizing in opposition to the *plan of separation* which had been offered in 1844. At the time the General Conference of the Methodist Episcopal church met in 1848, feelings of hostility between southern and northern branches of the church were running high. The *plan of separation* was repudiated by a large majority of the Convention and they also refused to receive the fraternal delegate sent to them from the Methodist Episcopal church, South.[38] Eighteenth hundred and forty-eight to the opening of the Civil War was a period of growing bitterness between the two branches of American Methodism.

The Other Churches

Practically all of the churches had at one time or another placed themselves on record as wishing that slavery did not exist. Next to the Quakers the Unitarians were among the early Christian opponents of slavery. Nearly all of the more prominent abolitionists in New England belonged to this school of thought. Some of the most vigorous abolitionists, particularly just before the war, held membership in the Congregational church. In 1850, the northern Presbyterian church under strong Congregational influence took a stand against slavery, although not absolutely condemning it under all circumstances. On the other hand, all of the denominations in the southern states were inclined to maintain the legal right of the South to its peculiar culture, including chattel slavery. The Lutheran church in the southern states organized a separate synod in 1862. This was not because of slavery differences, but it was assumed that the South would be able to maintain its independence. Fraternal relations were always maintained between the northern and southern branches of this church. The Episcopal church refused to permit the war to split its unity, and retained all of the churches of the south until peace was restored. The Roman Catholic church did not divide its churches into northern and southern wings over the slavery issue and the Civil War.[39]

MORE REFORM OVERTURES

The period of 1825 to 1860 witnessed considerable activity in both anti-slavery and temperance movements by the religious sects. This was due to a number of developments; among them the uniting of temperance and anti-slavery forces in some of the religious denominations. Of all the reforms relevant to the anti-slavery crusade, none cast a larger net than temperance. In 1826, when the American Society for the Promotion of Temperance was formed, a number of significant agencies concerned with spiritual and physical well-being were inaugurated. The American Temperance Society and others sought to instill Christian principles into Americans. This society was an offshoot of some of the other missions, but temperance possessed a characteristic quality of reform that none could match— that combination of zeal with a program for change. One of the remarkable features of the temperance movement was its influence on the anti-slavery crusade and the fact that it embraced a great number of groups and classes which otherwise were opposed to each other. The World Temperance Convention which met in New York in 1853 furnished a good example of this point. Attending this Convention were supporters of women's suffrage, abolition, and temperance. All believed that the fight against liquor was essential to the progress of their particular cause: that women suffered by the intemperateness of their men, that Negroes should practice sobriety for the advancement of the race, and that drinking was part of the moral corruption which sustained slavery. There were also dedicated southerners, to whom slavery was justified by religion. They sought to array their fellow patriarchs in the moral armor of temperance as well as to curb the drinking habits of their Negroes.[40] Between 1825 and 1860, the winds of reform furiously shook the United States. There were more causes than before, and in this era of the rise of the common man, they affected more people. In such an atmosphere of unrest, reform, and religious fervor slavery and temperance increasingly became pre-eminent issues with the denominations. With the support of the religious groups the temperance movement was near to achieving its aims when its progress was stopped by the Civil War. With prohibition activity at its height, the moral reform forces of the nation were diverted to the slavery question. This issue reached its crisis in the war of 1861-1865.

THE CIVIL WAR

During the Civil War, the temperance issue received little attention from the religious bodies. The people, North and South, were more concerned with the developments of the war. As a result of the long agitation carried on in the churches over the slavery issue, the members of the major denominations were prepared to take a stand when the Civil War began. The war received unanimous support from the churches. During the war, the members of the churches prayed for the army which represented the section in which they were located. Although the war had been brought about as a result of the slavery crisis, there was very little the church could do about the situation. It is possible that the cause of vital religion suffered as a result of the war. Membership in the churches generally showed a decrease during the war years. Some of the ministers expressed concern over the difficulties of sustaining the institutions of religion. It was also believed by some ministers that interest in the church and religion had been pushed into the background. As the war progressed some changes came and the spirit of religion again asserted itself. By the end of the war considerable damage had been done to the religious institutions of this country. As one writer stated, "the brutalizing effects of the four bloody years, the resulting increase of drunkenness and human selfishness generally, were to exercise their blighting influence upon the nation for years to come."[41]

The Civil War was considered by church people in both the North and the South as primarily a moral and religious struggle,

74

and it appealed more strongly to religious zeal than any war in modern times. The northern churches believed that they not only had a right, but that it was their duty to take a hand in the solution of Reconstruction problems. The missionary work began in the South by the northern churches during the war and was carried forward with increasing momentum during the period of Reconstruction. The Presbyterian and Congregational societies were particularly active in their educational work. This resulted in the intellectual and moral uplift of the freedmen. These two denominations, however, did not win large numbers of these newly freedmen to their own churches. On the other hand, the Methodist Episocopal church, through their Freedmen's Aid Society, soon had many schools in operation and by 1869 had formed ten new Conferences in the former slaveholding states. These Conferences worked among Negroes and whites.

The southern churches recognized their obligations to their ex-slaves and they attempted to meet them. In 1865, the Alabama Baptist Convention, because of the conditions among Negroes, made a strong appeal to the sympathy of every Christian heart and demanded at the hands of all who loved the Savior, renewed exertions for their moral and religious improvement. They also recommended the establishment of Negro Sunday schools and that means be provided for more adequate preaching of the gospel. The Protestant Episcopal church took similar action that year. In his pastoral letter, the Bishop of North Carolina urged the formation of Negro congregations in the towns and that means be provided for the religious training of Negro children. The members of the Methodist Epsicopal church, South, recognized their obligations to Negroes and by 1866, had outlined a plan for their colored members. The Negroes were to be formed into separate charges with their own quarterly Conferences and colored people were to be licensed to preach. Where conditions justified, colored districts were to be organized, and subsequently to be formed into annual Conferences. After two or more annual Conferences, they were to be assisted in forming a separate church. In 1870, the Colored Methodist Episcopal church was organized. It consisted of the Negro members who remained in the Methodist Episcopal church, South.[42] The efforts of the southern churches were more or less in vain. The Negroes were now free and many of them were anxious to separate themselves from the churches of their former masters. In many cases the Negroes were suspicious of the intentions of the southern churches in which they had worshiped under the eyes of their white masters, with the result that the Negro membership of the old southern churches rapidly decreased.

NEGRO CHURCHES

Before the Civil War, there were scattered beginnings of separate Negro churches; the result of resentment of free Negroes in the North at segregation and other discriminatory practices. After the war independent Negro churches emerged on a large scale. The Civil War and Emancipation removed the restrictions which had fettered independent Negro organizations and released the energies of the former slaves. The newly emancipated Negroes carried out the work of separation and independent organization of churches with astounding energy and success.[43] The Negro church grew rapidly after the war. In 1865, the Negro members of the white Primitive Baptist churches of the South established a separate organization called the Colored Primitive Baptists in America. In 1866, the African Union First Colored Methodist Protestant church of America was established by merging the African Union church with the First Colored Methodist Protestant church. In 1869, the General Assembly of the Cumberland Presbyterian church organized its membership as the Colored Cumberland Presbyterian church.[44]

The older Negro churches entered a new stage of growth following the war. The African Methodist Epsicopal church, which was formed in Philadelphia in 1816, and until the Civil War had existed only among northern Negroes, by 1880 had nearly 400,000 members, mostly in the South. The African Methodist Episcopal Zion church, organized in New York in 1820, in ten years after the war grew from 26,746 members to nearly 200,000. After the war, the large body of Negroes were not attracted by the Methodist church, but by the Baptist. The freedom, which even prior to Emancipation had meant so much in the growth of the Baptists, was thereafter a still greater cause for their expansion. The ease with which a Baptist church could be organized largely accounted for the greater number formed among Negroes. While the Methodists were debating

76

over what recognition should be allowed the Negroes or whether they should be set apart as a separate body, the Negro Baptists were realizing their new freedom which made possible the enjoyment of greater democracy in the church. It was also easier for a man to become a prominent figure in the Baptist church.[45] The church was the first social institution fully controlled by Negroes in America. The churches gave them an opportunity to develop qualities of leadership, and it is no coincidence that many outstanding Negroes have been ministers. From their experiences in the church, many of the ministers, bishops, and lay leaders moved into politics and education. In these areas, they gave a good account of themselves and many effectively represented their race.

POSTWAR PROBLEMS

CORRUPTION

From 1865 to the end of the century, the United States was picking up the threads of her social, political, and economic life so abruptly cut in 1861, and attempting to tie them together in a new pattern. During this period vast changes were taking place in the lives of the people. In fact, a revolution had taken place. The coming of industrialism, attended by all the roar and rattle of affairs; the shrill cries of millions of new voices that came among us from overseas, the going and coming of trains, and the growth of cities had worked a tremendous change in the lives and in the habits of thought of the American people. These changes were accompanied by graft and corruption; both North and South. Lowering of standards of conduct in both public and private life was one of the unfortunate consequences of the Civil War. The country's wealth increased rapidly in the midst of the political and social confusion. The war brought to prominence a class of rough, unscrupulous men with low standards of personal conduct who too frequently were permitted to gain leadership in both business and politics. Out of such a general background came an era of unwholesome corruption in politics which affected every section of the nation and every department of the government. Corruption in business was even more common, if possible, than in government. Even the business of the church did not entirely escape the corruption of the time and serious frauds were uncovered in the conduct of the great publishing business of the Methodist Episcopal church.[46]

The manufacture, sale and use of alcoholic beverages, which had been considerably checked in the 1840's and 1850's by the opposition of groups and the adoption of prohibitionary legislation by a number of the states, attained greatly increased proportions during and following the Civil War.

THE W. C. T. U.

The federal tax on liquor, which had been enacted as a war measure for the purpose of revenue, was continued after the war and gave to both liquor drinking and the liquor business added respectability. This situation, along with the increase in the amount of capital invested in liquor caused considerable alarm and concern among the supporters of temperance and prohibition. In 1874, a convention of Christain women met in Cleveland, Ohio, and formed the Women's Christian Temperance Union. This organization from the start was closely allied with the churches and was a powerful influence in the temperance cause.

The temperance movement in America drew its membership, its energies, and its moral code from organized religion. In the final quarter of the nineteenth century, much of the tone of temperance was permeated by the spirit of Christian concern for humanitarian justice and sympathy. From 1875 to 1920, a number of church organizations were active in the temperance movement. In 1895, the year following its organization, the Women's Christian Temperance Union declared its objectives:

RESOLVED, That whereas, the object of just government is to conserve the best interests of the governed; and whereas the liquor traffic is not only a crime against God, but subversive of every interest of society; therefore, in behalf of humanity, we call for such legislation as shall secure this end; and while we will continue to employ all moral agencies as indispensable, we hold prohibition to be essential to the full triumph of this reform.[47]

From 1875 to 1920, the Union exerted considerable influence upon the social, political, religious, and educational activities of this country. The Union was non-partisan until the Presidential campaign of 1880. The organization and activities of the Women's Christian Temperance Union were significant be-

78

cause they demonstrated for the first time in the history of the nation, the possibilities and potentialities of organized Christian womanhood in a crusade on behalf of moral reform. The Union proved to be one of the greatest moral forces in social reform that the world has ever seen.[48]

THE ANTI-SALOON LEAGUE

The same year the Women's Christian Temperance Union movement was organized in Cleveland to get rid of the saloon by means of prayer and visitation, in Oberlin,[49] Ohio, a League was formed to deal with a crisis in the local temperance situation. The organization was devoted to the complete suppression of the traffic in and the use of intoxicating liquors. The League differed from most of the pledge-signing temperance bodies of that day in that it sought from the outset to suppress saloons. In 1893, in Oberlin all of the state temperance forces were united into a single Anti-Saloon League. The dramatic tactics and success of the League attracted attention in other states. In 1895, a convention of the Anti-Saloon League was held in Washington, D. C. A second convention was held in 1896 and 557 attended. A third convention was held in Columbus, Ohio, in 1898 at which the attendance rose to 848 and the number of affiliated societies to 190. After the first convention the League grew steadily.[50]

The League was thus launched during what might be called the second great wave of prohibitionist sentiment; the first having occurred in the early decades of the same century. With the development of the Anti-Saloon League two major reform movements were now in the picture. Each, in its different way, attacked the problem of how to curb or abolish the excessive use of alcoholic beverages. The temperance movement became part of a broader attack on behalf of the Protestantism of the traditional rural areas and small towns against what they conceived to be the evils of the developing urban-industrial-commercial centers. Most of these were in the northeastern section of the country, though Pittsburgh, Chicago, and Cleveland were also beginning to burgeon as metropolises.

Since most of the immigrant Catholics pouring into the country settled in the northern urban centers, especially

79

Boston, New York, and Philadelphia, and the European Catholics brought with them no moral or theological strictures on drinking, the temperance forces found themselves lumping together Catholicism, urbanism, and drinking as all part of the same evil. Even politics were affected to the extent that urban Catholics moved overwhelmingly into the Democratic party, because they were seriously courted, not always by the most ethical devices, by big city professional organizations. The members of the temperance societies became allied with the Republican party. By contrast the Anti-Saloon League intent upon physically demolishing the saloons and suppressing all public drinking, identified with the church in urban environments where the vast majority of saloons were located. Its members did not get so closely allied with politics, religion, or socioeconomic classes or sections. They simply attacked the saloons directly as a social evil. To be sure many Evangelical Protestants saw this evil as inspired by the devil, and felt that by striking a blow for social good they were also attacking God's and Christ's enemy. But by and large, the Anti-Saloon League's crusade was social and moral rather than political or religious, sectional or partisan.

The League was organized to give church people an effective political organization to fight the liquor traffic. The Women's Christian Temperance Union had laid the groundwork for an attack on the liquor traffic by a national church-sponsored group. It was believed by the members that by working through the organized church, the League could reach every part of the country. The churches were to constitute the backbone of the League; the League was dominated by the Protestant churches. Not all of the churches cooperated with its program. The Protestant Episcopal and the Lutheran churches gave only tepid support. The Jewish and Catholic churches on the whole opposed prohibition and supported temperance. The Methodists were the most militant of all churches.[51]

The League set out to turn the floodlight of publicity upon the saloon and liquor traffic. Its object was not so much to form opinions as to mobilize for political action an already existing opinion. The League went a step further than the Women's Christian Temperance Union by concentrating on the saloon.[52] The need for some reform of the saloon was acknowledged and recognized by the brewers, distillers, and the general public. The League, however, refused to accept and be satisfied with the reform of the saloon. The propaganda with which it proceeded to arouse the public conscience leaves little room for doubt that it regarded the institution as hopelessly beyond reform or repair.

Within the various denominations of the churches there were considerable differences and variations of opinions concerning the programs and financing of the activities of the Anti-Saloon League. The 12 largest states had no prohibition laws, but had more than one-half of the church members. An attempt by the League to foster national Prohibition in the country by closing the saloons, appeared to be persecution of the large states by the small ones and of the city churches by the country churches. The populations of the largest eastern cities included a great number of immigrants who were not Protestant and considered the saloons necessary to their existence. The seven major religious bodies which supported the Anti-Saloon movement could not muster more than one American out of five behind their banners. For every churchman who was a Dry, there was another who was a Wet. The struggle between the Protestant churches and the saloon was based on different views of the role of God and man in society. It was also bound up with the nativist fears of the Roman Catholic church and the corruption which the liquor trade had brought to politics and life in the cities.[53]

In the South the Anti-Saloon League did not hesitate to use the menace of the drunken Negro as propaganda:

> The primitive Negro field hand, a web of strong sudden impulses, good and bad, comes to town or settlement on Saturday afternoon and pays his fifty cents for a pint of Mr. Levy's gin. He absorbs not only its toxic heat, but absorbs also the suggestion subtly conveyed that it contains aphrodisiacs. He sits in the road or in the alley at the height of debauch, looking at the obscene picture of a white woman on the label, drinking in the invitation it carries. And then it comes . . . opportunity . . . Then follows the hideous episode of the rape or the stake. Is it plain now? The secret of many a lynching and burning in the South?[54]

Terrible stories were told of the effects of alcohol on Negroes in other sections of the country. For sheer terrorism the following story is difficult to match. The people of Grayville, Illinois had voted dry. The saloons were about to close:

Two negroes who worked on the section here, Paul Thomas and James Burress, got the section boss' speeder and went down to Grayville last night. . . . Their bodies were found on the track this morning. Burress lay close to the demolished speeder surrounded by beer bottles, some of which were broken and others filled with the liquid devil. Burress's skull was crushed and both his legs broken. Thomas was carried some distance down the track before he was ground under the wheels. His body was cut in two just above the hips, and one arm was cut off. Bits of flesh and his entrails were strung along the track. He had been a hardworking fellow and but for drink would have made a good living for his wife and five little children who mourn his loss . . . Another fellow from Griffen, Indiana, was also at Grayville and was killed by an Illinois Central train . . . This makes eight for the Grayville saloons in twelve months.[55]

Between the founding of the Anti-Saloon League and the passing of the Volstead Act, the saloon was the most popular legal drinking place in the South as well as the North. In industrial cities, the saloon was often what the church was in a village. It was a center of faith and tradition, political rather than religious. Membership in the right saloon brought social prestige and good jobs, as did membership in the right church. When the church and temperance forces attacked the saloons, the saloonkeepers in the North and other sections of the country attempted to use the free lunches provided for the customers as a defense. Many of them claimed that the free lunches were a means of feeding the poor. The free lunch was vastly overrated as a means of feeding the poor; the saloonkeeper was in business to make money. Free lunches were not provided in southern saloons, because Negroes ate too much and the whites would not eat out of the same dish as Negroes. In the large cities of other sections of the country, bouncers threw out of saloons any who ate more than his money's worth of drink. Only in the Far West, where food was abundant and cheap, were free lunches provided without restrictions.[56]

THE TWENTIETH CENTURY

PROHIBITION

At the beginning of the twentieth century, the forces of prohibition were on the march. A long list of churches had rallied to the support of the Anti-Saloon League. Practically all the Protestant religious leaders spoke out against the liquor

82

traffic and the saloon. To thousands of the clergy and to millions of the lay Protestants the need for prohibition was to all practical purposes an article of faith. The case for temperance had ceased to be expounded by the foes of alcohol in the first decade of the twentieth century. References to seemingly Biblical support for temperance, rather than prohibition, were overlooked. The good and sincere people who were deeply religious and politically powerful in the rural West and dominant in the South had no faith in temperance. As in the 1850's, when abolition was to some the primary objective of reform, so now millions were so fully committed to prohibition that there was no place in their hearts for any other reform, temperance included.

Prohibition was among the social issues important to the American people at the beginning of the twentieth century. Between 1901 and 1920, "The Progressive Movement came as a reaction to a long period of conservatism during which time the nation had undergone a rapid transformation from a predominantly rural to an urban industrial society. The Progressive Movement embarked upon a wide variety of individual reforms. Prohibition was one of the more important. The movement was nourished on a belief of moral law; so was prohibition which sought to remove from commerce an article that was believed to despoil man's reason and undermine the foundation of religion and representative government. . . By the time the Progressive Movement got underway, American Protestantism was firmly committeed to temperance reform."[57] This had not always been the case during the early history of the country. The churches had not played a significant role in the reform. It was not until the first quarter of the nineteenth century that the Protestants took up the cause of prohibition and became its most arden supporter. The greatest Evangelical revivals of the nineteenth century prompted American Protestantism to become intensely concerned with the problem. The Evangelical Protestant churches often implied that drinking was wrong. They were also critical of and condemned those who participated in the liquor traffic. Unlike the individual drinker, the liquor seller incited others to drink, sometimes excessively. The seller of liquor was directly responsible for the evils arising from the traffic. In the eyes of the Evangelical churches, the liquor business was morally reprehensible and ought to be abolished.[58] Thus Evangelical Protestant churches gave up temperance reform and advocated total abstinence and prohibition.

The moral, economic, social, and political aspects of the liquor question were sufficiently compelling to provide the reform with a faithful following at all times, but it was only when special conditions existed to give the liquor problem unusual urgency that the temperance movement became an object of concern to the public at large. During the early years of the nineteenth and again during the early years of the twentieth century such conditions arose with particular force. In each case the temperance revival coincided with a nationwide reform movement.

The alcohol problem influenced the activities and programs of most of the Protestant churches between 1900 and the enactment of the Eighteenth Amendment in 1917. Although there was considerable effort on the part of the churches to develop a sweeping revival to fight for prohibition, they failed to do so. They were unable to bring about a religious revival; they enjoyed, however, unprecedented success at promoting temperance reform itself. Many Protestants believed that the church, while fulfilling its mission to save men's souls, could best solve the social problem by generating another great religious revival. They also believed that a religious revival could only succeed if accompanied by a temperance revival, for drinking and the liquor traffic were making it increasingly difficult to win men to Christ. Some Protestants were persuaded that America would never experience another general religious awakening until the liquor traffic was wholly eradicated. And so Protestants put considerable zeal behind the temperance movement because of faith in temperance reform as the prerequisite to a successful revival and in revivalism as the solution to the social problem.[59]

In the case of temperance, the church had depended largely on the American Temperance Society before the Civil War and the Prohibition party and the Women's Christian Temperance Union after the war. By 1900, however, the church was beginning to rely increasingly on the Anti-Saloon League and thereafter repeatedly encouraged its members to back the League's efforts. Some churches not only endorsed the League as a "sane, safe, and effective organization in the advancement of the great cause of temperance, but some of the churches went further; not only did they endorse the Anti-Saloon League, but entered into an organic relationship."[60] The League dominated the anti-liquor crusade everywhere in the United States, and came to be recognized as the real agency through which the church was directing its fight against the liquor traffic. Many years of difficult and patient endeavor were necessary to line up the churches on the right side of this movement.

The League coordinated and centralized the work of the Evangelical denominations and their various temperance organizations, and pushed them deeper into politics than they had ever been before.

American Protestants supported a program of revivalism and direct temperance measures. Alongside the doctrine of individual salvation, they placed the doctrine of social redemption which became known as the Social Gospel.[61] Prior to 1900, the Social Gospel was preached by only a few clergymen; the majority of them were theological as well as political liberals. With the rise of the Progressive Movement, the Social Gospel gradually found its way into the mainstream of orthodox American Protestantism.

The Social Gospel was very much concerned with the liquor problem. Social Christianity's most influential spokesman, Walter Rauschenbusch, believed that "American Capitalism was generally unchristian because of its selfishness, greed, and irresponsibility, and some businesses were particularly vicious because they not only put profits above humanity, but sold products that were actually harmful. The prime example of this was the liquor industry. Interested only in expanding its market and increasing its sales, the liquor business never hesitated to break down any barrier of law or morals that sought to restrict its profits."[62] He also stated that "it was difficult enough to wean a nation from drink, but the task of reform was made unusually hard by the malignant and fighting power of the liquor industry. The private industry that has invested its money in the wholesale and retail liquor business is seeking to fasten upon an angry people a relic of barbarism which the awakened conscience and the scientific intellect of the world are combining to condemn."[63]

The Social Gospel's concern with the liquor problems made clear that the prohibition movement was no longer a phenomenon of rural Protestantism, but was also a product of urban Christianity and was pushed as one remedy for the problems created by industrialism, labor, and the growth of cities. The prohibition movement had an urban as well as rural foundation, a fact which partly accounts for its great strength and its success in eventually drying up some of the larger cities prior to the adoption of the Eighteenth Amendment. Along with the Social Gospel movement the Federal Council of Churches of Christ in America became active in the temperance movement.

The Federal Council of the Churches of Christ in America, after 1912, began to support temperance. Through its Commission on Temperance organized that year, the Federal Council representing constituent denominations and 17 million communicants, devoted itself to the task of arousing public opinion and enlisting churchgoers in behalf of total abstinence and prohibition.[64] The most important of the Federal Council activities in this direction was to coordinate and stimulate the work of existing denominational temperance committees and to encourage the formation of additional committees among the church bodies. Although the Council worked with the Anti-Saloon League, its Commission on Temperance conducted a campaign of agitation and propaganda. From 1914 to 1916 it published and circulated a considerable quantity of temperance literature and used its staff and special speakers to present the message throughout the country.

The Council's Commission on the Church and Social Service also drew up a social creed, which called for equal rights and justice for all men. The creed stated that "the liquor problem was inextricably bound up with the general problem of establishing the Kingdom of God on earth and called for the protection of the individual and society from the social, economic, and moral waste of the liquor traffic."[65]

Recent studies of the temperance and prohibition movements have revealed the tremendous influence exerted by middle-class Protestants. There are some who believe that social class played as important a part as religion in bringing about national Prohibition. According to one author, "temperance represented the efforts of urban native Americans to consolidate their middle-class life styles and those of the immigrant, and the marginal laborer or farmer."[66] The essential fact about the prohibition movement was not that it was rural or urban, but that it was a middle-class reform that won the support of middle-class Protestants in the country and city. There was little in country life to make rural Protestants any more abstemious from drinking than their urban counterparts. From the early history of the country, the farmer had been notoriously fond of hard liquor, especially in the days before Evangelical revivals and the beginning of temperance movements. On the other hand, there was nothing inherent in city life to prevent Protestants living in urban areas from supporting a movement for total abstinence and prohibition. The city offered greater opportunities to drink and fostered a more worldly and tolerant attitude toward private morality; prudential consideration could always become strong enough to cause urban Protestants to give up drink and to accept prohibition. Another important similarity between country and city life was the factor that many Americans shared in common, a middle-class faith with its historic source in a fusion of free enterprise, capitalism, Evangelical Protestantism, and political democracy. As a characteristic expression of this middle-class faith, prohibition secured a firmer lodging in a rapidly industralizing America than it had in a more rural America.[67] There are other writers on alcoholic beverages who support this thesis of the importance of the middle class in the prohibition movement. One writer has stated that prohibition was a struggle between the rural voters and the rising power of the city. It was fundamentalist religion reacting to immigration and the flourishing Roman Catholic communion. It was middle-class American morality and the traditional folkways aligned to a fast changing technology. It was Ku Klux Klan and the lodges and vocal women. The determining factors were war hysteria and the super political maneuvering of the corps of the grand cyclops of the Klan, who headed the Anti-Saloon League.[68]

Along with other-world salvationism and a desire to realize the American dream of life, liberty, and happiness, another element entered into the thinking of Protestants. This was the expectation of the coming of the Kingdom of God on earth and this belief provided prohibition with its full driving force. Nineteenth century Evangelical Protestantism was looked upon

87

as a progressive advance toward the Kingdom of God and toward the final judgment and fulfillment of Christ's second advent. As this view became dominant, American Protestants turned increasingly from the expectation of heavenly bliss to the hope of a future on earth.[69] From 1900-1920, the Protestants were inspired by this vision of the future and threw themselves into the work of reform. The sense of mission of American Protestantism found expression in many reforms, but nowhere more clearly than in the prohibition movement.[70]

As a result of the vigorous efforts of the WCTU, Anti-Saloon League, Protestants and other groups, the Eighteenth Amendment was passed in 1917. It was ratified by the states in 1918, and national Prohibition became the law of the land. There have been many theories and conjectures as to the reasons the American people adopted Prohibition. One of the most obvious reasons was that they wanted it. For more than a hundred years they had been indoctrinated with the idea that the destruction of the liquor traffic was the will of God and would provide the answers to most of the problems of mankind.

Prohibition came to the United States out of a desire to revitalize and preserve American democracy. Middle-class Americans turned to Prohibition as one means of achieving their goal; the same middle-class groups who defined the place and treatment accorded the Negro in American society. A large segment of the middle class, especially in the South, believed that alcohol, foreign immigrants, and Negroes provided a great threat to the moral and religious life of America.

THE NEGRO

When the twentieth century arrived, the Negro had been effectively and firmly relegated to the status of second-class citizenship. The public symbols and constant reminders of his inferior position were the segregation statutes or *Jim Crow* laws. Along with these, policies and practices developed which lent the sanction of racial ostracism to practically every area of contact between blacks and whites in the South.[71] Since the deletion of the word slavery, there had been little change since Civil War days in the white man's arguments of superiority. The treatment of the Negro by whites, North and South, was in contrast to the principles of Christianity. It did not adhere to the American dream in which the people of this country so zealously and religiously believed. "The American dream is based upon Christian foundations, and the active presence of Christian faith has given a great strength and sustaining courage to millions of unremembered men and women. Christian teachings have inspired many of the great reform and humanitarian movements in the nations' past."[72] Between 1900-1920, the forces of religion found themselves fighting to abolish the use of alcohol and caught in a dilemma about the place of the Negro in society. Many of the church leaders of that period believed that racialism was the foremost issue confronting the Christian church.

Religious activities and sentiment did help to improve the position and conditions affecting Negroes. The Social Gospel movement permeated the great Protestant sects in the early years of the twentieth century. The breach between the estranged northern and southern branches of Methodism and the other churches healed more firmly in the 1930's. In the North, the Social Gospel included concern for the Negro. Some of the followers of the Gospel in the South were also concerned with the wrongs done him. The Roman Catholics much more highly and solidly organized, moved in the same direction. By the 1940's some of the most advanced pronouncements regarding the Negro's plight to be heard in the South were coming from Catholic groups.[73]

The Ku Klux Klan, in the first quarter of the twentieth century, was revived and developed into one of the most dangerous movements in the history of this country, because of its vicious racial and religious intolerance and flaunting of the Bill of Rights. Protestantism was notoriously connected with the Klan. "By 1925, there were possibly four or five million white Protestant native-born patriots engaged in tacitly supporting acts of intimidation, terror, and torture against their Negro, Catholic, Jewish, and foreign-born neighbors. They justified these acts on the grounds that America was in dire peril and could be saved only if it remained predominantly white, Protestant, native-born, and Anglo-Saxon. Professing to be a Christian organization and composed of Protestants, the Klan became an extremely powerful force in American life, especially in the South West, Middle West, and Far West."[74]

In the South, the Negro was the prime victim of Klan atrocities. This was due largely to the small number of Jews, Catholics, and foreign-born. As in other sections of the country, many of the ministers and their congregations were members of the Klan. "In practically all of the southern states, except Virginia and North Carolina, the rural clergy belonged to the Klan or had traffic with it en masse . . . In many towns throughout the South and everywhere the great body of the ministers either smiled benignly on it or carefully kept their mouths shut about it."[75] Many of the ministers and church members took leading and active roles in the Klan.

As early as 1919, the Administrative Committee of the Federal Council of Churches issued a special statement urging justice for the Negro. In addition, a Commission on the Church and Race Relations was organized in 1921. This later became the Department of Race Relations. It was through this Department that the Federal Council attempted to achieve some positive gains in race relations in the 1920's and 1930's. The Department of Race Relations held a large number of interracial conferences, sought the birth of interracial committees, encouraged the exchange of pulpits, printed thousands of posters and pamphlets, sent out speakers, and established Race Relations Sunday and Brotherhood Month. Race Relations Sunday was first observed in 1923.[76] At one time, this group was headed by a Negro and seemed to rely on education to lessen friction between the races.

POLITICS

Alcohol, race and religion were the issues that split the Democrats in the 1924 National Convention and election and again in 1928. Alfred E. Smith, the reform Governor of New York, backed by Tammany Hall, the Wets, the Roman Catholics, and the northern immigrants was defeated in his attempt to secure the nomination for President. He was defeated because of his religion and strong opposition to Prohibition.[77] In 1928, Smith was nominated by the Democrats as their candidate for the President of the United States. Many of the leaders of the Democratic party in the South opposed his nomination. Although a Wet, a Catholic, and on good terms with Negroes in New York, Smith managed to win the nomination. This was a significant development in a country which was predominantly

Protestant, Dry, and committed to keeping the Negro in a second-class position.

In the 1928 Presidential campaign religion was occasionally linked with the anti-segregationist stand of the Catholic church. A common theme of this campaign was the threat to white supremacy supposedly inherent in a Smith victory. The Republican and Democratic parties exploited the race issue. Some of the clergy in both parties loudly proclaimed and advocated the maintenance of racial segregation. The Methodist church, through its Board of Temperance, Prohibition and Public Morals, and Research Secretary, put up a not just southern but nation-wide fight to defeat Smith. Herbert Hoover, the Republican party's candidate, defeated Smith by an overwhelming majority. It is impossible to distinguish the religious campaign against Smith from the dry campaign against him. They were part and parcel of the same attitude. The pretense of the Drys that Prohibition had everything to do with Smith's defeat and religion very little, is questionable. There were also economic aspects to Hoover's victory. Smith lost by some six million votes largely because of the issue of prosperity. The Republicans had claimed so often to be the architects of good times that the Democrats were associated with bad times.[78] It is possible that in the 1928 election, the people voted more for Hoover and against Smith than for the dry cause or the religious factor. The campaign was the last great battle fought by the Drys. The candidacy of Smith had forced the Anti-Saloon League into a policy of what appeared to be religious bigotry and partisan politics. From this point, the importance of Prohibition as a major religious issue began to decline. The status of the Negro, however, continued to be a major issue of the church and religious bodies.

THE NEGRO AND THE CHURCHES

It was previously pointed out that the pattern of segregation has been more obvious and more adamant in the Protestant churches of the United States than in any other institutions. In 1928, southern Presbyterians in general went on record as being in favor of interracial goodwill and understanding. This was done after carefully segregating the Negro delegates.

In 1929, the minister of St. Matthews Protestant Episcopal church, Brooklyn, informed the Negroes in his congregation that they were not welcome. When an Episcopal minister in New York insisted upon permitting Negroes to worship, the members of his vestry, by a vote of 11 to four, had the church closed for repairs and locked. Segregation at church meetings has been and continues to be a problem.[79]

During the 1930's the major Protestant demoninations expressed concern over the plight of the Negro. This was done largely through statements of the various national and regional bodies. In 1931, the World Service Agencies of the Methodist Episcopal church issued a New Year's message which contained a strong statement on race relations. A more significant action took place at the 1932 General Conference. The northern Methodists adopted a resolution that approved the General Conference meeting only in cities where there were sufficient numbers of hotels to accommodate the delegates. It was necessary for the owners or operators of the hotels to agree in writing to the following conditions:

1. No segregation of specific groups in room assignments.
2. No discrimination against any delegates in the use of hotel entrances, lobbies, elevators, dining rooms, and other hotel services or facilities.
3. Specific instruction of hotel employees by the hotel authorities regarding the interracial character of the conference and the treatment of all delegates with equal courtesy.[80]

The southern Methodists were also concerned with the Negro problems. As early as 1919, the Committee on Temperance and Social Services called for cooperation and helpfulness between the races. In 1930, the bishops issued a strong condemnation of racial pride. Four years later (1934) the bishops again expressed their beliefs that Negroes deserved and should have equality before the law, social, civil, and industrial justice, equitable educational, community, and religious advantages, and a human chance at the finer spiritual realities of American life. The Conference (Methodist Episcopal, South) also adopted a social creed calling for justice, opportunity, and equal rights for all regardless of race.[81] In the local conferences, the southern Methodists, now and then, championed racial tolerance. It was the General Conference of the church, South, that assumed the leadership in this area of activity. The experiences of the Baptists with the Negro were similar to the Methodists. The northern Baptists were articulate on the so-called "Negro problem." As early as 1922, the northern Baptist Convention adopted a resolution objecting to unchristian discrimination and favored legislation to remedy matters. In 1925, the American Baptist Foreign Missionary Society held that the most ominous sign on the world horizon was the apparent growth of race prejudice. In the same year, the Convention (northern) expressed a belief that America could not survive if racial lines continued to separate the nation into groups that misunderstood and were hostile to one another. During the opening year of the Depression decade, (1930) the northern Baptist Convention termed race prejudice the greatest hindrance to the establishment of the Kingdom of God on earth. In 1935, the members of this Convention voted to hold future meetings in only those cities where accommodations would be available to all delegates regardless of race or color. From time to time local Baptist groups of this Convention took a strong stand against racial intolerance.[82]

The approach of the southern Baptist Convention on the Negro issue was similar to that of the Conference of the Methodist Episcopal church, South. The southern Baptist Convention was not silent on lynching, but excepting this, there was little to indicate concern with the Negro problem. In 1937, the Home Missions Board made a report that emphasized the infinite worth of personality, regardless of color. The report flatly stated that the Negro was not divinely doomed to perpetual subordination. It listed specific disabilities which must be removed in education, housing, the courts, and labor. It was not until the report of the Home Missions Board that southern Baptists began to speak with vigor and in 1939 the southern Baptist Convention adopted a very vigorous resolution calling for the end of inequalities. Occasionally, Baptist state and district Conventions assumed an advanced position on the Negro.[83]

The Presbyterians (North and South) moved forward faster than other Protestant denominations. In 1919, the General Assembly condemned mob violence. A resolution of 1922 urged Presbyterians to aid the Negro in securing better education, health, housing, recreation, and all other necessities of a Christian community. The 1938 General Assembly adopted a strongly worded protest against racial intolerance.[84] From all indications, northern Presbyterians exerted considerable influence on the

93

breaking down of racial barriers. Although southern Presbyterians did not reveal a deep sense of guilt concerning the treatment of Negroes in America, they were perhaps a shade in advance of the general thinking of their section.

During the 1940's, all of the Protestant denominations, along with many of the Catholics and Jews, began to speak out strongly against the treatment of the Negro. The Protestant churches with smaller memberships—Lutheran, Congregational, and Episcopal—had not divided into northern—southern bodies as the Baptists, Methodists, and Presbyterians. As a result, they were able to maintain closer ties and relations with those members of their denominations in the South. Practically all of these denominations had a history of speaking out against the treatment accorded the Negro. In 1925, the Congregationalists adopted their famous social creed that requested the elimination of racial discrimination. In 1934, the General Council of the now United Congregational and Christian churches stated that racial prejudice was rooted in a competitive economic order. The Protestant Episcopal church frequently spoke against lynching and mob violence and forwarded race relations through the American Church Institute for Negroes, the authorized agency responsible to the General Convention.

The magnificent showing and progress made by the churches, Catholic and Protestant, on desegregation in the forties and fifties drew strength from the precedents established in the twenties and more especially the thirties. By 1960, all major religious bodies in the United States had made pronouncements officially favoring desegregation. In spite of sporadic opposition and failure of denominational recommendations to be accepted on the congregational level, more and more church members challenged segregation on moral and spiritual grounds. Integration within church congregations, as well as church-related colleges, theological seminaries, and hospitals also progressed significantly during the past decade.[85]

During the Depression years, the majority of people were so much concerned with earning a living that they did not go on religious crusades or social reform causes. Occasionally, here and there a new wave of dry sentiment appeared to be forming but in most communities, what had been a lively issue in 1933 had dropped almost completely out of the focus of public attention by 1939, as if settled once and for all. The influence of religion and the church decreased during the years of the Depression. One might have expected that in such a period a great number of people would have turned to the consolation and inspiration of religion. Yet, this did not happen; at least in the sense in which the clergy in innumerable sermons had predicted.

During World War II, from December 1941 until August 1945, practically all of the religious denominations and groups were so engrossed in supporting the war effort that they diverted little or no time or energy to the issues of alcohol and the Negro. On a small scale there continued to be some agitation in behalf of the treatment of Negroes by religious groups. In mid-1940, there appeared a major shift in the thinking of the people of this country about religion. The Federal Council of Churches made a statement that: "For at least half a century Americans have been drifting away from religion. But at the present time all signs—the cheap and the reverent, the serious and the trivial—lead only to one conclusion. Americans are going back to God."[86] During the Korean War years, much of the nation was restlessly, irritably seeking to break through the sense of frustration as a result of the war. In their search for deliverance from the war and other restrictions, they turned to religion. The influence of alcohol and the Negro on religion and the activities of the church were not evident in the mounting religious interest of the country.

As the people of the United States entered the 1960's, the place of the Negro in society continued to be a burning issue. The voice and actions of the church played and will continue to play a dramatic role in solving this issue. The alcoholic beverage issue is no longer of major importance in most parts of the country, and from all indications it will not reach the magnitude of influence in religion and activities of the church as it did a half-century ago.

1 William Warren Sweet, *The Story of Religion in America,* (2d rev. ed.; New York: Harper & Bros., 1950), pp. 2, 8, 13, 26.
2 Will Herberg, *Protestant — Catholic — Jew: An Essay in American Religious Sociology* (New York: Doubleday & Co., 1955), p. 23.
3 *Ibid.,* pp. 151 and 213.
4 Herbert Asbury, *The Great Illusion* (New York: Doubleday & Co., 1950), p. 6.

5 *Ibid.*, pp. 16-17
6 *Ibid.*, p. 16.
7 Ernest Cherrington, *The Evolution of Prohibition In The United States of America* (Westerville, Ohio: The American Press, 1920), p. 28.
8 John A. Krout, *The Origins of Prohibition* (New York: Alfred A. Knopf, 1925), p. 51.
9 Asbury, *op. cit.*, pp. 13-14.
10 Cherrington, *op. cit.*, p. 65.
11 Krout, *op. cit.*, p. 114.
12 Gerald Carson, *The Social History of Bourbon* (New York: Dodd, Mead, & Co., 1963), pp. 146, 263.
13 The Prohibition movement did not begin as such, but as a temperance movement, directed at the task of winning converts by persuasion rather than by law.
14 Cherrington, *op. cit.*, p. 75.
15 Joseph R. Gusfield, *Symbolic Crusade* (Urbana: The University of Illinois Press, 1963), p. 41; and Cherrington, *op. cit.*, p. 93.
16 Krout, *op. cit.*, pp. 114-116.
17 *Ibid.*, p. 119.
18 Kenneth M. Stampp, *The Peculiar Institution* (New York: Alfred A. Knopf, 1956), p. 156.
19 Benjamin E. Mays and Joseph W. Nicholson, *The Negro's Church* (New York: Institute of Social and Religious Research, 1933), pp. 1-3.
20 Herberg, *op. cit.*, p. 127.
21 Stanley M. Elkins, *Slavery: A Problem in American Institutional and Intellectual Life* (Chicago: University of Chicago Press, 1959), pp. 59-60.
22 Herberg, *op. cit.*, p. 116.
23 Stampp, *op. cit.*, pp. 157-158.
24 Sweet, *op. cit.*, pp. 286-287
25 James Benson Sellers, *Slavery in Alabama* (Tuscaloosa: University of Alabama Press, 1950). p. 294.
26 Charles S. Sydnor, *Slavery in Mississippi* (New York: Appelton-Century Co., 1933), p. 55.
27 Elkins, *op. cit.*, p. 60.
28 Sydnor, *op. cit.*, p. 55
29 Ulrich Bonnell Phillips, *American Negro Slavery* (New York: D. Appelton & Co., 1936), p. 421.
30 John Hope Franklin, *From Slavery to Freedom* (New York: Alfred A. Knopf, 1947), p. 189.
31 Sydnor, *op. cit.*, p. 60.
32 *Ibid.*, p. 61.
33 W. E. B. DuBois, *The Negro Church* (Atlanta: Atlanta University Press, 1903), p. 21.
34 Fred A. Ross, *Slavery Ordained of God* (Philadelphia: J. B. Lippincott Co., 1857), p. 135.
35 E. Franklin Frazier, *Black Bourgeoisie* (Glencoe, Illinois: The Free Press, 1957), p. 135.
36 Sweet, *op. cit.*, pp. 298-301.
37 *Ibid.*, p. 301.
38 *Ibid.*, pp. 301-305.
39 Thomas Cumming Hall, *The Religious Background of American Culture* (Boston: Little, Brown, & Co., 1930).
40 Louis Filler, *The Crusade Against Slavery, 1830-1860* (New York: Harper & Row, 1960), pp. 38-40.
41 Sweet, *op. cit.*, p. 326.
42 *Ibid.*, pp. 328-329.
43 Herberg, *op. cit.*, p. 127.
44 Carter G. Woodson, *The History of the Negro Church* (Washington, D. C.: The Associated Publishers, 1921), p. 192.
45 *Ibid.*, pp. 196-197.

46 Sweet, *op. cit.*, p. 333.
47 Peter H. Odegard, *Pressure Politics: The Story of the Anti-Saloon League* (New York: Columbia University Press, 1928) p. 38.
48 Gusfield, *op cit.*, pp. 72-73; and Cherrington, *op. cit.*, pp. 172-175.
49 This city was one of the major strongholds of the abolitionists and later became a major stop on the Underground Railroad.
50 Odegard, *op. cit.*, pp. 2-5.
51 Andrew Sinclair, *Prohibition: The Era of Excess* (Boston: Little, Brown, & Co., 1962).
52 Odegard, *op. cit.*, p. 38.
53 Sinclair, *op. cit.*, pp. 68, 69, 81.
54 Quoted from *Collier's*, June 6, 1908. The reference here is to gin sold by Lee Levy & Company, of St. Louis, whose bottles bore labels with gaudy pictures of nude white women in various seductive poses.
55 Odegard, *op. cit.*, p. 63.
56 Sinclair, *op. cit.*, pp. 76, 77.
57 James H. Timberlake, *Prohibition and the Progressive Movement, 1900-1920* (Cambridge: Harvard University Press, 1963), pp. 1-5.
58 *Ibid., pp.* 12-13.
59 *Ibid.*, pp. 17-18.
60 *Ibid.*, p. 20.
61 *Ibid.*, p. 23.
62 Walter Rauschenbusch, *Christianizing the Social Order* (New York: The Macmillan Co., 1912), pp. 125, 156, 180.
63 *Ibid.*, pp. 209, 288-289, 276.
64 Timberlake, *op. cit.*, p. 21.
65 Charles H. Hopkins, *The Rise of the Social Gospel in American Protestantism, 1865-1915* (New Haven: Yale Studies in Religious Education XIV, 1940), pp. 316-317.
66 Gusfield, *op. cit.*, pp. 36-37.
67 Timberlake, *op. cit.*, p. 30.
68 Carson, *op. cit.*, p. 204.
69 H. Richard Niebuhr, *The Kingdom of God in America* (Chicago: Willett, Clark & Co., 1937), pp. ix, x, 45-46, 99, 105, 128-130, 141-157.
70 Timberlake, *op. cit.*, pp. 36-37.
71 C. Vann Woodward, *The Strange Career of Jim Crow* (New York: Oxford University Press, 1955), p. 7.
72 Robert Moats Miller, *American Protestantism and Social Issues, 1919-1939* (Chapel Hill: The University of North Carolina Press, 1958), pp. 301-302.
73 Woodward, *op. cit.*, p. 112.
74 Miller, *op. cit.*, p. 137.
75 W. J. Cash, *The Mind of the South* (New York: Alfred A. Knopf, 1941), p. 304.
76 Miller, *op. cit.*, p. 304.
77 Edmund A. Moore, *A Catholic Runs for President* (New York: The Ronald Press, 1956), pp. 22, 58.
78 Sinclair, *op. cit.*, p. 303.
79 Miller, *op. cit.*, pp. 299-300.
80 *Ibid.*, p. 305.
81 *Ibid.*, p. 306.
82 *Ibid.*, p. 308.
83 *Ibid.*, p. 309
84 *Ibid.*, p. 311.
85 David O. Mosberg, *The Church As A Social Institution* (Englewood Cliffs, New Jersey: Prentice-Hall, 1962), pp. 451-452.
86 Eric F. Goldman, *The Crucial Decade* (New York: Alfred A. Knopf, 1956), p. 43.

BOOTSIE By OLLIE HARRINGTON

Courtesy The Pittsburgh Courier

"Yaas, Brother Bootsie, I know 'bout them scientists, too, who writes books 'bout how you're supposed to see visual apparitions if you drinks good whiskey, but, Brother, you reckon we has had THAT MUCH good whiskey?"

Economics—Alcohol
and the Negro

CHAPTER THREE

ECONOMICS—ALCOHOL—AND THE NEGRO

COLONIAL DAYS

BEGINNING with the early history of this country, the manufacture and use of alcoholic beverages and the peculiar situation of the Negro have exerted considerable influence upon our economic institutions. The first commercial brewery in the New World was built in 1625 on the southern tip of what is now Manhattan Island, in the Dutch Colony of New Amsterdam.[1] The colonists who were interested in the development of commerce, encouraged and supported the manufacture and use of alcohol. The shrewd trappers used alcoholic beverages as bargaining media to secure riches from their fur trade with the Indians. Many of the ambitious settlers found the use of alcohol potent in suppressing Indian claims to choice tracts of land which they desired. "The fortunes made from furs were piled up alongside the drunk and dead bodies of the Indians."[2] In controlling the fur trade with the Indians rum was indispensable. Wherever the Indians had pelts for sale, there the independent traders or merchants' agents were to be found, usually with a stock of liquor to be used as a medium of exchange. Some of the New England colonists believed that any restrictions on the use of alcohol in the fur trade would end the prosperity for those engaged in this important branch of Colonial commerce.[3] The Colonial statutes also created a climate conducive to the sale and use of alcoholic beverages and the enslaving of the Negro.

LICENSES

A number of the Colonial statutes were plainly intended to encourage the keeping of inns, and the brewing and distilling of alcoholic beverages. Prospective innkeepers were granted a special license by the King's Proprietor or his representative, conferring on the licensee a monopoly for the sale of liquors in his district. The idea of selling the liquor monopoly within a definite district at a high price, either to raise revenue or to limit the number of licensees, was not evident, however, in the early legislation. A small clerical fee usually constituted the only charge made for a license. But as the trade became more profitable and the establishments more numerous laws were enacted to charge higher fees. These fees were graduated according to the profits of the dealers; they were higher in New England than in the colonies to the south. The disposition of the revenue from licenses caused a great deal of friction and conflict between local and provincial authorities. The Colonial officials were not primarily interested in an efficient administration of a license system or in enforcement or regulatory measures. Their chief concern was to raise revenue from the liquor traffic.[4]

In the seventeenth century, licenses to operate taverns or inns were granted only to men of good character and reputation. The tavernkeeper operated the only public place in the town or village; he enjoyed great prestige and high social standing. The increased use of alcoholic beverages changed the picture; when drinking became more profitable, the issuance of a license was determined by political and other considerations. A lower class of men gradually acquired control of the trade and a new type of drinking establishment began to appear; the dram shop and the gin mill, housed in rude shacks, attracted thieves, prostitutes, ruffians, and others of a lawless class.[5]

There was considerable drinking in the colonies, largely due to the lack of other entertainment and to the promotion by the tavernkeepers of a profitable business. The character of the taverns declined. There was so much quick money to be made in the sale of liquor that other features of the inns, taverns, or public houses were neglected.[6] Along with these conditions, the arrival of the Negro also influenced the economy of the colonies.

THE ECONOMIC VALUE OF THE NEGRO

The introduction of the first 20 Negroes to Jamestown, in 1619, and their legal enslavement in 1661; the distillation and exportation of rum in New England; and the increased demand for labor to clear and work the sugar, tobacco, rice and other crops had a profound impact upon the economy of this country. As mentioned earlier, Negroes in Virginia were considered as indentured servants. During this period, the bulk of the

101

agricultural laborers coming into the colonies were white servants whose terms were to become more and more definitely fixed by indenture, and the Negroes so far as the law was concerned were regarded as servants like the rest. There was no articulated legal structure in the colonies to impede their becoming free after a term of service and entering society as artisans and holders of property.[7] The use and economic value of Negro slaves varied in the colonies.

The middle colonies—New York, New Jersey, Pennsylvania and Delaware were more interested in slaves as commodities of commerce than laborers. The West India Company, which fostered the Dutch interest in the slave trade, owned large plantations in New Netherland (New York) and these areas were cultivated largely by Negro slaves. Negroes contributed to the economy of New York through their labor and profits were made by the merchants who bought and sold them. New York had the largest slave population of any northern colony, but found the institution of slavery economically unprofitable. There was an adequate supply of white labor and a lack of extensive farming as in the southern colonies.[8] Nor was it profitable in New Jersey which had the second largest slave population of the northern colonies. The English were responsible for the growth of slavery in New Jersey; the early Dutch and Swedish settlers were indifferent to slavery and imported few Negro workers into this colony. The Negroes contributed to the economy through their work in farming, mining, lumbering, and maritime duties.[9] In Pennsylvania, the white artisans, shopkeepers, and small farmers did not feel any special need for slaves and were opposed to their presence. They believed the non-slaveholders suffered in competition with those who held slaves, and as the institution was not profitable, slave labor was not widely used.[10]

Beginning in 1638, only a limited number of Negroes were brought yearly into the New England colonies to be sold because neither Indian nor Negro slavery was profitable; it was unsuited to the diversified agriculture of these colonies. The immediate successor of the Indian was not the Negro but the poor white. These white servants included a variety of types. Some were indentured servants; they signed a contract, indented by law, binding them to service for a specific period of time in return for their passage. Others were known as redemptioners; they

102

arranged with the captain of a ship to pay their passage on arrival or within a specified period of time; if they were unable to do so they were sold by the captain to the highest bidder. Others were convicts sent out by deliberate policy of their home government.[11]

During the seventeenth century, Colonial New England became deeply involved in the slave trade. Massachusetts took the lead in the slave traffic and laid the basis for the economic interdependence of Colonial New England and the West Indies. Prior to 1664, Massachusetts merchants had occasionally brought Negroes from the West Indies, but in that year, Boston traders attempted to import slaves directly from Africa when an association of business men sent three ships there for gold dust and Negroes.[12] By 1700, Boston traders were supplying other New England colonies with Negroes. Although New England's share in the slave trade was small in the seventeenth century, by the eighteenth century her merchants had laid the foundations for a lucrative commerce. They had already begun the triangular slave voyages and had learned the West Indies offered the best market for Negroes. Comparatively few Negroes (slaves) were actually brought to New England; the traders in these colonies made their profits as carriers and not exploiters of Negro labor.[13]

The New England slave trade attained its greatest development in the eighteenth century. This was mainly due to the increased demand for Negroes in the sugar islands of the British and Spanish West Indies and the growing employment of Negroes in the tobacco and rice growing colonies of the South. As the New Englanders were prevented by climate and soil from reaping rich returns from agriculture, they were attracted by prospects of profits greater than could be realized from the land, and early began to engage in commerce, the fishing industry and trade in Negroes. As a result, of these factors, the New England colonies in the eighteenth century became the greatest slave-trading section of America. There came into being the famous triangular slave trade with New England, Africa, and the West Indies as its focal points.[14]

In the triangular trade, ships from New England carried food and other commodities to the West Indies. These cargoes were exchanged for rum and the ships would proceed to Africa. There they bartered their rum for slaves which they transported

103

to the West Indies, where they disposed of them for rum, sugar, molasses and other tropical products. (When rum was unobtainable in the islands, the ship captains bartered their wares for sugar, cocoa, molasses or other products.) The sugar and molasses were carried to New England, distilled into rum, and along with other trinkets, bar iron, beads and light-colored cloth, carried to Africa and exchanged for Negroes. In the beginning of the triangular slave trade, the dealers on the African Slave Coast sold a "prime" Negro for a few gallons of rum, but as rum became cheaper and more plentiful, the price of slaves rose to 250 gallons each and the business became unprofitable. During these years preceding the American Revolution more than 600,000 gallons were shipped abroad annually and large quantities were sold for domestic consumption.[15] Sugar, rum, and molasses were vital to the slave trade as well as to New England's economy.

THE ECONOMIC VALUE OF ALCOHOLIC BEVERAGES

The first rum used in this country was imported from the West Indies. The domestic distillation began on a large scale when a shipload of molasses was brought to Rhode Island in the seventeenth century. Soon afterwards distilleries were in operation throughout New England. The distillation of millions of gallons of molasses from the British Islands or the West Indies was the basis of a liquor industry of such magnitude that the making of rum became New England's largest manufacturing business before the Revolution. There were a large number of distilleries throughout the New England colonies with more than 30 in Rhode Island and 63 in Massachusetts. Rum was primarily linked with the Negro trade and immense quantities of the liquor were sent to Africa and exchanged for slaves.[16]

The popularity of New England rum and other alcoholic beverages was challenged after the middle of the eighteenth century by a distilled product of the West—whiskey. It soon became a favorite beverage with a high commercial value. Distilled whiskey represented concentrated value and was readily salable. It even passed in some districts as an acceptable substitute for currency. In whatever branch of trade the merchant invested his capital he relied upon rum or some other form of ardent spirits to earn profits for him. Since the alcoholic beverage traffic was consistently profitable for all who engaged in it, the public accorded it that approval which attaches to most things indispensable to the business world.[17]   On the eve of the Revolution spirituous liquor was one of the greatest factors in moving Colonial commerce.

The sale of alcoholic beverages enriched the merchants and some of the colonies as well.   The government licensed tavernkeepers not only as a measure of control and regulation of the sale of alcoholic beverages, but as a source of revenue.

All of the colonies levied import duties on foreign and excise taxes on domestic alcoholic beverages.   Some of the colonists defended the alcoholic beverage traffic on the basis that it provided revenue for the support of local government.   The Massachusetts Colony was the first to place a tariff on the importation of wines and spirits and a small excise tax on local production for sale.   In 1644, New York levied an excise tax on beer, wine, and brandy and in 1710 an excise tax was enacted for liquor sold in retail outlets.   New York, in 1714, required retailers of potent liquors to pay a special tax which was appropriated for the support of the Colonial government.   In 1720, a duty was placed on imported wines and distilled liquors.[18]   Maryland, in 1704, enacted legislation that levied an import duty upon a number of items, including rum, wine, and liquor.   The revenue derived from the alcoholic beverages was used to repair courthouses, prisons and to increase the salaries of justices.[19]   Education in Connecticut received considerable impetus from the sums accruing to the treasury in the form of custom duties and excise taxes from alcoholic beverages.   In 1650, Connecticut placed a heavy duty upon all imported liquors and an excise tax on all manufactured liquors at home.   In 1721, a rector's house was built for Yale College from these taxes, and six years later, the assembly voted that the rum revenue appropriated for one year be used to benefit and support the college and its clergymen and teachers. An Act of 1766 awarded the excise money to the towns to be used for benefit of the local schools.[20]   In 1706, Pennsylvania passed a law which levied a tax on retailers of foreign spirits. This law was extended in 1772, to include rum, brandy, and domestic spirits.   This revenue was set up as an emergency fund to meet extraordinary expenses, insuring the government against too frequent financial embarrassment.[21]

Along with revenue derived from the sale of alcoholic beverages, the sale of slaves provided income for the Colonial governments. The initial import duty on servants and Negroes, in Virginia, was enacted in 1699 and remained in force until 1701. That this was not purely a revenue act is shown by the fact that a rebate of three-fourths of the duty was given when the Negroes were transported out of the Dominion within six weeks. The importation of Negroes remained unchecked and the only advantage Virginia reaped was a large revenue for her public works. In 1704, the council of Virginia imposed an extra duty of two shillings per slave for the alleged purpose of rebuilding William and Mary College, which had been burned. The duty imposed upon slaves was also used to replace the Statehouse which had been destroyed by fire; this source of revenue was used to avoid an extra poll tax. An Act of 1699 imposing a duty on slaves and servants expired by limitation in May 1707, after raising a revenue of 4,000 pounds. Out of this amount, 3,000 pounds were expended to construct a house for the governor of the colony.[22]

The Carolina colonists in 1719 levied a duty of ten pounds per head on Negroes imported from Africa and 30 pounds on all Negroes imported from the Islands. In 1722, a duty was laid on Negroes brought from other colonies. There was concern by some Carolinians about the economic consequences to the colony of large slave importations. They feared that the prosperity in the slave traffic would result in economic disaster. Before the middle of the eighteenth century the rice planters of Carolina were running the dangerous risk of over-investing in slaves and of thereby destroying their economic gains.[23]

In 1704 Maryland passed a revenue act which was unique. It imposed a duty upon rum, wine, brandy, Negroes, and Irish servants. The primary purpose of this legislation was to raise revenue.[24]

In 1700, a duty of ten shillings was levied on every Negro brought into the Pennsylvania Colony. By 1705, this duty had been doubled. The assembly of 1712 enacted a law preventing the importation of slaves under any condition. The law was changed in 1715 and a duty of five pounds was placed on each slave that was imported. This was rescinded and seven years later, in 1722, was levied again and then reduced to two pounds in 1729. Finally in 1761, the duty on each slave was increased to ten pounds where it remained until the importation of slaves was totally forbidden in 1780.[25]

The first import duty levied on slaves by the colony of New York was in 1702. The law required a payment of 15 shillings for each slave imported directly from Africa and 30 shillings for all others. In the same year, for slaves not imported directly from Africa, the duty was increased to three pounds per head. Between 1709 and 1732 there were other laws enacted concerning import levies on slaves. On two occasions, slaves were taxed as property in New York. In 1709, chimneys, fireplaces and slaves were taxed; a levy of two shillings was placed upon each Indian slave and Negro slave. The assembly, in a period of depression, enacted an annual levy of "two penny weight and twelve grains of plate or one shilling in bills of credit, upon slaves between 14 and 50 years old for ten years."[26]

New Jersey followed the pattern of New York and the other colonies in enacting laws that levied a duty for bringing Negroes into the colony. A duty of ten pounds was imposed on all slaves brought into the colony between 1713 and 1716 under a law passed in 1713.[27]

The levy of a duty on all Negroes imported into the New England colonies was initiated by Massachusetts. This colony enacted a law in 1705 which placed a tax of four pounds on every Negro. In 1711, Rhode Island followed with a similar enactment imposing a duty of three pounds a head.[28]

The influence of the revenues derived from the duties and taxes levied upon the slave trade and liquor traffic upon the economic institutions of the colonies is not known. They provided funds to support various activities of local governments which were designed to meet the needs of the people. The economic value of slavery resulted from the fact that ownership made cheap labor available for all types of work, especially farming in the South. On the eve of the American Revolution, traffic in human beings was an integral part of Colonial economy and prosperity.

107

THE NEGRO AND THE CONSTITUTION

Following the War of Independence, the leaders of the country called a Constitutional Convention to meet in Philadelphia in 1787, to stablize and strengthen the government and to stem the tide of social revolution. Some of the leaders—George Washington, Benjamin Franklin, Thomas Jefferson, John Jay, and Alexander Hamilton—considered slavery an evil inconsistent with the principles of the Declaration of Independence. The signers at the Constitutional Convention pledged not to import slaves nor to purchase those which had been imported.[29] It was natural that slavery became an important issue in the Convention. The opponents of slavery hoped that the Constitutional Convention would act to stop this evil. Although there was considerable sentiment against the traffic in human beings, it was not abolished. The Northwest Ordinance of 1787, which forbade slavery in the Northwest Territory, divided the United States into two well-defined and sharply contrasted sections, one having slavery and the other devoid of this institution. The South also won another victory at the Convention in 1787. After the Convention had granted Congress the power to levy direct taxes and had provided for a lower house elected according to population, the question of slavery arose. The slaves, according to the North, should be counted as property in levying direct taxes, but not as people in determining the basis of representation. The result of the debates was a three-fifths compromise, providing that three-fifths of the slaves be counted for purposes of both representation and taxation. Other compromises were effected between the slave-holding, free trade South and the North. Congress was not to interfere with the slave trade for 20 years and could lay no import tax in excess of ten dollars a slave.[30] The oratorical battle which decided the struggle, was led by men from South Carolina and Georgia. They threatened that their states would not join the Union if foreign slavery was abolished. In the North there were also many powerful supporters of slavery in the persons of ship-owners. Many of the slave ships which carried their cargoes of blacks from Africa to America sailed from such northern ports as Salem, Massachusetts and Newport, Rhode Island. The capitalistic shipowners added their support to the demands of the southern states. In a compromise to prevent the formation of a southern union, slave trade was to be permitted only until 1808.

The framers of the Constitution gave serious attention and consideration to the economic life and future of the country. "The fathers of the Constitution were dedicated to the proposition that 'government should rest upon the dominion of property'. For the southern fathers this meant slaves, just as surely as it meant commerce and industry for the northern fathers."[31] The protection of this property by the Constitution had given recognition to the institution of human slavery and it was to take about 75 years to undo that which was done in 1787.

THE SLOW DEATH OF SLAVERY

The extent to which slavery had been influenced by the humanitarian philosophy of the War of Independence and the framing of the Constitution would largely be speculation. Immediately following the war, slavery began to die slowly in these former colonies. In 1777, Vermont abolished the institution of slavery; Massachusetts followed suit in 1780; and New Hampshire, in 1783. These states accomplished the abolition by means of constitutional provisions. The Pennsylvania legislature passed an act in 1780 which provided for the gradual emancipation of slaves. A similar action was taken by Rhode Island and Connecticut in 1784, by New York in 1799, and New Jersey in 1804.[32]

In the years following 1780, the areas where the slaves were concentrated experienced a severe depression. The tobacco plantations were plagued by soil exhaustion and a glutted market. Rice and indigo production brought little profit to the planters of these commodities. The price of slaves was declining and there was reason to believe that the institution would completely deteriorate. The planters did everything they could to mitigate their losses and continue the institution until a solution could be found to their problem.[33] They did not have long to wait. The initiation of one of the most influential features in the economic and social history of the South was to give slavery a reprieve and/or new life—the development of a cotton culture. The raising of cotton had made little progress during the Colonial period, for superior profits from tobacco, a lack of market, and other factors had discouraged its production. The American Revolution interrupted the importation of foreign fabrics and the planters turned their attention to the possibilities of cotton. The Industrial Revolution provided an insatiable market. At the same time, the declining profits from the worn-out tobacco fields made the planters experiment with new crops; cotton was one of them. Prior to the Civil War, cotton became the largest single export of the country and the greatest commercial crop of the South. At the same time, the Industrial Revolution sealed slavery upon the South. Distinctly on the decline after the American Revolution and subject to caustic criticism by many southern leaders, slavery seemed to be doomed. According to one writer, "Cotton-culture, however, was ideally suited to the crude and wasteful methods of ignorant slave labor, and the black man, whose economic value had been on the decline, suddenly took on new importance."[34]

Between 1790 and 1830, a revolution in southern agriculture took place which influenced the entire country, and especially the value of slaves. In England, the systems of producing cotton textiles had undergone revolutionary changes. With the inventions of spinning and weaving machinery, the manufacturing process was so cheapened that the demand for cotton goods was greatly stimulated. The invention of the cotton gin by Eli Whitney in 1792 made profitable the growing of the short staple cotton in the South. A few years after the invention of the cotton gin, the South began to make the economic transition which the new development induced. The cultivation of cotton required little capital and many farmers began to shift from the cultivation of rice, indigo, or tobacco to cotton. Production increased, new lands were cleared, and Negro labor was employed exclusively in the cultivation of cotton instead of the tedious job of seeding it. Between 1791 and 1795, 5,200,000 pounds of cotton were produced in the United States. In 1860, cotton constituted 57 percent of the nation's exports compared to 22 percent in 1820. In 1790, a "good" Negro might be purchased for $300.00. The same Negro in 1830 would bring $1,200.00 and $1,500.00 by 1860. The increase in the production of cotton was accompanied by a demand for more slave labor. Slavery was very important to the South and to the nation as a whole between 1830 and 1860, due to the fact that cotton was the primary product; it made up more than one-half of the total exports of the country.[35]

Coincident with the rise of the cotton culture in the Atlantic states was the development of sugar cane growing in the delta lands of southeastern Louisiana. The major sugar cane producing area—Florida, Texas, and Louisiana—depended upon slave labor for the cultivation of their crops. In fact, sugar was as important a product to the economy of Louisiana—the largest producing area—as tobacco, rice, indigo, and cotton were to the other states of the South. The ante-bellum sugar industry required a large number of laborers. This need was supplied by Negro slaves; in fact, they composed the overwhelming majority of the working force in the sugar economy. Louisiana, as did some of the earlier colonies and other states, attempted to solve its labor problem by indenturing white servants and enslaving Indians. Both of these solutions failed, and success came only with the introduction of African Negro slaves in 1712.[36]

Sugar cane was the foundation of the economy of Louisiana and a small area of eastern Texas. It provided the wealth for the planter society; it furnished the sustenance for thousands of slaves and indirectly contributed enormously to the economic well-being of thousands of non-sugar folk of the area, who in one way or another were tied to the sugar economy until the Civil War. The expansion of the sugar industry brought about an increased demand for Negroes. It was rare for a sugar planter to sell any of his slaves. Occasionally a planter would dispose of a Negro who constantly ran away or caused trouble. The farmers and sugar plantation owners had substantial financial investments in slaves. A cholera epidemic hit Louisiana in 1832 and killed hundreds of whites and Negroes. "A contemporary estimate placed the pecuniary loss of Louisiana planters from slave deaths of $4,000,000."[37]

DOMESTIC SLAVE TRADE

In 1808, the Congress of the United States outlawed the slave trade as per the Constitutional agreement. This had been the major source of cheap labor to farm cotton, sugar cane, and other crops. As a result of the termination of the slave trade, there was an increase in the value of slaves. Between 1808 and 1860, with the supply from Africa shut off, those needing slaves had to depend on the domestic supply resulting from normal increase. With the official closing of the African slave trade in 1808, inter-state slave traffic began to assume the aspect of a regular business, though for some years it continued on a small scale and was often merely incidental in character.[38]   After 1808, many business firms that dealt in farm supplies and animals frequently carried a line of slaves. Auctioneers who disposed of real estate and personal property sold slaves along with their other commodities.   Planters who were abandoning their farms or were undergoing some kind of retrenchment either passed the word around or advertised in the newspapers that they had slaves for sale.   Benevolent organizations frequently sold slaves by lottery.[39]

The heyday of the domestic slave trade came in the time of peace and migration from 1815 to 1860.   By 1815, about the time of the great population movement into the cotton kingdom, trading in slaves had become a major activity.   The years immediately following the War of 1812, witnessed an un-paralled movement of the population westward.   Into the Gulf region went large numbers of settlers to clear the rich lands and cultivate extensive crops of cotton.   Not only did cotton give to the South a great staple crop and preserve slavery in that region, but it hastened at an astonishing pace the occupation of the South West.   Slavery lived in part by exploiting the soil, and the land hungry planters gathered their slaves and possessions and pushed into the South West.   The expansion of the country increased the demand for slaves and created considerable concern among the planters whether the supply would last.   One of the ways in which the slaveholders guarded against exhausting the supply was the systematic breeding of slaves.   Although there have been denials and apologies by students of the history of American slavery, there are no doubts that many slaveholders deliberately undertook to increase the number of salable slaves by encouraging prolificity in every possible way.[40]

The high point in slave sales in the domestic market was reached just before the panic of 1837 when Virginia reported that in the previous year she had exported about 120,000 slaves into the lower South.   Thereafter, the flow was held in check, first by the hard times in the cotton belt and then by an agricultural renaissance in Virginia.   After the panic, the slump in both prices and demand became so pronounced that some traders were forced to return to Virginia and Mary-land with their slaves and sustain staggering losses.[41]   Accord-

112

ing to one historian, the cost of rearing slaves had no practical bearing upon the market price for the reason that the owners could not, or at least did not, increase or diminish the production at will.[42] The prices of slaves in domestic trade reflected all the forces operating to create supply and demand in American society. The increase in the number of slaves was not sufficiently rapid to keep pace with the opening of fresh land to cotton, and the demand for slave labor was greater than supply. An able-bodied fieldhand who sold for $300 before the cotton gin or $750 in 1845 might bring from $1,500 to $2,000 in 1860. Slaves seemed to be the one type of property that inevitably increased in value. A slave owner had but to devote reasonable care to his slaves, and his wealth would expand.[43]

Closely allied with slave trading was the practice of slave hiring. This practice prevailed extensively all over the South. Owners had various reasons for hiring out their slaves instead of selling them. Slaves were hired by the day, the month, or by the year, to engage in all kinds of work. The rates varied considerably depending on the skill of the slave as well as the supply. In 1800, a slavehand brought $100 per year in the lower South. By 1860, he brought $200 or more. Slave trading and hiring were essential parts of the economic and social fabric of the South.[44] On the eve of the Civil War, the North had developed an economy based upon trade and industry. In the South, the economy and wealth were largely invested in agriculture and the owning of slaves. Along with the issue of the Negro and slavery, the use and sale of alcoholic beverages continued to be a controversial issue.

THE WARS AND ALCOHOL

The War of Independence served to increase the use of alcohol. The military records reveal the important role alcohol played in the economy of those who fought, and those who sold supplies. Each colony attempted to provide its militia with the best liquor available. The Continental troops were allowed either one-fourth or a half-pint of whiskey a day, if available. The desire of the men in the army for liquor was so keen that the Quartermaster-General was authorized to allow one sutler to each brigade to sell whiskey, rum, gin, brandy, and cordials.[45] These strenuous efforts to provide sufficient quantities of liquor were an indication of the widespread use of the product of the still during the war.

Following the war, distillation from grain became more popular in all parts of the country. Domestic production was augmented in 1790 by the importation of 3,678,000 gallons of spirits. In rural communities throughout the country little work was done wihout the use of intoxicants. Wages were quoted in terms that included a daily allowance of rum; few laborers cared to accept more money in lieu of the liquor. In many places, merchants carried larger stocks of wet goods than dry goods. No grocer seemed to prosper unless he kept a barrel of spirits on tap and treated his customers whenever they settled their accounts.[46] Between the Revolutionary War and the last of the eighteenth century the manufacture and sale of alcoholic beverages had become an important part of the American economy.

In 1791, the newly founded government of the United States was confronted by financial problems, as a result of the war. Alexander Hamilton, Secretary of the Treasury, proposed that the United States should meet fully and promptly its financial obligations including the assumption of the debts contracted by the states in the struggle for independence. The money was partly to be raised by placing an excise tax upon distilled spirits. The news of the enactment of this measure was greeted with a roar of indignation in the back country settlements. The duty was laid uniformly on all the states, as the Constitution provided.[47]

This tax survived the next 11 years. In 1802, the laws laying duties on stills and domestic distilled spirits were struck from the statute books. The formal declaration of war in 1812, forced the President to call a special session of Congress in 1813 to reinforce taxation revenue. The war had endangered receipts from custom duties and the excise on spirituous liquors. The internal revenue system was readjusted to correct the financial balance of the country by placing a direct tax on real estate, slaves and a duty on spirituous liquors. The duty was levied in the form of a license to be paid by distillers. With the end of the emergency, four years later, this tax was eliminated. Congress concurred and from that time to the beginning of the Civil War, there was no attempt to levy an additional excise

tax on liquor or any other domestic product.[48]   Along with
the revenues raised by placing a tax on slaves, the slaves helped
the war effort as workers.

THE WARS AND THE NEGRO

During the war, Negroes made substantial contributions to
the economy of the country. In the South, they were a fundamental element in the agricultural economy of the Confederacy
and an important factor in making possible the feeding of
soldiers and civilians. In fact, the slaves and free Negroes of
the Confederacy constituted a great reservoir of labor, which
made it possible for a large number of whites to serve in the
army.   In 1860, there were about 3,500,000 slaves in the 11
Confederate states.[49]   The non-industrial South presented a
desperate picture attempting to wage war by home industries.
The isolation of the South resulted in almost every plantation
becoming a manufacturing unit in which Negroes were laborers
and white women the supervisors.[50]

In addition to laboring in these home industries, slaves
were valuable in agriculture and in military service.   They
worked as teamsters, cooks, body servants, hospital attendants
and in labor battalions. In 1862, there developed considerable
support for the use of gunboats by the Confederacy. Some
leaders advocated that the government impress 15,000 or more
slaves and put them to work building these engines of destruction. By 1864, there was a great demand for them to work in
armories, munition factories, and other industries where they
served as wheelwrights, blacksmiths, harness makers and shoe-
makers. As the war moved toward a climax, almost every industry was competing for Negro labor.[51]

THE CIVIL WAR

When the Civil War began, the North had a more diverse
civilization and economy than the South. The stimulation of
business and the military drain upon manpower produced a
labor shortage. Negro labor was also used in the North; the
white workers, however, showed open hostility to their presence.
They feared that the emancipation of slaves would cause a
general exodus of Negroes to the North and that competition

115

between whites and blacks for work would depress wages and increase unemployment. The results were riots and fights when Negroes sought work. One ugly aspect of the labor situation was seen in the race riots which occurred in 1863 in Brooklyn and Cincinnati, when white laborers objected to the employment of Negroes. Longshoremen in Chicago, Detroit, Cleveland, Buffalo, New York and Boston fought Negro workers whenever they were brought on the job.[52] Even in the face of the conflicts and the resistance of white laborers, Negroes were of economic value to the North. As laborers, they produced goods and services thus contributing to the war effort. Many of the Negro slaves deserted the South and served in the Union army and they performed all kinds of services. Although the economies of the North and South benefited from the efforts of Negroes, both were confronted by problems in financing the war; both turned to alcoholic beverages for additional funds.

Although whiskey had been taxed since 1791, it was not until 1862 that the first federal beer tax was levied. The revenue derived from this tax was to help finance the mounting costs of the Civil War. Both the North and South adopted excise taxes for the manufacture and sale of alcohol to support the war effort. The Civil War compelled the federal government to create a most extensive and complicated system of internal taxes upon incomes, commodities and distilled spirits. It has been pointed out before that a federal act imposed a tax of 20 cents per proof gallon on distilled spirits of domestic manufacture effective August 1, 1862, which continued in force until March 7, 1864 when the rate was raised to 60 cents. The excise tax on the output of whiskey was increased several times during the war. Taxes were also placed on the processes of mixing and compounding spirits and licenses were required for selling them wholesale. The number of gallons on which taxes were levied increased from 16,149,953 in 1863 to 85,295,392 in 1864. The available evidence seems to indicate that excises provided considerable revenue for the Union to carry on the war.[53]

Attempts to secure revenue for war purposes in the South were confronted by many problems. The distilling of alcoholic beverages was encouraged by the government. Early in the war, the Confederacy passed acts to discourage drunkenness and to conserve grain supplies necessary to feed the armed forces.

116

It also prohibited the importation of alcoholic beverages, to conserve space for war supplies on incoming ships. These restrictions on the use of alcohol became burning issues in the Confederacy; both were the enforced products of war conservation policies. The acute shortage and restricted supply sharply reduced the revenue collected from the manufacture and sale of alcoholic beverages in the states of the Confederacy. The situation was further exacerbated because large quantities of alcohol and alcoholic stimulants were required for the maintenance of the army, which placed additional demands on the limited supply. To supply the public services with alcohol, contracts were made by the War and Navy departments with the states and private distillers. The Confederate government, during the last two years of the war, because of its inability to control the manufacture and sale of liquor by contract with private distilleries, had to establish its own distilleries and abolish the contract system.[54]

RECONSTRUCTION

THE NEGRO

At the end of the Civil War, the slaves were set free by the federal government. The South suffered great losses. The greatest single possession the southerner lost was his property in Negroes. The money value of the slaves was estimated at from one to four billion dollars.[55] Along with this there was destruction everywhere—towns and cities, railways, bridges, forests, fields, factories, livestock, homes, and personal belongings.[56] As the people of the South attempted to rebuild, the only help available was the Negro. Many were convinced that when freedom came to the slaves, they would not work. There was almost a universal preference among black belt landlords for Negro tenants and workers. "White labor is totally unsuited to our methods, our manners, and our accommodations, declared an Alabama planter; No other laborer [than the Negro] of whom I have any knowledge, would be as careful or so contented on four pounds of meat and a peck of meal a week, in a little log cabin 14 x 16 feet with cracks in it large enough to afford free passage to a large sized cat." A Mississippi planter echoed, "Give me the nigger every time. The nigger will never strike if you give him plenty to eat and half clothe him. He will

117

live on less and do more hard work, when properly managed than any other race of people . . . we can boss him and that is what we southern folk like."[57]   Negro farm workers contributed greatly to the economic recovery of the South. As free workers, however, they gained but little. The wages paid to them, in most cases, were lower than those that had been paid to hired slaves. When they attempted to sharecrop, the cost of maintenance was so great that at the end of the year the freedman was indebted to his employer for most of what he made, and sometimes it was more than he made.[58]   In fact, the perpetual indebtness of the Negro tenant farmer bound him to the land almost as a slave.

The mass of Negro labor became less concentrated in farm work. Freedom brought to a large number of Negroes a greater variety of work than they had engaged in as slaves. The almost universal practice of employing Negroes for menial work at low wages was justified by the firm conviction that they were lazy, shiftless, and unreliable in the highest industrial callings. The Negroes were worsted by white labor in competition for better types of employment. Between 1865 and 1890, Negroes fell from a position of dominance in the skilled crafts— carpenters, brick and stone masons, painters, plasterers, and machinists—to unskilled jobs. They were excluded from the textile industry except for a few thousand entrusted with the heaviest or most disagreeable tasks. Negro males were freely employed in such poorly paid occupations as railroad building, brickmaking, street-cleaning, and sewer-digging. The lumber, iron, and tobacco industries made use of them as unskilled laborers. A large number of Negroes were employed as domestic servants; about one-third of all employed Negroes in 1890 were to be found in this category. Negro females were engaged for the most part in domestic service and received the low pay associated with those occupations.[59]

In some respects, the Negro was worse off in the South in 1890, than he had been in 1860. In spite of these conditions, the economic opportunities for southern Negroes surpassed those of the North. So bitter was the hostility of the northern working classes to the employment of Negroes that between 1880 and 1890 as many as 50 protest strikes were held. When Negroes were imported as strikebreakers the antagonism deepened.[60]

In 1900, there were not quite nine million Negroes in the United States and they were overwhelmingly concentrated in the South. Nearly nine-tenths of the Negroes were to be found there, but almost three-fourths of the total were to be found in the rural South. The war and Emancipation had destroyed the plantation South. Many of the whites, however, were interested in building a labor organization as similar as possible to slavery. The old plantation system re-established itself as the years passed. A considerable number of the plantation owners were killed in the war, went bankrupt or left the land for other reasons. Much land was forfeited to creditors and tax authorities. As cotton prices soared, it was profitable for anybody who could secure cash to buy land and hire Negro labor. In spite of much wandering Negro labor was available. After some attempts at a wage system, sharecropping became the labor pattern into which the Negro, and later on, poor whites were pressed.[61] There were and continue to be considerable differences in the economic status and degree of dependency between the several types of tenants. Highest on the ladder are the renters and cash tenants, who rent their farms for a fixed sum of money. All other kinds of arrangements entitle the landlord to certain shares of the main cash crops, for instance, one-fourth, one-third, one-half, and sometimes even as much as three-fourths. These tenants who receive one-half or less of the crop are sharecroppers. The cash tenants usually furnish all the work, stock, feed, fertilizers, and tools themselves. The other groups generally furnish less and less of these things. Those lowest down on the scale have little or nothing but their labor to offer.[62]

Over a period of years, there had been a tendency for Negroes to migrate northward. It was not until 1915 that the northward migrations reached flood proportions. The increased demand for unskilled workers in northern industry by the World War I boom accelerated this movement. And it grew as word spread through county after county and city after city, in the South, that friends and relatives were eating regularly and living better and voting. That schools were better than those at home and that sanitary conditions were less primitive.

The migration of the Negro to the North was important because: (1) behind this movement there was a dissatisfaction with conditions from which they had come, and (2) the promise of improvement in another area. The dominant "push" in the Negro migration, in this period and later, was the inability to earn a satisfactory living in the South. The principal "pull" was the greater aspect of economic opportunities in industry.[63] In his exodus from the South, the Negro was hoping for relief from the harsh conditions he left behind; this, however, was not going to be the case. As the migration to the North and Midwest increased, hostility grew. As the Negro moved from the rural areas to the cities in the South and migrated to the North, he developed a greater feeling of freedom. The migration of Negroes between World War I and the 1920's had great implications for the group. The Negro migrated for the best possible reasons: because life in the South had become intolerable; because he glimpsed the horizons of freedom elsewhere. Many of these migrants had ambitions for a better life which could not be realized in the South. The healthy—physically and mentally— and better educated or trained moved to the North and Midwest in search of economic opportunity at a youthful age when they could make a maximum contribution to the urban labor force.

ALCOHOL

From 1865 to the twentieth century more than seven million immigrants entered the United States, and nearly 50 percent came from Ireland and Germany. Immigration was one of the factors which accounted for the increased use and growth of the liquor traffic. Many of the immigrants were accustomed drinkers and expanded the market for liquor. Between the Civil War and the Volstead Act, the saloon was the major legal dispenser of alcoholic beverages in the United States. In the cities, a number of the saloons were staffed by individuals who were not Anglo-Saxon and Protestant. They were Irish, German, Italian and others, who were members of the Roman Catholic church. There were some who believed that the increase of non-Protestant foreign speaking people and the rapid growth of the cities created new liquor problems. By the early 1870's, the liquor traffic, particularly the brewing industry waxed prosperous. The majority of the newly arrived immigrants were largely beer drinkers. Prior to Prohibition the big money in the alcoholic beverage industry was in beer. During the 60 years

120

from 1850 to 1910, the per capita consumption of beer increased 1,000 percent.[64]

In 1875 and 1882 there were two events which had considerable influence and impact upon the alcoholic beverage industry; both related to federal revenue laws and policies. In 1875, when the federal tax was raised to 90 cents per proof gallon, spirits on hand were exempted. This legislative windfall put profits into the pockets of distilling interests and their friends in Congress. Playing a leading role in this legislative profiting was the notorious "Whiskey Ring," which had been organized to evade taxes and license fees on spirits. Its headquarters were located in St. Louis; its sphere of influence and participation embraced officialdom from local supervisors, collectors, and storekeepers to the officers of the Internal Revenue Bureau, and persons occupying a confidential relationship to President U. Grant. The distillers in various parts of the country thus conspired with the federal and local officers to defraud the government of untold millions of dollars in taxes on whiskey and to secure protection through political campaign funds.[65] Although these events were responsible for considerable criticism and public discussion of liquor, it did not seem to influence its use or consumption.

Between the Reconstruction period and the twentieth century, Negroes along with other members of the population consumed considerable quantities of alcoholic beverages. Whether they used alcohol in excess of their numbers in the total population was and continues to be a moot question among many people. Negroes were unable to engage in the large scale production and sale because of inadequate financial resources. In the North, Negroes were confronted by problems in their attempts to secure licenses to operate saloons. Many of the distillers were of foreign extraction—largely German and Irish—and they were partial in their support of their fellow countrymen who were saloon operators. The distillers and brewers subsidized the saloonkeepers with loans, which provided the necessary monies for the payment of heavy license fees. Where elected officials were in charge of the issuance of licenses, the liquor industry attempted to control the local political machine or made heavy campaign contributions to control and influence them.[66] But in spite of all of these obstacles confronting them a few Negroes were able to secure the necessary capital and licenses to operate saloons.

In 1876, an investigation in the city of Philadelphia, revealed that intoxicating liquors were being sold in 8,034 places. Engaged in the retail sale of liquor were: two Chinese, 18 Italians, 140 Spaniards, 106 Welsh, 205 white Americans, 265 Negroes, 285 French, 497 Scotch, 568 English, 2,179 Germans, 304 Irish, and 672 of unknown nationality.[67] In the South, Negroes had more opportunities to operate saloons that catered to the members of their group than in the North. Some of these drinking places were patronized by both white and colored customers. Until 1890, saloons operated by Negroes served both races in Mississippi.[68] The 1880 census revealed that there were four times as many drinking places as churches, nine times as many liquor sellers as ministers and 12 times as much paid for liquor as for the gospel in the United States.[69] The expenditure for alcoholic beverages in this country has never been totally known because of the illegal manufacture and sale of alcohol. In 1865, users of alcoholic beverages spent $18,731,422.45 for distilled spirits and wines, and $3,734,928.06 for malt beverages, a total expenditure of $22,466,350.51. This compares with a total expenditure of $109,868,817.00 for distilled spirits and wine, and $73,550,754.00 for malt beverages, for a total of $183,419,-571.00 in 1900.[70] This substantial increase in revenue for all alcoholic beverages leaves no doubt that the manufacture, sale and use of alcoholic beverages exerted considerable influence on the economy.

The liquor business—brewers, distillers, vinters, wholesale and retail dealers—underwent rapid growth and expansion during the early years of the twentieth century. From 1900 to 1914, the total consumption of alcoholic beverages (distilled spirits, wines, and beers), increased from 1,349,732,435 gallons to 2,252,272,675 gallons respectively. The per capita consumption for this period was as follows:[71]

Alcoholic Beverages	1900	1914
Distilled spirits	1.28	1.44
Wines	.39	.53
Beer	16.06	20.69

The total of distilled spirits was not used for human consumption; a considerable amount was converted to industrial purposes.

For the purpose of illustrating the impact of alcoholic beverages on the economy of the country, the year 1910 provides a good example. That year the American economy was expanding rapidly because of trade, inventions, and industrialization. It was also seven years before World War I and the enacting of legislation to prohibit the sale of whiskey to the armed forces. The 1910 census listed 70,000 wage earners engaged in the manufacture of beer, wine, and spirits; 68,000 saloonkeepers and 101,000 bartenders. The distillery business alone was estimated to be about $91 million.[72]

By 1915, the alcoholic beverage industry ranked fifth in invested capital among all manufacturing industries in the United States. The brewing industry enjoyed the most spectacular gains and was by far the richest and most powerful. Between 1890 and 1914, the capital invested in brewing rose from approximately $415,000,000 to $793,000,000 while the annual value of its product increased from $237,000,000 to $442,000,000. In the same period capital invested in distilling (liquor) grew from $33,000,000 to $91,000,000. The annual value of the distilled product rose from $73,000,000 to $207,000,000. The relatively small wine industry also grew rapidly increasing its capitalization in the same period from $10,000,000 to $32,000,000 and the annual value of its product from $7,000,000 to $17,000,000. By 1915, the combined capital of the liquor industry was $916,000,000.[73] Between 1870 and 1915, the liquor tax provided between one-half and two-thirds of the whole internal revenue of the United States, providing some 200 million dollars each year after the turn of the century. With the introduction of the federal income tax by the Sixteenth Amendment, the Eighteenth Amendment became possible. Income and excess-profits taxes provided the vast bulk of the federal revenue in the five years before 1920. The entry of the United States into war with Germany in 1917 had increased the demands for revenues. The new size of the federal budget had made the liquor tax less important to the government, although the wealthy people of America began to realize for the first time that the loss of the liquor tax would be made up by higher taxes on themselves.[74]

PROHIBITION

With the enactment of the Volstead Act and the Eighteenth Amendment the brewers, distillers and others connected with the alcoholic beverage industry suffered large financial losses. The other great legal loss of property in America occurred with the emancipation of the slaves.[75]

The Prohibition law had not been long on the books before people began to flaunt it right and left. Soon a great many men and women, who had always considered themselves law-abiding and respectable citizens, began to patronize bootleggers or attempted to manufacture some type of alcoholic beverage at home. The five main sources of illegal alcoholic beverages were imported liquor, diverted industrial alcohol, moonshine, illicit beer, and wine. The first two sources supplied most of decent liquor available in the early twenties. If this condition had continued into the late twenties, there might have been some hope of adequate enforcement of Prohibition. The production of moonshine, beer and wine in the homes decentralized the making of bootleg liquor to such an extent that enforcement became almost impossible.[76]

The distillation of rum and brandy was never stopped, although, the manufacture of both was considerably curtailed after 1918. The shortage of alcohol created by the Eighteenth Amendment gave the criminal a new commodity to peddle. The market was strong for the commodity; the product was not too difficult to secure; and the entrepreneurs were plentiful. The gangsters organized the illicit manufacture, distribution, and sale of alcoholic beverages on the same principles as other large American businesses. The big profits from the illegal alcoholic traffic did not come from a still in the cellar, turning out a few gallons for sale to the neighbors. The large incomes and profits came from the giant breweries servicing one or several cities, a state or larger territories. No large city escaped the ravages of the gangs, but nowhere else did they attain such power as in Chicago. All of the evils of Prohibition came to a head in this city, and they were symbolized in the person of Al Capone.[77] A New York hoodlum, he moved to Chicago in 1920 and began a bootlegging business. By 1927, he had a 60 million dollar business with a private army of nearly 1,000 gangsters to protect the market and raid other territories.[78] Capone became the richest, best-known, and most powerful of the American gang leaders, but he was not the smartest. Another gangster, Johnny Torrio, was probably the most efficient organizer of large scale criminal enterprise that this country has ever produced. It was Torrio who created Chicago's bootleg empire and ruled it for five years and then turned it over to Al Capone as a going concern doing a gross business of more than 70 million dollars a year.[79]

The economic claims of those who were against Prohibition were as biased and false as those who supported it. Neither the losses nor gains of Prohibition can be calculated in terms of dollars and cents. There are not any reliable statistics on the volume and worth of the liquor trade. Nor can there be any statistics available of the exact value of Prohibition in helping to continue the period of prosperity throughout the twenties. In strictly economic terms, according to the testimony of social workers, Prohibition helped the poorer people. The social workers were practically unanimous in their statements that "during the first few years of Prohibition, the health and wealth of America increased and their drunkenness decreased."[80] On the other hand, Prohibition did nothing to help the middle class or to enrich the wealthy. They turned against Prohibition, except in those rural areas where the prohibitionists were still strong. The increase of the federal income tax and the elimination of the liquor tax made very seductive the argument that Prohibition was costing the country two million dollars a day in taxes.[81] The loss of revenue from alcoholic beverages as a result of Prohibition made heavier levies necessary upon personal and corporate incomes. From 1900 to 1929, there were between 87,589 and 111,589 persons with incomes over $25,000 per year. They paid 85 to 93 percent of the individual income tax respectively. Upon the wealthy class fell the main burden of replacing the major proportion of the taxes lost by alcohol.[82] There were very few, if any, Negroes and lower-class whites with incomes in this cagetory.

Negroes have never figured significantly in the ownership or managerial functions of the economic institutions of the United States. During the Prohibition era, Negroes were unable to operate distilleries and breweries and engage in the manufacture, transportation, and sale of alcoholic beverages on a large scale. This was because of their lack of knowledge and experience to establish and operate large business enterprises; their inability to secure the necessary capital; lack of political influence or connections to operate safely; and no organization of forces to protect their property and market. As a consequence, Negroes had to limit their operations to the manufacture and sale of small amounts of alcoholic beverages. This was confined largely to the South because in the North and Midwest, they faced competition from the Sicilians, Irish, Jews and others. The economic gains and profits derived by Negroes from illicit alcohol traffic in the 1920's were relatively meager and not too rewarding compared with other groups. Those engaged in the manufacture and sale of illicit liquor in the South were not exposed to as many dangers or hazards as those in the North. In the South, they had only to elude the officers of the law to operate, but in the North crime was so organized that if the law enforcement officers were eluded or a political bribe arranged, there was always the danger of having the distillery or brewery destroyed and of being killed by rivals.

Prohibition was profitable in the backwoods of the South. The sharecroppers, tenant farmers, fishermen of the bayous, dwellers on the mudbanks of the Mississippi all found the marketing of illegal alcohol or the selling of rum more profitable than the cultivation of the overworked soil. Between 1920 and 1925, corn whiskey averaged five dollars a pint and West Indian rum brought more. The illicit liquor trade became almost respectable as well as profitable. A student put himself through a southern theological seminary by selling bootleg liquor to congressmen. Even the poor Negroes benefited, from the owners of speakeasy cabins to bellboys and porters at southern hotels.[83] Negroes did not play as important a role in the sale of alcohol in the North as they did in the South. They were great consumers in all sections of the country, and especially in the larger cities. Along with others in the country, Negroes shared the economic prosperity prior to the Depression of the 1930's.

October 29, 1929, the stock market crash signaled the Depression which finally broke the back of the dry Prohibition camel. The Wets exploited this national disaster to the utmost. Their trained economists declared that the Depression was altogether due to the Prohibition. In every conceivable medium of propaganda the Wets belabored the obvious fact that legalizing liquor would create thousands of much-needed jobs and greatly increase dwindling federal revenues.[84]   They made this an issue in the Presidential campaign of 1932.

REPEAL

With Franklin D. Roosevelt the Democratic candidate for the Presidency of the United States, the campaign slogan was "A New Deal and a pot of beer for everyone."[85]   Roosevelt was elected by a landslide victory partly due to his declared "wetness."

Following repeal of national Prohibition there was considerable state legislation aimed at taxing malt beverages.   Prior to this time no excise taxes had been levied by the individual states on the sale of beer.   Within three months after 3.2 percent beer became legal—April 7, 1933—only tobacco and the income tax produced more revenue for the federal government than beer.[86]

THE DEPRESSION

By the end of the winter of 1934-1935, although a great deal had been done by the Roosevelt Administration to help relieve the distressing economic situation, there remained much to be viewed with concern.   About 11 million workers were without jobs, and the relief situation, although improved, still left millions of people in desperate and deplorable conditions.[87] Unemployment among Negroes far exceeded that of whites. It was estimated that 1.5 million of the 5.5 million Negroes capable of work, or 27 percent, were jobless.[88]   The Depression's economic effects upon the Negro were disastrous.   In periods of prosperity, Negroes had by no means fully shared in the benefits of good times; with hard times came more than their share of economic want.   All over the country, jobs that had once been reserved mostly for Negroes—menial, dirty, backbreaking—came to be filled by the unemployed whites.[89]

During the Depression, a number of law-abiding people violated the alcoholic beverage laws.   Their need for money encouraged them to illegally manufacture and sell alcohol. Without statistical proof, there are reasons to believe that Negroes engaged in this practice all over the country.   In many of the larger cities, Negroes gave "house-rent parties"; parties to raise money to pay the rent, and to buy food and meet other needs.

127

At some of the parties, a small admission fee was charged, which entitled the payee to a drink of alcohol. Usually whiskey, homebrew, or beer-like drinks, and fish, chitterlings, pigs feet, cole slaw, potato salad, and other foods were sold. Whiskey was 25¢ a drink and up. For a number of Negroes, the income or revenue from this type of activity was their only means of support during the Depression years. But the pattern began to change with the coming of World War II.

WORLD WAR II

The advent of this war in Europe, in 1939, had far-reaching effects upon the economic institutions and relationships of people around the world. Despite a great deal of prejudice directed against them, Negroes in general improved their position in American society during the war years. The main improvement in Negro relations was economic. The large number of cash-paying jobs available stimulated Negroes to move. From the farms, they moved into southern towns and cities, and from there they moved on to northern and western industrial centers. The migration of Negroes in World War I was minor compared to the 1941-1945 conflicts, and Negroes crowded into New York City, Philadelphia, Chicago, and Cleveland.[90] Negroes streamed to the West Coast—Los Angeles, San Francisco, San Diego, Portland—to secure employment in the new industries. The great shipbuilding centers of Charleston, Hampton-Roads, and Mobile had a need for laborers and Negroes filled it.

THE SIXTIES

The prosperity and full employment that accompanied World War II and the years following were shared by the American Negro. The Negro's affluence was reflected in their purchase of clothes, houses, automobiles and other consumer goods. Living in this country for over 300 years, Negroes had become indoctrinated with the culture of America. They shared the values and goals of the other members of society. The purchase of consumer goods by Negroes was similar to those of other groups. The purchase of automobiles, clothing, household furniture and alcoholic beverages out of proportion to their incomes or financial resources has been a criticism of the Negro over a period of years. There have been many theories relative to the quantity of alcoholic beverages consumed by Negroes. Statistics on the use of alcoholic beverages and amounts of money spent by race are inadequate.

On December 12, 1961, John H. Johnson, President of Johnson Publishing Company discussed the "Negroes Role in the Marketing Revolution," before the Association of National Advertisers Workshop on Selected Markets, in New York City. Johnson pointed out that: "It is estimated that there are about 19 millon consumers in the Negro market with a total purchasing power of some $20 billion." The Negro market and income have a far-reaching influence upon the economy of this country. The amount and types of goods and services they purchase and consume have implications and a great impact upon the production and distribution of goods. According to Johnson, "the prime white buyers of Scotch (whiskey) are in the $8,000 and above bracket; yet Negroes buy 57 percent of the total Scotch consumed in the United States." A survey revealed that urban Negroes spend more for alcoholic beverages per household than the general population. Among all income classes betweeen $2,000 and $10,000, the average Negro family spends substantially more for alcoholic beverages than the white family.[91] *The Pittsburgh Courier*, in an editorial on July 18, 1959, stated: "Proportionately the greatest beverages market in the United States is the Negro community, as attested by the increasingly large number of Negro salesmen employed, although few colored are hired on the production line."

Urban families spent an average of $5,390 for annual living expenses in 1960-1961. Their expenditures for the purchase of alcoholic beverages were 1.7 percent. The urban Negro families spent 2.0 percent of their incomes for alcoholic beverages and the white families 1.6. Families residing in rural nonfarm areas had an average money income after taxes of $4,700. The white average was $4,835, which was almost double that of the $2,455 of Negroes. Rural nonfarm white families spent the same amount as the national average of 1.2 percent for alcoholic beverages and the Negro families was lower, .8 percent

In 1960-1961, the expenditures for alcoholic beverages by race were as follows:[92]

Regions	Percent	White	Negro	Other
Western	1.8	1.8	1.5	1.6
Southern	1.1	1.0	1.5	.0
Northeastern	2.0	1.9	3.0	1.2
North Central	1.7	1.7	2.0	2.5

The expenditures of Negroes for alcoholic beverages exceeded those of whites in all regions excepting western—possibly due to the small Negro population in this area.

From the preceding data, one basic conclusion emerges. Negroes expend a larger percentage of their incomes than whites for the purchase of alcoholic beverages.

Prior to World War I, Negroes were largely employed in the unskilled and lower paying jobs in the manufacture, distribution, and sale of alcoholic beverages. After World War II, there were some indications that there would be an attempt to improve the economic relationship of Negroes to the alcohol industry. In 1959, the National Negro Licensed Beverage Association, Inc., was founded in Philadelphia. This organization attempted to secure the membership of all Negro-owned bars, package stores and taverns in the United States; increase the economic power of the Negro community; and to enhance its bargaining power.[93] Among other services provided by the Association to improve the economic position of the Negro were the following: the purchase of liquor, beer and wine at fair competitive prices; securing bar equipment and supplies at considerable discounts; making available successful sales and merchandising ideas to all of its members; and the participation in local or national political action to help the interest of tavern or package store owners.[94] The impact of the National Negro Licensed Beverage Association, upon the liquor industry is not yet known, but Negroes have made some important employment gains in the alcoholic beverage industry. They have been employed in increasing numbers in sales, public relations, clerical and stenographic positions. The past two or three years have witnessed the advancement and promotion of Negroes to managerial, supervisory, and administrative positions in this industry. In December 1963, a Negro was made a vice-president of Schenley Distillers.

As noted previously, from the early history of this country until the present the places where alcoholic beverages were sold by the drink were required to have a license or pay to operate. The tavern or tippling house of the Colonial period was later replaced by the saloon. From the Civil War to the Volstead Act, the saloon was the legal drinking place. With the repeal of national Prohibition the states assumed the responsibility for the regulation of the sale and consumption of alcohol. Popular opinion and state laws outlawed bars and saloons in favor of bottle sales by special shops, drugstores, or grocery stores. The public serving of alcoholic beverages became the role of cocktail lounges, beer gardens, nightclubs and restaurants. These retail outlets provide a lucrative source of revenue for state and local governments and those who own or operate them.

In the states where the retail alcoholic beverage business operates as private enterprise, through a system of licensing, Negroes own a relatively small number of outlets. The proprietors of a large number of the retail outlets—bars, taverns, cocktail lounges, and package stores—in Negro areas are usually white. In the large cities of the North, the Midwest, and West, the retail sale of alcoholic beverages is controlled by organized groups. They own the majority of the bars, taverns, and package stores. Usually, they are managed or operated by Italians, Irish, Greeks or Jews. The Negroes in the North own between ten and 20 percent of the retail outlets in their neighborhoods or areas. In the South, they own from 70 to 90 percent. Because of outside control Negroes own fewer retail outlets in Miami, Florida than any other place in the South. The highest percent of retail outlets owned by Negroes is in New Orleans, and the smallest is in New York City.[95]

There are a number of reasons why Negroes do not own and operate more retail liquor outlets. The ability to secure a license and the necessary capital may become formidable barriers at times. A good example of problems encountered in the North and the South are provided by New York and South Carolina respectively. In a 1963 investigation of the alcoholic beverage license system of New York, members of the State Liquor Authority were accused of taking bribes from applicants for licenses and licensees. At the present time, the state issues only one type of license for the on-premise consumption of liquor; a restaurant license. The off-premise sale of whiskey and wine, in New York, is handled by the package store. "The state has not issued a new package store license in 15 years."[96] The South Carolina laws are stringent in connection with the securing of a license to operate an off-premise or package store. The applicant must have no prison record, a "good character," and the endorsement or recommendation of a person of influence, usually political. Along with this, he or she must have a minimum of $2,000.00. Federal, state, and city taxes and licenses totaling about $800.00 have to be paid. The licenses and regulations of this state have a tendency to reduce the profits and make the off-premise operation of a retail outlet a financially precarious venture and this is especially so for Negroes. The securing of a license to sell beer for consumption on the premises is not as difficult and it does not require such a large financial outlay.[97] The inability of Negroes to secure the necessary capital to finance and operate a retail liquor outlet continues to be a problem. There is a trend, however, toward increasing ownership by Negroes of retail on- and off-premise outlets throughout the country. This has come about because of increased opportunities to borrow money and better financing arrangements for these types of businesses.[98]

The Negro has and continues to engage in the illicit sale of alcohol. The amount of money earned through the illegal sale of alcohol, largely whiskey, cannot be determined. An examination of the newspapers of the southern and border states will reveal that a large number of the individuals arrested, convicted, and sentenced to prison for violation of the alcoholic beverage laws are Negroes. A large number of the Negroes arrested for the illegal sale of "moonshine or corn" and tax-paid whiskies are women. Because of the low wages of these women and their legal or common-law husbands, and the inadequate financial aid received from social welfare agencies, these women frequently engage in the illegal sale of whiskey to supplement their incomes. For some Negroes, the illegal sale of whiskey is their only income or source of support. They purchase two or three gallons of corn or white liquor and/or several pints or fifths of tax-paid whiskey and sell them by the drink. A drink usually sells for 25¢ and up, depending on the quality of the whiskey. A substantial profit is made from the illicit sale of liquor, if the seller does not get caught by the law.   The low and inadequate incomes among a large number of Negroes, the laws regulating the amount and time when whiskey may be purchased encourage "bootlegging" and illegal sales.   In many of the monopoly states, the smallest amount of whiskey that can be purchased is a half pint in a package store.   In the states where mixed drinks are sold at bars, taverns, and cocktail lounges, some are economically unable to purchase whiskey by the drink.   All of the state laws prohibit the sale of whiskey on credit; the bootleggers, however, are able to extend credit to many of their customers.   Negroes have very few exclusive places—social and country clubs, where they hold membership and have access to the purchase of alcohol at most times.   This is especially true of the Negroes in the South, although some of the national fraternal organizations for Negroes have local affiliates or branches, where members may purchase whiskey by the drink and take friends.   Since World War II, there has been an increase in the number of private clubs established and operated by Negroes.   The membership of these clubs is composed largely of the Negro middle and upper classes. The members of the fraternal organizations are from the lower classes with a sprinkling of middle and upper class members for business and political reasons.

Incomes of Negroes and revenues derived from the alcohol industry have influenced and continue to influence the economy of this country.   It is not possible to determine the extent of their influence upon the total economy.   The total annual purchasing power of the Negro was estimated to be about 20 billion in 1961.[99]   There were approximately 70,000 persons employed in the manufacture of malt beverages alone in 1962.   The direct payment of salaries to brewing industry employees amounted to over $467,000,000.   "The brewing industry causes more than five billion dollars to flow each year through the channels of American trade and commerce.[100]   The alcohol industry employs a large work force of persons in the manufacture alone, and this does not include the number engaged in the transportation and retail products or those engaged in the manufacture of necessary goods such as grains, cans, bottles, labels and machinery.   A tremendous amount of money is invested or expended in capital stocks, machinery, raw materials, packaging, distribution, advertising, and retailing processes.   The alcoholic beverage industry also contributes to the economy through taxes and license fees. Public revenue from alcoholic beverages during the calendar year, 1962, amounted to $4,871,299,170: federal $3,453,418.00; state $1,290,764,105; and local $127,117,065.[101]

The distribution of these revenues varies widely. There is no specific designation for the use of federal revenues from alcoholic beverages. In some states all of the revenues go into the general fund; in others, a part is allocated to counties or municipalities. There is a tendency for the states to use portions of the public revenues from alcoholic beverages for specific educational and social purposes.[102] Some states earmark revenues from alcohol to the general fund as follows: public welfare, old age pensions, public assistance, crippled and disadvantaged children, public schools or educational, charitable institutions, social security, workman's compensation, relief and hospitalization. The states pay much toward the support of mental illness. Funds from alcohol revenue contributed to the general fund are used for the custodial care of alcoholics among the mentally ill. Relatively small sums are also designated for educational work by state liquor control authorities.[103] License fees frequently revert to the municipality where the outlets are located. All 50 of the states and the District of Columbia allocate funds from revenue, licenses and fees from alcohol, for public programs of benefit and value to the members of the total population. Without the revenue from this source, real estate and other local taxes would have to be raised to support educational, welfare, and other public programs.

In spite of the large amount of revenue produced by the alcoholic beverage industry, many questions could be raised in connection with the social cost of its use. There were approximately 5,000,000 alcoholics in the United States in 1963. Alcoholism ranks fourth among the major health problems of the country after mental illness, heart disease, and cancer. The cost of the problem in economic terms of work time lost, accidents, welfare payments, is two billion or more dollars a year. Alcoholism is responsible for multiple problems of varying proportions—psychological, social, physical.[104]

1 *The Brewing Industry in the United States* (New York: United States Brewers Association, Inc., 1963), p. 6.
2 Gus Tyler, *Organized Crime in America* (Ann Arbor: University of Michigan Press, 1964), p. 44.
3 John Allen Krout, *The Origins of Prohibition* (New York: Alfred A. Knopf, 1925), pp. 44-47.
4 *Ibid.*, pp. 6-18.
5 Herbert Asbury, *The Great Illusion* (New York: Doubleday & Co., 1950), p. 8.
6 Foster Rhea Dulles, *America Learns to Play* (New York: Appelton-Century Co., 1940) p. 17, and Asbury, *op. cit.*, p. 8.
7 Stanley M. Elkins, *Slavery: A Problem in American Institutional and Intellectual Life* (Chicago: University of Chicago Press, 1959), p. 38.
8 Samuel McKee, Jr., *Labor in Colonial New York, 1664-1776* (New York: Columbia University Press, 1935), pp. 120-121.
9 Henry Scofield Cooley, *A Study of Slavery In New Jersey* (Baltimore: The Johns Hopkins Press, 1896), p. 36.
10 Edward Raymond Turner, *The Negro In Pennsylvania, 1639-1861* (Washington, D. C.: The American Historical Association, 1911), pp. 113-114.
11 Lorenzo Johnston Greene, *The Negro in Colonial New England* (New York: Columbia University Press, 1942), p. 31, and Eric Williams, *Capitalism and Slavery* (Chapel Hill: The Universiy of North Carolina Press, 1961), pp. 9-19.
12 There will be no attempt to go into a detailed presentation of various companies of the English and Dutch which engaged in the slave trade.
13 *Ibid.*, pp. 22-23.
14 *Ibid.*, pp. 24-25.
15 Asbury, *op. cit.*, p. 7.
16 Greene, *op. cit.*, pp. 24-25; and Williams, *op. cit.*, pp. 51-52.
17 Krout, *op. cit.*, pp. 50, 60.
18 Ernest Cherrington, *The Evolution of Prohibition in the United States of America* (Westerville, Ohio: The American Press, 1920), pp. 22, 28, 32, 38.
19 Jeffrey Brackett, *The Negro in Maryland: A Study of the Institution of Slavery* (Baltimore: The Johns Hopkins Press, 1889), pp. 102-103, and Krout, *op. cit.*, pp. 18-19.
20 Krout, *op. cit.*, p. 19.
21 Cherrington, *op cit.*, pp. 36-38.
22 James Curtis Ballagh, *A History of Slavery in Virginia* (Baltimore: The Johns Hopkins Press, 1902), pp. 11-15.
23 John Hope Franklin, *From Slavery to Freedom* (New York: Alfred A. Knopf, 1947), p. 79.
24 Brackett, *op. cit.*, pp. 102-103.
25 Turner, *op. cit.*, pp. 32, 113-114, 141.
26 McKee, Jr., *op. cit.*, pp. 120-121.
27 Cooley, *op. cit.*, p. 36.
28 Greene, *op. cit.*, p. 50.
29 Henry Wilson, *The History of the Rise and Fall of Slavery in America* (Philadelphia: J. R. Osgood & Co., 1872), Vol. I, p. 3.
30 Harold Underwood Faulkner, *American Political and Social History* (7th ed.; New York: Appelton-Century-Crofts, 1957), pp. 153-154.
31 Franklin, *From Slavery to Freedom*, p. 143.
32 Albert B. Hart, *Slavery and Abolition*, Vol. XVI of the *American Nation* (New York: Harper & Bros., 1906), p. 153.
33 Franklin, *From Slavery to Freedom*, p. 146.
34 Faulkner, *op. cit.*, pp. 350-351.
35 William Warren Sweet, *The Story of Religion in America* (New York: Harper & Bros., 1950), p. 294.

36 J. Carlyle Sitterson, *Sugar Country: The Sugar Cane Industry in the South, 1753-1950* (Lexington: University of Kentucky Press, 1953), pp. 60, 89.
37 *Ibid.*, pp. 93, 111, 180-181.
38 Ulrich B. Phillips, *American Negro Slavery* (New York: D. Appleton & Co., 1936), p. 189.
39 Franklin, *From Slavery to Freedom*, p. 174.
40 Phillips, *op. cit.*, pp. 360-361; and Franklin, *From Slavery to Freedom*, pp. 176-177.
41 *Ibid.*, pp. 189, 371.
42 *Ibid.*, p. 361.
43 Faulkner, *op. cit.*, p. 354.
44 *Ibid.*, pp. 190, 371.
45 Krout, *op. cit.*, p. 60.
46 *Ibid.*, pp. 62-63.
47 Gerald Carson, *The Social History of Bourbon* (New York: Dodd, Mead, & Co., 1963), p. 12.
48 Tun Yuan Hu, *The Liquor Tax in the United States, 1791-1947* (New York: Columbia University Press, 1950), pp. 2, 32-33; and Fred Albert Shannon, *Economic History of the People of the United States* (New York: The Macmillan Co., 1934), pp. 301-302.
49 E. Merton Coulter, *The Confederate States of America, 1861-1865* (Baton Rouge: Louisiana State University Press, 1950), p. 254.
50 Bell Irvin Wiley, *Southern Negroes, 1861-1865* (New Haven: Yale University Press, 1938), p. 54.
51 Coulter, *The Confederate States of America*, p. 258.
52 Franklin, *From Slavery to Freedom*, pp. 274-275.
53 *The Brewing Industry in the United States*, p. 8, and Hu, *op. cit.*, pp. 37-41.
54 William M. Robinson, "Prohibition in the Confederacy," *The American Historical Review* 37 (1931-32), pp. 37, 50-58.
55 E. Merton Coulter, *The South During Reconstruction, 1865-1877* (Baton Rouge: Louisiana State University Press, 1947), p. 1.
56 *Ibid.*, p. 5-6.
57 C. Vann Woodward, *Origins of the New South* (Baton Rouge: Louisiana State University Press, 1951), p. 208.
58 Franklin, *From Slavery to Freedom*, pp. 307-308.
59 Coulter, *The South During Reconstruction*, pp. 93-95; and Francis Simkins, *A History of the South* (New York: Alfred A. Knopf, 1963), p. 507.
60 Simkins, *op. cit.*, p. 516.
61 Gunnar Myrdal, *An American Dilemma* (2d ed.; New York: Harper & Row, 1962), p. 224.
62 *Ibid.*, p. 237.
63 Louise Venable Kennedy, *The Negro Peasant Turns Cityward* (New York: Columbia University Press, 1930), pp. 11, 41.
64 Sweet, *op. cit.*, p. 334; Andrew Sinclair, *Prohibition: The Era of Excess* (Boston: Little, Brown, & Co., 1962), p. 6; Carson, *op. cit.*, p. 188 and Asbury, *op. cit.*, pp. 67, 116.
65 Hu, *op. cit.*, p. 46.
66 D. W. McConnell, "The Liquor Traffic," *Encyclopedia of the Social Sciences* (New York: The Macmillan Co., 1933), p. 508.
67 Cherrington, *op. cit.*, p. 197.
68 Wilmouth A. Carter, *The Urban Negro in the South* (New York: The Vantage Press, 1961), pp. 47-48; and Vernon Lane Wharton, *The Negro in Mississippi, 1865-1890* (Chapel Hill: The University of North Carolina Press, 1947), p. 128.
69 Cherrington, *op. cit.*, p. 206.
70 *The Brewing Industry in the United States, op. cit.*, p. 89.
71 Herman Feldman, *Prohibition: Its Economic and Industrial Aspects* (New York: D. Appelton & Co., 1927), pp. 28-29.

72 Henry Lee, *How Dry We Were* (Englewood Cliffs, New Jersey: Prentice-Hall, 1963), p. 52.
73 James H. Timberlake, *Prohibition and the Progressive Movement, 1900-1920* (Cambridge: Harvard University Press, 1963), p. 102.
74 Sinclair, *op. cit.*, p. 101.
75 Tyler, *op. cit.*, p. 52.
76 Raymond G. McCarthy and Edgar M. Douglass, *Alcohol and Social Responsibility* (New York: Thomas Y. Crowell Co., 1949) pp. 36-37.
77 Asbury, *op. cit.*, p. 291.
78 David A. Shannon, *Twentieth Century America: The United States Since the 1890's* (Chicago: Rand McNally & Co., 1963), p. 283.
79 Asbury, *op. cit.*, pp. 292-293.
80 Sinclair, *op. cit.*, p. 397.
81 *Ibid.*, p. 397.
82 Hu, *op. cit.*, p. 62.
83 Sinclair, *op. cit.*, pp. 289-290.
84 Asbury, *op. cit.*, p. 328.
85 Kenneth Allsop, *The Bootleggers and Their Era* (New York: Doubleday & Co., 1961), p. 37.
86 Lee, *op. cit.*, p. 235.
87 David A. Shannon, *op. cit.*, p. 335-336.
88 Simkins, *op. cit.*, p. 533.
89 David A. Shannon, *op. cit.*, p. 38.
90 *Ibid.*, p. 481.
91 *Study of Consumers, Expenditures, Incomes and Savings* (Philadelphia: University of Pennsylvania, 1957), Vol. 27, p. 52.
92 United States Department of Labor, *Survey of Consumer Expenditures 1960-1961*, Bureau of Labor Statistics Reports, 237-34; 35; 36; April 1964, and 237-38, May 1964.
93 *The Pittsburgh Courier*, (Pittsburgh, Pennsylvania: July 18, 1959).
94 "Why Stand Alone? The Story of How the NNLBA, Inc., Can Help You," published by the National Negro Licensed Beverage Association, Philadelphia, Pennsylvania.
95 This information was provided by William J. Curtis, Executive Director, National Negro Licensed Beverage Association, Inc., in a conference with author, December 4, 1963.
96 Michael F. Keating, "Rockefellow Reforms in Liquor Laws," *New York Herald Tribune* (February 11, 1963).
97 This information was secured through a personal interview with an individual who operated a package store in one of the larger cities of South Carolina.
98 This information was provided by William J. Curtis, December 4, 1963.
99 John H. Johnson, President, Johnson Publishing Company, made this estimate in an address before the Workshop on Selected Markets, Hotel Plaza, New York, December 12, 1961.
100 *The Brewing Industry in the United States*, p. 3.
101 *Annual Report Distilled Spirits Institute*, 1962, p. 4.
102 McCarthy and Douglass, *op. cit.*, p. 67.
103 Benson Y. Landis, "Some Economic Aspects of Inebriety," *Alcohol, Science and Society, Discussions As Given at the Yale Summer School of Alcohol Studies*, (New Haven: published by Quarterly Journal of Studies of Alcohol), pp. 216-220.
104 Gertrude Samuels, "In Search Of A Cure For The Alcoholic," *The New York Times Magazine*, (Sunday, Sept. 27, 1964).

BOOTSIE
By OLLIE HARRINGTON

"Somebody ought'a report that cat to the FBI. I just peeked over his shoulder to see what he was laughin' an' gigglin' about, an' man . . . he was readin' about how them African natives is chasin' nice white folks aroun' with clubs an' spears!"

138

Politics—Alcohol
and the Negro

CHAPTER FOUR

POLITICS—ALCOHOL AND THE NEGRO

F ROM the Colonial period until the present time, the regulation of the manufacture, sale, and use of alcoholic beverages
and the social and legal status of the Negro have been political
issues in America. Bernard De Voto stated, "Our political institutions were shaped by our whiskeys, would be inconceivable without them, and share their nature. They are distilled not only from
our grains, but from our native vigor, suavity, generosity, peace-
fulness, and love of accord."[1] The Negro has also influenced
our political institutions, simply by being present. In the North,
Midwest, and West, the Negro has not been a political issue of
primary and lasting importance, except insofar as he has constituted an issue in national politics. In the South, the issue has always been the Negro's status. In the earlier years of the country,
the issue was the South's struggle to widen the area over which
its concept of the Negro would prevail.[2] The attempt of the
Negro to vote and hold public office also became political issues
in the South.

As stated in the Preface, alcohol and the Negro were
issues as early as the Colonial period. To outlaw drunkenness,
the colonists initiated regulative measures. Through the device
of licensing, they attempted to achieve control of the liquor
traffic. In the seventeenth century, licenses to operate taverns
and tippling houses were granted only to men of good character
and reputation. The tavernkeeper operated the only place of
public resort in the town or village and he enjoyed great prestige
and high social standing. In most places, the tavernkeeper was
ranked above the local clergyman. As drinking increased and
the sale of alcoholic beverages became more profitable, the
issuance of licenses came to be determined by political and other
considerations.[3]

Likewise, the legal status of the Negro became a political
issue in the seventeenth century. The 20 Negroes who were left
at Jamestown, Virginia in 1619, occupied a position similar to
that of the white servants. Opposition to enslaving the Negro

early became a political issue. Some of the colonists expressed grave doubts about the placing of them in slavery. In fact, there was no statutory recognition of slavery in Virginia until 1661.[4] During the Colonial period slaves were not permitted to participate in politics nor hold public office.

The whites who used alcohol excessively were relegated to almost the political status of slaves. In 1658, the Plymouth Colony enacted a law disfranchising drunkards. Maryland prohibited drunkenness under penalty of confinement in the stocks for six hours or a fine of 100 pounds of tobacco (one-half to the informer); for the second offense the law provided a public whipping and a fine of 300 pounds of tobacco; and for a third offense the offender was disfranchised for three years. Virginia enacted a law which decreed that anyone convicted of drunkenness three times was a common drunkard; persons convicted were held incapable of being witnesses and holding office.[5] Many excessive drinkers were tried and convicted in the courts and stripped of their rights to vote and hold public office. Consequently, free Negroes, slaves, and the whites who were considered drunkards all found themselves in the same predicament when it came to voting and holding public office.

Wherever free Negroes found themselves, they lived somewhat precariously upon the sufferance of the whites, although their legal status was fairly high during the Colonial period. At various times free Negroes were permitted to vote if otherwise qualified, in each of the 13 original colonies. But before the colonies became states, disfranchisement of the free Negro was underway. Negroes and Jews were disqualified to vote in South Carolina in 1716. Virginia followed in 1723 with a law depriving all Negroes, Indians, and mulattoes of the right to vote in any election. Georgia restricted voting to white males in 1761. New York, in 1821, demanded of Negro voters a property qualification not required of white voters.

As the Colonial population grew, it became increasingly difficult for the representatives of the Governor or the Proprietor to select the persons to be favored with licenses, and so the selective power was generally placed in the hands of the county court. The selling of the liquor monopoly for a definite district at a high price to raise revenue or to limit the number of licenses; the conditions imposed upon the innkeeper; and scarcity of liquor

141

tended to make alcohol a political issue. The scarcity of liquor and the license system tended to place a virtual monopoly in the hands of a few dealers in each colony.[6] On the eve of the American Revolution, the use and sale of alcoholic beverages were among the main political issues confronting the people of this country.

By the middle of the eighteenth century slavery was a well-established American institution. There had been protests against the slave trade and some religious groups, notably the Quakers, had questioned the right of one man to hold another in bondage. But there had been no frontal attack upon the institution and even in the northern colonies, where there was no extensive use of slaves, the majority of the articulate colonists paid little attention to slavery. At the first Continental Congress in 1774, slavery did become an issue when an agreement was reached not to import slaves after December 1775.[7]

The test of the colonists' regard for slavery came in 1776 in their reaction to the Declaration of Independence when it was submitted to the Second Continental Congress by Thomas Jefferson. There was no forceful or direct slavery pronouncement in the Declaration of Independence, but rather indirection and inference. The sole reference to slavery was in the first paragraph. George Washington, Benjamin Franklin, Thomas Jefferson, James Madison, John Jay, Alexander Hamilton, and others considered slavery an evil inconsistent with the principles of the Declaration of Independence. Georgia and South Carolina led the agitation for the continuance of slavery and the slave trade. Virginia and Maryland often joined the North in advocating the end of the slave trade.[8]

THE CONSTITUTION AND THE NEGRO

With the end of the War of Independence in 1783, and the victory of the colonists, the doctrine of the equality of men was brought into the political sphere by the declaration that all men are born free and equal. The argument of the rights of man growing out of the political theory of the American Revolution led many people of this country to ponder the question of slavery. At the Constitutional Convention in Philadelphia in 1787, slavery became an issue. There had been and continue to be varying

142

opinions concerning the influence of slavery on the shaping of the Constitution. According to the abolitionists, slavery helped to shape the Constitution because it was the basis of the sectional conflict between North and South, and because the compromise of that conflict was the main work of the Constitutional Convention. One of the framers of the Constitution pointed out that the institution of slavery and its consequences formed the line of discrimination between the contending groups of states. Slavery was recognized as the basis of sectionalism; and it was not difficult to show that sectional conflict between North and South was the major tension of the Convention. One line of argument against this contention has been that the words slave and slavery do not appear in the Constitution. Another of the framers believed that the founders did not use the words slave and slavery because in 1783, when the Continental Congress changed Article VIII of the Articles of Confederation to include slaves in apportioning taxation among the states, the Congress had been ashamed to use the term slaves and had submitted a description. A member of the Virginia ratifying Convention expressed an opinion that the fugitive slave clause of the proposed Constitution did not use the word slave because of the particular scruples of the northern delegates. A representative of the Convention later advised a friend that the omission of the word slavery was to avoid any stain on the new government.[9]

While the Constitutional Convention was meeting in Philadelphia in 1787, the Congress operating under the Articles of Confederation enacted the Northwest Ordinance. The plan provided that the territory north of the Ohio River and west of New York should be divided into states and as states, be admitted into the Union on an equality basis with the original members. The outstanding provision was that there should be no slavery or involuntary servitude in the territory. This Ordinance divided the United States into well-defined and contrasted sections, one having slavery and the other devoid of this institution.[10]

At the 1787 Convention in Philadelphia, the South won another victory. This achievement was the result of bitter debate on slave representation. In the Constitutional Convention the question of representation was raised—whether slaves should be counted in computing state representation to the lower house of Congress. It was agreed that five slaves should count as three

143

white men or three-fifths of the slave population should be counted as "people" for the purpose of apportioning taxes and representatives among the states.[11] This meant that southern states could send more representatives to the lower house in Washington than northern states.

There is another point of view on the importance and influence of the slave issue on the framing of the Constitution. In 1903, in a paper delivered before the American Historical Society, one historian argued that in 1787 the slavery question was not the most important one. Ten years later he attacked the view that the important compromises at the Convention were those concerning slavery. According to his interpretation, the three-fifths ratio had been devised in 1783 and accepted by 11 states before the Convention met; it was not really a Convention compromise. The bargain over slave importation and commercial laws was a compromise of the Convention, but less important than a number of others, such as those concerning the admission of the new states and the method of electing the President.[12] From all indications the institution of slavery with its consequences was a potent force in the shaping of the Constitution. The abolitionist historians believed that a counterrevolution took place, but they perceived the victim to be the slave rather than the white artisan or farmer. They felt that John Adams would have been President in 1800 had the three-fifths clause not existed and they viewed the accession of Thomas Jefferson as a triumph for slavery[13]

There have been several theories relative to the South's acceptance of the provisions of the Constitution. At the crucial Virginia ratifying Convention (1788) there seemed no doubt that the South would soon be the most populous section of the country. But a difference existed between those who thought it safe to strengthen the federal government at once, and those who counseled waiting until the southern Congressional majority was achieved. Some of the leaders saw clearly that if the South were to agree to strengthen Congress, the plan that gave each state one vote would have to be changed in favor of the South. This basis of representation would allow representation by numbers as well as by states. Such a change was recommended to the eastern states by the actual superiority of their populousness, and to the southern states by their expected superiority. The irony was that the expected southern majority in Congress never materia-

144

lized; the Senate not the House of Representatives became the bulwark of the South.[14]

Although the South accepted the Constitution, it might not have ratified the document had not the proponents of the Constitution compromised with sectional feelings. They made concessions in favor of self-government by limiting federal authority to those powers delegated by the Constitution. Concessions were made to slaveholders by leaving the regulation of slavery to the individual states; making provisions for the return of fugitive slaves; counting slaves as three-fifths in the apportionment of Congressional representation, and for continuation of the foreign slave trade for 20 years.[15] After the American Revolution, slavery was never again accepted as a matter of course, as during the Colonial period.

As the new nation began to function under its Constitution, these controversies developed around the Negro that ultimately were to be resolved by the Civil War; the issue of abolition gained prominence as the abolitionist movement gained new life and organization; the status of the runaway slave was bitterly argued and contested, and the issue of slavery in the territories and new states threatened the nation's unity and development.[16]

Like slavery, alcohol became a political issue in the newly formed Union. In the First Congress of the United States, the Secretary of the Treasury proposed that an excise tax be levied on distilled spirits. The money from this tax was to be used to meet financial obligations created by the War of Independence. The tax became the law of the land in March 1791. The news of the passage of this measure was greeted with great indignation all over the country; especially in the back country settlements. The issues of slavery and alcohol involved states' rights in general, and in particular, the question of the possibility of solving both of them under the American form of government. It was necessary for the states' rights doctrine, which had already asserted itself in the South and North to be settled. The settlement of the West was to increase the tension and problems of the status of the Negro.

TERRITORIAL EXPANSION AND THE NEGRO

The westward expansion of the nation began with the acquisition of new territories. Newly populated areas applied for admission to the Union as states. In 1818, Missouri, part of the Louisiana Territory purchased from France in 1803, applied for admission to the Union. This created a controversey between the North and South. Northerners contended that prohibition of slavery should be a condition of admission. Southerners while not disputing Congressional power to regulate slavery in the territories, insisted that Congress had no power to place such restrictions on new states.[17]

The slave issue influenced the political activities of the North and South. The North was opposed to the opening of the western country to slavery. The North feared that its influence in national affairs would be diminished by the appearance in Washington of representatives from slaveholding states that would be carved out of the West. The South had reasons equally fundamental in demanding slavery for Missouri. A free Missouri would destroy the equality with the North which the South possessed in the Senate. The population balance between Slave States and free states was broken in 1820. At that time, the free states had over half a million more people than the Slave States. Under the system of apportionment by which only three-fifths of the population was counted, the free states had 105 members in the lower house of Congress to 81 for the Slave States. The balance, however, was maintained in the Senate where the 22 representatives of the states were matched by representatives of the 11 states.[18] Prior to May 13, 1913, the Constitution of the United States provided that the Senators from each of the states were to be chosen by their legislatures. After this date two senators from each state were to be elected by the people—Article XVII, Constitution of the United States.

The politicians stepped into the sectional chasm with the Missouri Compromise. It provided that Missouri as a Slave State should be balanced by Maine as a free state, and that in the remainder of the Louisiana Purchase the dividing line between slavery and freedom should be 36° 30', an extension of the southern border of Missouri.[19] The outburst of sectional feeling which had accompanied the Missouri crisis had introduced the anti-slavery issue into American politics.[20] By 1833, sectionalism had reappeared in a different and more menacing manner. The dissension occurred over whether planters should

146

carry their slaves into territories desired for free states. As in 1820 the statesmen of the country succeeded in delaying the threats of sectional breaks in 1833.

At the time the Constitution was drawn up free Negroes had the right to suffrage in all of the original states, except South Carolina and Georgia. The majority of the Negro people were held in slavery; as a result they were denied suffrage. As a political power the free Negroes were inconsequential, both in the South and in the North.[21] State after state restricted suffrage to white males; Georgia in 1761; Delaware in 1792; Kentucky in 1799; Ohio in 1803; New Jersey in 1807; Maryland in 1810; Louisiana in 1812; Connecticut (the only New England state) in 1814; Tennessee in 1834; and North Carolina in 1835, the last original Slave State to ban voting by free Negroes.[22] Sentiment against the disfranchisement of the free Negro was strong. This was especially the situation in the mountain counties of the West. The measure was barely passed by the Constitutional assembly of 1835, by a vote of 66 to 61. This Constitutional provision disfranchised several hundred men of color whose voting records had been acceptable to the whites. Their vote had been eagerly sought, and in some communities they were reported as holding the balance of power. Politicians had wooed the Negro vote as ardently as any other.[23] The newly admitted states, northern as well as southern banned Negro voting.

It has been pointed out that from 1830 to the opening of the Civil War may be termed the era of sectionalism. New winds were blowing over the American people in the thirties and forties. During this period, many of the anti-slavery and anti-alcohol groups joined forces. Political interest and activities related to slavery and temperance increased all over the country. The slave issue was especially predominant; it exerted influence upon political decisions from the local level to the Congress of the United States. As tension over slavery and states' rights increased, internal discord began to rack both political parties in the South. In those regions where Negroes outnumbered the whites, there was constant fear of rebellion and the overthrow of the established political order. It was during this period that political parties began to make platforms at their conventions.

Political platforms began in 1840, the year the Liberty party was organized. It was made up of former members of anti-slavery societies and abolitionists, and included an anti-slavery plank in its platform. The party nominated James G. Birney, a Kentuckian who had freed his own slaves, for the Presidency in 1840. Birney ran again in 1844; he was able to substantially increase his vote and he won enough support in New York to keep the Whig, Henry Clay, from carrying the state. Thereby, the Liberty party succeeded in placing the proslavery James K. Polk in the White House.[24]

TEMPERANCE PANGS

Even though slavery continued to claim the attention of large numbers of those interested in politics, the supporters of temperance continued to labor in the political arena. The temperance movement in the United States began with appeals to individuals to abstain from alcoholic beverages. As in the early agitation against slavery, it was believed that in a democratic country an appeal to the individual conscience was the surest and best way to counteract social evils. By 1840, there began to develop a conviction among some of the anti-alcohol forces that the temperance movement should stand for total abstinence.[25]

Between 1830 and 1840, a wave of indignation against the arrogance of the liquor dealer and the venality of local politicians was spreading throughout the nation. By the middle of the 1840's, strong temperance lobbies were busily at work in every state legislature and political pressure was being brought to bear on city officials and thousands of dry workers were gathering signatures to petition state legislatures. These supporters of anti-alcoholic beverage manufacture were morally and religiously inspired to total abstinence. During this era, the interest centered in Maine, which even in the early days was recognized as the bell-wether of American politics. Many dry leaders were convinced that if a strong prohibitary law could be passed in Maine, the other states would fall into line.[26]

In 1839, the people of Portland, Maine voted on an ordinance to make the traffic of liquor illegal. In connection with this election, Neal Dow, one of the most astute politicians produced by the temperance movement, developed the doorbell technique of electioneering which is still used effectively today. The temperance forces lost by a narrow margin of votes, but four years later, they won. Portland became the first important city to outlaw liquor by popular vote. This was largely accomplished through the efforts of Neal Dow. He devised a system of political maneuvering for Maine, which in later years was copied and carried to near perfection by other foes of alcohol. In every district the temperance forces endorsed a candidate for the legislature who promised to support prohibition, and urged the people to vote for him regardless of party ties.[27] The supporters of prohibition had learned by this time that petitions were not enough. They discovered that politics was required to achieve their goals. The strength of this early movement was so great that the agitation for temperance soon extended to prohibition and resulted in legislation. In 1851, Neal Dow influenced the legislature of Maine to pass the first liquor prohibition law in our history; a law that, except for the years 1856-1858 remained on the statute books until 1933. Using the Maine law as a model, 13 states, all north of the Mason-Dixon Line, attempted to restrict the sale of spirituous liquors. The movement had been rapid and the legislation more far-reaching than the preparation of the people. Practically everywhere popular opposition made enforcement a difficult and hazardous matter. Maine, New Hampshire, and Vermont were the only states in which early temperance legislation did not collapse. The early prohibition movement subsided in the 1850's and was almost obliterated by the slave issue and the Civil War.

SLAVERY

The shadow of slavery ranged over Congress, the platforms of political parties, elections, and even Presidential campaigns. The slavery debates were neither calm, consistent, nor logical. The issues were further accentuated by the annexation of the territories. Texas, for example pressed for annexation to the United States from 1837 until 1845. Anti-slavery politicians in Congress were opposed to the admission of Texas as a Slave State. In May 1844, a member of Congress warned the House of Representatives that if Texas were admitted to the Union, its delegate to Congress would hold the balance of power.[28] The status of Texas was politically important to the North and South. The South was interested in achieving a political balance and the North in maintaining political domination. In 1845, after protracted agitation, Texas was incorporated into the United States as a Slave State.

The South welcomed Texas as an addition to the body of Slave States and looked forward to the creation of others from the Mexican Territory. Enemies of the South saw in the Texas phase of the westward movement a conspiracy on the part of slaveholders to stake off new lands for their despised institution. Large segments of northern public opinion opposed the annexation of Texas. When the forces of expansion proved more compelling than opposition to slavery, a principle most irritating to the South was advanced. It was embodied in the Wilmot Proviso.[29]

In 1846, David Wilmot, a Democratic congressman from Pennsylvania, introduced in the House an amendment to an appropriation bill. The bill contained a proviso prohibiting slavery in the territory to be acquired to the west of Texas. The northern majority in the lower house of Congress carried the measure, but the Slave States prevented its passage. The South regarded the proposal as a diabolical conspiracy to overturn the balance between their states and the 15 free states which would exist after 1848 with the admission of Wisconsin as a free state. Had the proviso been adopted, the new area below the Missouri Compromise line would have been free territory.[30] The Wilmot Proviso became the symbol of northern opposition to slavery's new assault on the federal government.

The northern maneuver to stop the expansion of slaves culminated in the Free Soil Movement of 1848. In August, at Buffalo, a large number of anti-slavery leaders, representing all parties, launched the Free Soil party. The platform revealed the party's desire and determination to rescue the federal government from the control of slave power. The party's program to achieve this goal was inherent in the platform:

That It Is The Duty Of The Federal Government To Relieve Itself From All Responsibility For The Existence or Continuance Of Slavery Wherever That Government Possess Constitutional Power To Legislate On That Subject, And Is Thus Responsible For Its Existence.
The *only* safe means of preventing the extension of Slavery into territory now free, is to prohibit its existence in all such territory by *an act of Congress.*[31]

The ten years preceding the Civil War were filled with tense and crucial moments closely related to slavery. The period began with controversey over slavery in the newly acquired territory in the Southwest and the dominant political struggle during the 1850's was over the expansion of slavery into the territories of the West[32] In 1850 Congress thoroughly aired the questions related to this issue and desperate efforts were made to work out a solution that would diminish intersectional strife. After considerable debate by some of the leaders from the North and the South an agreement was reached which provided that (1) California should enter the Union as a free state; (2) the other territories should be organized without mention of slavery; (3) Texas should cede certain lands to New Mexico, and be compensated; (4) slaveholders should be better protected by a stringent fugitive slave law; and (5) there should be no slave trade in the District of Columbia.[33] The Compromise of 1850 was not satisfactory to all. Southerners agreed to remain in the Union only so long as there was strict adherence to the Compromise, especially in enforcing the fugitive slave act. The Compromise of 1850 disposed of the issue of the expansion of slavery, and destroyed the illusion of an all-conquering slaveocracy. The South's acceptance of the principle of limited power in the territories eliminated the element of fear from the anti-slavery crusade. The Compromise reassured the North that it could co-exist peacefully and profitably with the South within the confines of the American democratic process, and it split the purely free-soil from the more radical anti-slavery bloc in the North. It sent the moderate anti-southern groups of 1848 hurrying back to the Whig and Democratic organizations and compelled the genuine anti-slavery forces to retreat again to the single issue of abolitionism. The vast majority of northerners had no interest in this issue.[34]

In the 1850's there were politicians in both the North and South whose futures hinged on the slave issue. During this period anti-slavery politics came upon hard times. Some northern politicians believed that a broad anti-slavery coalition required nothing less than an issue which would resurrect the illusion of an aggressive slave power. Senator Stephen A. Douglas' (Illinois) Kansas-Nebraska Bill of 1854, provided the anti-slavery politicians with the legislative act to destroy the

Compromise of 1850. As finally passed Douglas' act provided that Kansas and Nebraska be organized as territories and that the question of slavery be decided by the territorial legislatures. The passage of the act precipitated a desperate struggle between North and South for the control of Kansas. The Missouri Compromise had been repealed and those forces that mustered the greatest strength in Kansas could win it. In the ensuing years abolitionists and proslavery factions fought and bled for Kansas; the land became a preliminary battleground of the Civil War. No longer was there much semblance of intersectional peace.[35] The Kansas-Nebraska Bill of 1854 crystallized anti-slavery feeling once more and at the same time augmented it.

In the 1850's, a third political party made its appearance—the American Know Nothing party. This party was organized because the Irish immigrants settled cities and German refugees took up land in the West. They competed with native Americans in the labor market or took land which Americans, a couple of generations removed from the immigrant steerage, thought they alone should have. The party represented anti-foreign and anti-Catholic movements and its members were largely Protestants and urban workers. As the Irish Catholic immigrants were chiefly Democrats, the new organization obtained most of its adherents from the disintegrating Whig party. Before the politicians of the older parties knew it, the Know Nothing party was winning victories at the polls.[36]

In 1854, the Know Nothings won complete control of Massachusetts, carried Pennsylvania and elected a number of congressmen. The next year the party split on the slavery issue and fell into the hands of southerners. In 1856, their candidate for President, Millard Fillmore, polled 875,000 popular votes and won Maryland's eight electoral votes. At this time, the Know Nothings were further splitting on the slavery issue, and Democratic strength in the North was rapidly declining. The Republican party offered an opportunity for some of the members of the Whig party of the North, and the anti-slavery group of the Know Nothings, and the Democrats to coalesce on the issue of slavery.[37]

The Kansas-Nebraska Act persuaded many anti-slavery sympathizers that political action was necessary to combat the relentless drive of the proslavery forces to extend slavery.

Northern Whigs, Free Soilers, and Democrats who had fought the passage of the Act came together, and out of their discussions arose the Republican party. This new political organization, unalterably anti-slavery in its point of view, profited by the mistakes of earlier anti-slavery parties and evolved a program broad enough to attract voters who were indifferent to slavery. The Republican platform of 1856 declared:

> The Constitution confers upon Congress sovereign powers over the territories of the United States for their government; and that in the exercise of this power, it is both the right and imperative duty of Congress to prohibit in the territories those twin relics of barbarism — Polygamy, and Slavery.[38]

James C. Fremont, Republican, opposed James Buchanan, Democrat, in the Presidential campaign of 1856. The Republican platform was largely concerned with the slave question. The Republicans made Kansas the main issue of the campaign; the Democrats countered by stressing the Union, pointing out the sectional character of the Republican party, and prophesying the breakup of the Union if Fremont was elected. Although it was its first Presidential election, the new party made an amazing showing. Buchanan won the election, but it was closely fought, and he was the last Democrat to win the Presidency for 28 years.

During the first year of the Buchanan Administration, one event after another opened up new areas of controversy, and underlying practically all of them was the issue of slavery. Among them was the Dred Scott Decision. This was a judicial assault upon the cardinal principle of Republicanism which provoked a storm in anti-slavery forces and strengthened their determination to rescue the federal government from its southern masters.[39] The fundamental question presented in the Dred Scott case was that of the legal status of slaves who had lived in free territory and subsequently returned to the state of their original owners. Dred Scott, a Negro slave, had been taken by his master into the State of Illinois, a state made free by the Northwest Ordinance, then into the northern part of the Louisiana Purchase territory made free by the Missouri Compromise, and finally back to Missouri, a Slave State. On the grounds that residence in free territory had made him a free man, he sued

153

for his freedom in 1846 in the Missouri courts. The Superior Court of the state ruled that whatever his status might have been in a free territory, his return to Missouri had again made him a slave. A new suit instituted in the United States Circuit Court brought the same ruling and finally the case was carried to the United States Supreme Court. This court upheld the decision of the other courts, and also insisted that since the Constitution recognized slave property, Dred Scott's status was determined by the law of Missouri and not that of Illinois.[40] This decision dealt a blow to the newly formed Republican party, which was founded on the thesis that the further extension of slavery might be prevented by Congressional action. At the same time it gave the Republicans an issue on which to fight and hastened the impending crisis.

Along with the Dred Scott Decision and other developments, there continued to be considerable debate over the slave issue in Kansas, which eventually resulted in civil war in that state. It was necessary for the President to send federal troops into the territory to quiet the civil war. In 1858, the convention meeting at Lecompton drew up a document guaranteeing property in slaves, and drafted a special clause that would have denied the prospective state both the power to emancipate slaves without consent of the owners and to forbid the entrance of slaves. The clause "constitution with slavery" or the "constitution without slavery" was the only one submitted to the voters.

The Buchanan Administration attempted to secure the admission of Kansas as a Slave State under the Lecompton instrument, but the House refused to concur. Under a later act, Kansas had an opportunity to obtain immediate admission by accepting the Lecompton constitution. She rejected it and the situation remained this way until 1861, when she joined the Union as a free state. Buchanan's support of the Lecompton constitution was responsible for an outburst in the North and another confused political situation. The most spectacular aspect of this affair was Stephen A. Douglas' bold revolt against the Administration (Democrat) and the resulting split in the Democratic party. The controversy also had some unsettling effects upon the Republicans.[41]

The campaign of 1858 was significant in several ways. It meant that the Republican party would carry on in spite of the

Dred Scott Decision and Douglas' break with the Administration. This campaign made Lincoln a national figure and it hopelessly split the Democratic party. The campaign gave rise to the famous Lincoln-Douglas debates in which slavery was the most prominent issue. Citizens flocked by the thousands to the great outdoor gatherings to hear the debates. The interest of the entire country centered on these debates, which saw an eloquent Democratic senator with aspirations to the Presidency pitted against a rising spokesman of the new Republican party. Lincoln's position was that the Republic could not exist forever divided into free and Slave States and that slavery must be accepted everywhere or done away with entirely. Lincoln lost the election that year but his party captured the Congressional election. Both gained national stature and momentum toward their Presidential candidacies in 1860.[42]

In 1860, the issue of slavery hovered over the nominating conventions of both the Republican and Democratic parties. According to one writer, "No American political convention has ever held so much meaning for party and nation as that conclave of determined Democrats which gathered in Charleston, South Carolina, in April 1860, to nominate a candidate for the presidential office."[43] There were many who believed that upon the decision reached at Charleston rested not only the future of the Democratic party, but also the continued existence of the Union. The convention was unable to nominate a candidate for president because of the sectional animosity that had built up between the factions of the North and South. When the convention adjourned, its business unfinished, the Democratic party had been reduced to a shambles and the fate of the nation had been sealed. It adjourned to Baltimore, where it later nominated Douglas for president and Herschel V. Johnson, of Georgia, for vice-president.

With the Democrats badly split, the Republicans' chance for victory was enhanced. When the convention met at Chicago, the nomination for the Presidency was generally conceded to William H. Seward, the best-known leader of the party, but his well-known affiliations with the moneyed interests of New York, his friendliness to Catholic immigrants, and his radical opposition to slavery weakened his position. By clever manipulation and lavish promises, the opposition to Seward consolidated behind Lincoln, who received the nomination on the third ballot. The nomination for the vice-presidency went to Hannibal Hamlin of Maine.[44]

By 1860, American politics had reached the dead end predicted for it by the very nature of the slavery issue. Dominant political elements of both the North and the South demanded of the nation what they could achieve only in defiance of the Constitution. "For American people there was no escape from the eternal predicament to which the politicians had consigned them."[45] Whatever disagreement there may be about the underlying causes of the Civil War, it is clear the conflict was precipitated in 1860-1861 by a series of momentous decisions which began with the election of a Republican president.[46] The issue of slavery in the territories gave birth to the Republican party; it had also spilt the Democratic party into northern and southern factions and prompted northeastern and border state conservatives to launch the Constitutional Union party to bind together the dividing nation.[47] The Civil War was largely a consequence of the political differences caused by the institution of slavery, between the North and South.

Lincoln's election marked the elevation to power of a party whose philosophy from the southern point of view was revolutionary and destructive. There was no place in the Union for states unalterably committed to the maintenance and extension of slavery. The reaction to Lincoln's election was swift. On December 20, 1860, a convention summoned by the South Carolina legislature met at Charleston and unanimously declared that the Union now subsisting between South Carolina and other states under the United States be dissolved. By the time of Lincoln's Inauguration on March 4, 1861, Georgia, Alabama, Florida, Mississippi, Louisiana and Texas had followed South Carolina into secession and the Confederate States of America had been formed.[48] Without slavery the question of the extent of federal authority in the territories would have remained academic, and could have been debated openly and peaceably. On the other hand, the humanitarian reform movement would have proceeded apace had there been no slaves, for temperance and women's rights would have received generous support throughout the country in communities where there was a tendency to assume civic responsibility.

156

It was pointed out earlier how the Maine prohibition law of 1851 was brought into being. The four years that followed the enactment of this law were among the most triumphant years, politically, in the history of the temperance movement. During that time, 12 states and one territory, in addition to Maine and Oregon, adopted prohibitary laws. Then suddenly and without warning, the onward march of dry reform came to an abrupt stop. The New Hampshire legislature passed a stringent version of the Maine law in August 1855, and that was the last of the string of victories; not for a quarter of a century did another state adopt prohibition. Many of the important dry leaders were deeply involved in the abolition movement, and after the middle 1850's the latter absorbed most of their time and attention.[49] During the 1850's the abolition movement worked against the dry cause. The northern Drys supported the abolition of slavery, while the southern Drys did not. Another factor responsible for the repeal of prohibition laws that had been enacted in several states was the partisan political turn which the prohibition movement took in the 1850's. Prohibition became a party issue; it was championed by one political party and opposed by another. As prohibition activity and legislation reached their height, the moral reform forces of the nation were turned to the slavery issue, which reached its crisis in the war of 1861-1865.[50] With the Civil War won by the North and the question of abolition of slavery settled, the temperance movement lost its lassitude of postwar times.[51]

RECONSTRUCTION

After four years of war against heavy military, technical, and financial odds, embittered throughout by internal dissension, the South in 1865 found itself in utter confusion—social, economic, and political. At the close of the Civil War the threat which the South had long feared was realized; the Negro slaves were emancipated without the consent of their masters. The stage was set for a social revolution. Whether or not it was to take place depended upon the manner of political reconstruction, and this was determined by northern policy.[52] Political reconstruction came in two stages. The first was Presidential Reconstruction and lasted from the end of the war until 1867. They were Lincoln's ideas and on his death they were carried out

157

under Johnson's supervision, with few conditions and no interference by national agencies. The second stage was Congressional Reconstruction, from 1867 to 1876 carried on by the Republican politicians of the national legislature.

During Reconstruction, the legislation was in the embrace of the so-called Black Codes. Between 1865 and 1867, eight states of the former Confederacy, enacted Black Codes. The Negro as a slave had been property; he had no rights, civil or political. The mere act of setting the Negro free still left him without these rights; he was still not a citizen.[53] The Black Codes made plain the intent to re-establish the status quo ante, to retain the conditions of slavery even after the abolition of the institution.[54] The Mississippi Code was the first, and the most elaborate and severe; Georgia and Alabama had few laws regarding Negroes, and Arkansas and Tennessee at first passed none whatsoever. The more elaborate of the Codes dealt with vagrancy, apprenticeship, labor contracts, and the civil status of the Negro. In no cases were Negroes allowed to sit on juries and in most states their testimony was not accepted in court, if a white person was the defendant.[55]

Congress angered by the South's Black Codes passed a Civil Rights Bill which was vetoed by President Andrew Johnson. Congress then brought forth a plan of its own which was submitted in the form of an amendment to the Constitution and ultimately became the Fourth Amendment in 1868. It embodied the Civil Rights Law and more. It defined citizenship, made the Negro a citizen, and gave him civil rights. Although it did not confer on him suffrage outright, it penalized any state which did allow him to vote.[56] On February 26, 1869, Congress proposed a Fifteenth Amendment to the Constitution of the United States. This Amendment provided that "the right of any citizen of the United States to vote, shall not be denied or abridged by the United States or by any State on account of race, color or previous condition of servitude." In less than one year ratification was completed, and in 1870, the Secretary of State certified that it had become part of the Constitution.[57]

From the day of Emancipation, officers of the Union army and the Freedman's Bureau inculcated political ambitions in the Negro. In the closing months of the war, the need for food, clothing, thousands of displaced persons, and the absence of civil authority, created a distressing situation in the South. The pleas of Negroes for relief from these conditions were largely ignored. There was need for a comprehensive and unified service for the freedmen. In March 1865, the federal government established the Freedmen's Bureau. With officials in each of the southern states, the Bureau aided refugees and freedmen by furnishing supplies and medical services, establishing schools, supervising contracts between freedmen and their employers, and managing confiscated or abandoned lands, leasing and selling some of them to freedmen.[58]

The attempt to protect the Negro through the Freedman's Bureau was nothing compared with efforts under the Reconstruction acts to raise his social and political status. As the freeing of the slaves progressed and the Negro turned for direction and leadership from his former master to the federal soldiers and Unionist officials, representatives of the Republican party pressed in to organize the Negroes. The Union League of America became in the South the political organization into which the Negro was enrolled. The League became the spearhead for southern Republicanism. Since Negroes were the largest enfranchised group, the League depended on them for the bulk of Republican strength. One of the most noteworthy accomplishments in the history of American politics occurred during Reconstruction, the creation among Negroes of an enthusiastic desire to register and vote. The freedmen, despite their ignorance, poverty and lack of social and political training, were impressed with the necessity of engaging in political activities along with their former masters.[59] Most of them, however, were without the qualifications to participate effectively in a democracy. In the elections held in the former Confederate states, appeals were made to Negroes to join the Democratic party. These appeals won few converts among Negroes. The whites failing to entice Negroes into their ranks took a stand against Negro suffrage.

In the immediate postwar years, the former Confederates refused to support the Reconstruction program backed by Congress. The white southerners were politically unable to check by legal methods and elections the advancement of Negroes in voting and the holding of public office. As a result, they turned to illegal and violent means to regain control, and thus added dis-

159

order and bloodshed to the difficulties of the period. The Ku Klux Klan and similar organizations came into being in the South, and assumed the function of a guerilla police. Their methods were secrecy, menacing warnings, tar and feathers, and whippings. Although their approach was unofficial, it was frequently effective. Everywhere in the South these acts were committed, chiefly against Negroes. It has been claimed by some writers that the Klan organizations had no political motives. The rituals of the various secret societies pledged the membership to combat Negro domination and participation in politics.[60]

The real stimulus to the growth and expansion of Klan activities was not the attacks on innocent white families by Negroes and others, but the apparent determination on the part of Negroes and their radical friends to assume and wield political power. The years 1869-1871 were the heyday of the Ku Klux Klan activities. The Klan was responsible for the election of some Conservative state officials, in these three years. It also assisted the Conservatives in some states to regain control of the political machineries in the counties. By 1870, the entire radical Reconstruction program—less than three years old—was on the brink of collapse in many parts of the South and the rights of freedmen were seriously jeopardized. Violence and lawlessness had reached such proportions that every semblance of political and economic stability in the South was rapidly destroyed. It became manifest that without additional federal action, the new Constitutional Amendments would be merely words on a piece of paper. In May 1870, Congress passed a law designed to protect Negroes exercising the franchise. This was our first Civil Rights Act. It stipulated that persons hindering, obstructing, or controlling qualified electors in their efforts to vote were to be fined and imprisoned. The Klan, or others who interfered with anyone in the enjoyment of his Constitutional rights were to be found guilty of committing a felony. Federal district and circuit courts were to have jurisdiction, and federal marshals and other officers were to enforce the law.[61]

Although radical leadership brought about changes in the fundamental law of the land, resulting in national suffrage for the Negro from 1870 on, it failed to cope with the mounting of southern opposition to the exercise of the franchise by Negroes. The increasing strength and intimidating activities of the Klan served as a deterrent to Negroes voting and holding office. In order to relieve these conditions, Congress in February 1871, amended the Enforcement Act of May 1870. Under the new legislation, supervisors of elections were appointed by federal courts and interference with the discharge of their duties became a federal offense. Federal courts were given jurisdiction over the election supervisors and their work. A new flood of outrages, numerous altercations and riots in the South were called to the attention of the President of the United States. His concern that life and property were insecure and that the carrying of the mails and collection of revenue were being endangered made him recommend legislation to Congress to facilitate his endorsement of the Enforcement Act. Congress responded by drawing up a bill known as the Third Enforcement Act, which became law on April 20, 1871. The new law was known as the Ku Klux Klan Act.[62] It gave the President the authority to suspend the privilege of the writ of Habeas Corpus and proclaim marshal law in areas where two or more persons gathered to obstruct the equal administration of civil rights or franchise laws.[63] Because of the hardships encountered in attempting to vote, the Negro electorate declined steadily in state after state. The full force of the Klan came forward to supervise elections where federal troops failed to supervise.

The Negroes who had watched political developments began to entertain serious doubts about the Republican party. Those who had fought for effective civil rights legislation in 1874 and 1875 were not satisfied with the law that finally passed. In 1875, Congress enacted the most far-reaching civil rights legislation ever considered. The preamble to this act proclaimed Congressional recognition of the "equality for all men before the law," and recognized the responsibility of government to "mete out equal and exact justice to all of whatever nativity, race, color, or persuasion, religious or political."[64] The Negroes had no active political support and no federal officials willing to enforce the Constitutional Amendments and the laws to protect them. These conditions were responsible for fear and despair among Negroes for their future.

The entrance of the Negro into the political arena as voter and office holder was the most revolutionary aspect of the Reconstruction program. Prior to Reconstruction no Negro was taken seriously as a voter nor as a candidate for public office. During Reconstruction, Negroes did hold public offices in the southern states. They sat in the legislatures and assisted in enacting laws. In South Carolina, they wielded the greatest influence. There were 87 Negroes and 40 whites in the first legislature. From the outset the whites controlled the state senate and in 1874 the lower house. There were white governors at all times; therefore, at no time were Negroes in control of South Carolina.[65]

Negroes were not significant in the leadership of Alabama during Reconstruction. Very few Negroes held office in the new government of Virginia. Negroes were never powerful enough to determine any policy of the government, except on a few occasions where they held the balance between militant factions. As far as the exercise of influence is concerned the same thing could be said of Negroes in Texas, Tennessee and Arkansas.[66]

By 1870, Congressional Reconstruction was in full sway in the South. In these states, Negroes had been elected[67] to the offices of Lieutenant-Governor, Speaker of the House, Secretary of State, State Auditor, State Superintendent of Education, and Justice of a state Supreme Court. Negroes acted as governors in Mississippi and Louisana. It was natural and important for them to aspire to federal elective offices.[68] Between 1869 and 1880, two Negroes served in the Senate and 14 in the House of Representatives. Both of the Senators represented Mississippi—Hiram R. Revels and Blanche K. Bruce. Revels was appointed to fill the Senate seat previously held by Jefferson Davis in 1870-1871. "He was the first Negro in national politics; he blazed the way, and it was easier for the others to follow."[69] The next Negro to serve in the Senate had a distinction of his own. Blanche K. Bruce, elected to the Senate in 1874, was and continues to be the only Negro in American history to serve a regular term in the United States Senate.[70]

It was in the Forty-first Congress, in 1869, that three Negroes first appeared in the federal legislature. J. H. Rainey of South Carolina was elected to fill a vacancy. He was the first member of his race in the House of Representatives. Rainey and Robert Smalls, both of South Carolina, led all Negroes in length of service in Congress. They served five consecutive terms. Negroes had a better chance of being elected to any

162

and all offices while Reconstruction was in progress and while all the state election machinery was controlled by their political party. Of the 20 Negroes serving in the House of Representatives of Congress, South Carolina sent the largest number of eight and North Carolina followed with four. Most of the Negroes in Congress had some experience in public service before going to Washington. Although they were chiefly interested in civil rights and education, their efforts were by no means confined to the Negro.[71]

THE TEMPERANCE FORCES

During the dismal decade of the 1860's, while the storm raged over the Negro as a political issue, the dry leaders were able to extract hope and comfort from three things. One was the organization of the National Temperance Society and Publication House at Saratoga Springs, New York, in 1865. Publication House became the principal outlet for temperance propaganda. Another event from which great things were expected was the organization of the national Prohibition party in 1869. Thirdly, this was also the year the first Negro was elected to the House of Representatives of Congress and the Ku Klux Klan were increasing their efforts to disfrancise the Negro. The Prohibition party failed to fulfill its promise; it was never able to exert any appreciable influence upon the American political scene, or to become more than a small minority party.[72] "With chattel slavery abolished through the Civil War and presidential action; certain reformers wanted to abolish rum slavery by similar means."[73] Since neither the Republican nor the Democratic party would take a stand against the saloon, those who believed in prohibition had to find another party. The National Prohibition party marked an epoch in the history of the temperance reform movement in America. It pioneered the path of political activity for the prohibition movement. It helped clear the way for non-partisan political activity, which in later years, succeeded in securing what the party as such could not achieve—Prohibition.[74]

Up to 1870, the prohibition issue had been of relatively minor importance as a political issue. It had been overshadowed by slavery and the status of the free Negro. Most of the prohibition activity had been in local, county, and state elections. The

Democratic and Republican parties had been requested by religious denominations and temperance groups, to take a definite
stand on the issue, but neither had done so.[75] In the 1870's the
Negro continued to be a political issue and create conflict between the North and South. The conditions surrounding the
sale of liquor continued to worsen. Since this was a period
of social reform, it was natural that alcohol would develop into
a major political issue at this time. The Prohibition party presented its first candidate in a Presidential election in 1872. The
party ran its candidate on a platform advocating constitutional
prohibition and universal suffrage.[76] This was the first time in
the history of this country that a national party had supported
constitutional prohibition and the enfranchisement of the total
population in a political platform.

DISFRANCHISEMENT

1876

In the election of 1876, both alcohol and the Negro were
national issues. This was the famous contest in which Rutherford
B. Hayes won the Presidency of the United States by a single
vote in the Electoral College. Hayes' opponent, Samuel J. Tilden,
the Democratic nominee, received a majority of the popular vote.
The Prohibition party again ran candidates for national office
and their candidate for president aroused great interest in his
advocacy of nationwide prohibition, but the temperance people
failed to cast their ballot for him. Both the Democrats and Republicans made strenuous efforts to get the dry vote.

In 1876, what remained of radical Reconstruction[77] was
practically eliminated by a controversial election. After 1876,
the southern whites gained full control of the area. There were
no limits to which certain elements in the South would not go
to eliminate the Negro as a political factor and to restore as
nearly as possible the old order. Reconstruction had been
fervently opposed because it gave the Negro opportunities in
the important field of political action. In the opinion of most
whites, a system that tolerated such behavior, even if only a few
Negroes voted was a disgrace and they protested continuously
against it. Following the disputed Hayes-Tilden Presidential
election of 1876, a deal was made between northern Republicans

and the white southern leadership. Included in the terms of the deal were the withdrawal of federal troops from the South and permission to handle the question of Negro rights and suffrage in their own fashion. The most effective means of maintaining white supremacy was through political unity under the Conservative party, as the Democratic party was called for a generation.[78] According to one writer, "The southern experiment in democracy was doomed by the fateful compromise of 1877; a compromise between northern and southern white folk, with democracy and the Negro as sacrificial victims."[79] After 1876, the 11 Confederate states segregated themselves from the rest of the Union by their faithfulness to the Democratic party until 1959. "Marriage to the Democratic party was an expedient and useful arrangement for the white southern leadership for many decades. It provided an escape from the excesses of the Negro dominated reconstruction government in the South. At the origin of the southern one-party system stood the single figure of the Negro."[80] In the South from 1877 until 1910, all public issues were subordinate to white supremacy.

The blackout of the Negro's political activity in the South did not descend suddenly and dramatically. Negroes did not surrender the ballot at once and without a fight. From 1876 to the first years of the twentieth century, the Negro suffrage problem was met first by a series of statutory disfranchising devices enacted during the seventies, eighties, and nineties.[81] Immediately after 1876, the redeemed South devoted its energies to minimize the Negro vote. It could not at once sweep the Negro out of the political arena; it had to devise adequate machinery to do so. Negroes could still vote and hold office. They continued to hold remnants of political power in South Carolina, Florida, Louisiana, in parts of North Carolina, in Texas, Tennessee, and Virginia.[82] A number of Negroes were elected to Congress after Reconstruction. George H. White of North Carolina, was the last Negro to serve in the Congress for over a quarter of a century. His term ended March 4, 1901.

1884

The Presidential campaign of 1884 was one of personalities and vituperation. Religion and alcohol were injected into this election between James G. Baline, Republican, from Maine, and

Grover Cleveland, Democrat, from Ohio. As election day approached, observers felt that New York, where the parties seemed evenly divided, held the key to the outcome of the contest and that the Irish voters in New York City probably held the balance of power in the state. In the closing days of the campaign, the Reverend Samuel Burchard, in a speech in New York said that the Democrats were the party of Rum, Romanism, and Rebellion.[83] This statement was circulated in an attempt to arouse the Catholic voters in New York. The phrase was equivalent to a charge that the Democratic party was composed of saloon-keepers; the kind of priest depicted in anti-Catholic cartoons; and rum-soaked politicians of Irish extraction. The Irish voted as usual for the Democrats and Cleveland carried New York. New York's electoral votes provided him with a sufficient majority to insure victory. Out of this campaign came one of those historical slogans—"Rum, Romanism, and Rebellion"—that attained almost the weight of a new historical cause.[84] The incident was a by-product of the campaign. There is no reason to doubt that this slogan backfired in New York to the extent that it was enough to elect Cleveland. For the first time, the Prohibition party and the dry issue had tipped the balance in a national election by taking votes from a major candidate. Prohibition played a trick on American politics as slavery did in 1860.

1888

In the 1888 Presidential election, the Republican nominee Benjamin Harrison barely defeated Grover Cleveland the Democratic candidate. Harrison received a minority of the popular vote. If he had not received the greater number of the one-fourth of a million votes of the Prohibition party, he would not have won the election. Again the Prohibition party seemed to hold the balance of power in a national election. The Republican party paid the Drys compliments by mentioning their cause in their platform in 1888.[85]

1892

While his participation in politics had declined sharply by 1890, the Negro as a political issue in southern politics tended to gain importance as the years passed. Negro disfranchisement again became a leading issue from 1890 onward. The elimination of the Negro from the political picture created circumstances that brought him back in the picture again. In 1892, the People's party nominated a candidate for the Presidency of the United States. The People's party began in the grain-growing states and spread into the South. "Agricultural Wheels and Farmers Alliances joined forces with money reformers who wanted greenbacks and free silver with Knights of Labor who favored one big union to launch a national party."[86] In 1892, the People's or Populist party attempted to win the Negro vote in most of the southern states. In many instances the party resorted to desperate means to seek the franchise for Negroes in communities where it had been prevented by custom and practice for a period of time. The Democrats became alarmed, desperate, and made overtures to the Populists. But they were not successful in their attempt to solicit the support and cooperation of the Populists. In some communities Negroes were forced to vote for Democrats by the very people who had denied them the exercise of the franchise only a few years before. Many Negroes stood by the Populists, who advocated political if not social equality. A number of Negroes were killed in Georgia and riots broke out in Virginia and North Carolina.[87]

The three years following the Presidential election of 1892 were fateful and important ones for the supporters and opponents of prohibition. Both groups had attempted to influence local, state, and national political parties over a period of years. In March 1870, the Temperance Alliance had been organized in Oberlin, Ohio to become the most highly organized and influential body striving for prohibition. In 1879 the distillers had provided the first organized opposition against the temperance movement through the United Brewer's Association. The Brewers used the methods which the Drys had developed in Maine and other places. They attempted to influence elections and control political machines. They went a little further; they put forth very powerful efforts in Washington, D. C., and attempted to influence the legislative and executive departments of the federal government.[88]

At the time the temperance movement became the Ohio Anti-Saloon League in 1893, a similar League was getting underway in Washington, D. C. Then, in December 1895, the Washington League took the initiative in calling a convention for organization of what was to become the Anti-Saloon League of America. The League was a powerful influence in the progressive stages leading to the adoption of the Eighteenth Amendment.[89] From the beginning, the League emphasized its non-partisan political activities. It refused to form affiliations with any political party or to place in nomination a ticket of its own. Its plan was to make selections of the most available candidates placed in nomination by existing parties, and to invite persons of all political parties to unite in securing their election. The original and basic plan of the Anti-Saloon League was to dry up the United States in steps—first the towns and the villages, then the counties, then the states, and finally the nation.[90]

1894

The year 1894 opened with the political air tenser in many areas of the nation, though it was not a Presidential election year. In North Carolina, the Populists and the Republicans combined forces and with the Negro vote, they gained control of the legislature and many local offices went to colored men. Populist-Republican fusion meant the race question had entered the stage of party politics.[91] This aroused southern democrats to allow Negroes more access to the polls, provided they voted for the Democratic party. There was a temporary upsurge of Negro political influence in some parts of the South. White conservatives witnessed the political resurgence of the Negro in North Carolina, Georgia, and other southern states with deep resentment. As the Negro returned to prominence, either as an elector or an election issue, sentiment against his participation grew. The Democrats, failing to control the Negro vote, were concerned about the return of black Republicanism. Even when they controlled him, it was believed that the Negro made for corruption in politics. Although the Populists could have the Negro vote, they preferred not to bother with it because of fear of the Democrats. The election laws could be turned against poor ignorant whites, if the Democrats became vindictive and sought to disfranchise the Populists as well as their Negro allies. "It was much better to have clear-cut constitutional disfranchisement of the Negro and leave the white groups to fight elections out among themselves."[92] The time during which all

168

three parties bid for the Negro vote was brief. After the collapse of the agrarian revolt in 1896, the movement for complete disfranchisement of the Negro helped to reunite the white South.

Since the white factions competed for the Negro vote, this frequently gave the Negro the balance of power. As a result, the southern whites decided it was time for the complete disfranchisement of the Negro. Most southern whites agreed that this should be done, but they differed over the method. In 1886, Mississippi called a convention to change its constitution: the primary purpose being to disfranchise the Negro. A suffrage amendment was written which imposed a poll tax of two dollars, excluded voters convicted of bribery, burglary, theft, arson, perjury, murder, and bigamy, and also barred all who could not read any section of the state constitution or understand it when read, or give a reasonable interpretation of it. South Carolina followed Mississippi in 1895. A clause was added to its constitution which called for two years residence, a poll tax of one dollar, the ability to read and write the constitution or to own property in the amount of $300, and the disqualification of convicts. This clause effectively disfranchised the Negro. In 1898, Louisiana invented a legal device destined to spread in the South —the Grandfather Clause. The law declared eligible for the ballot only those men whose grandfathers or fathers voted prior to 1867. This meant that freedmen or sons of former slaves (i. e., Negroes) were kept off the registration books. By 1910, the Negro had been effectively disfranchised by constitutional provisions in North Carolina, Virginia, Georgia and Alabama.[93]

THE TWENTIETH CENTURY

At the beginning of the twentieth century, the American people were in a reform mood and renewed their efforts to eliminate the use of alcohol. This was to be one of the major issues in the first two decades of this century.

THE PROHIBITION FORCES

Between 1900 and 1910, prohibition as a political issue increased in importance all over the nation. Fights and controversies developed over prohibition in local, state, and national political campaigns. When the Anti-Saloon League entered the temperance field in the 1890's, the groundwork had been laid. "The League set out to turn the flood light of publicity upon the saloon and the liquor traffic. Its object was not so much to form opinion as to mobilize for political action on already existing opinion."[94] The League insisted that its campaign was against the saloon and not for prohibition. Its propaganda, however, made little effort to keep the issues distinct. "The thing that made the saloon a hellish thing was liquor, and it was this that the League was gunning for."[95]

The forces opposed to alcohol were convinced that the root of the problem was the saloon. The liquor industry became thoroughly involved in political corruption through its connection with the saloon. Their illegal activities enabled saloons to make a profit; they also put them at the mercy of the politicians. A formidable alliance arose between the liquor interests and political machines, especially in the cities. For the privilege of breaking the law, saloons delivered to the politicians both money and votes. As the chief social center of the lower classes, the saloon was a natural and convenient political unit. The political power of a saloon varied with the class it served. Those that catered to the respectable middle classes were unusually unimportant politically, but those that served the lower classes were quite powerful at election time. The most valuable saloons were those that were always able to deliver a dependable bloc of votes. As a social and political center, the saloon was headquarters for the precinct. In the larger cities, a key link in the alliance between the saloon and politics was the saloonkeeper. Usually, the saloonkeeper was a friend and confidant of the working man. He was a person of considerable prestige among the immigrant population; therefore, the average saloonkeeper commanded the loyalty and respect of his neighbors and was able to exert considerable influence over them. Many saloonkeepers used their positions to enter politics.[96]

For a number of years, the League devoted its efforts almost entirely to local option. Statewide and national prohibition movements were discouraged on the ground that the country would not be ready for them until the drying up of the towns and counties or at least a sizeable majority of them had been accomplished. During the first decade of the 1900's, the opposers of the liquor traffic discovered that there were omnipartisan methods of supporting candidates for office and they

170

controlled the legislatures of half a dozen states. During the Progressive era, 1900-1920, the League increased its efforts to secure state prohibition in several areas. The success of these tactics was soon apparent. In the South, where it was claimed that the use of alcoholic beverages contributed to racial tension, seven states went dry in the years between 1907 and 1915, and four others in the Middle and Far West quickly followed suit.[97]

The wave of statewide prohibition was begun by Georgia in 1907 when the legislature passed a dry law; that same year a majority of the people of Oklahoma voted for a state consitutional prohibition amendment. Mississippi and North Carolina adopted statutory prohibition in 1908; Tennessee did the same in 1909; and in 1912, a similar type amendment was added to the constitution of West Virginia.[98]

Despite repeated victories in rural areas of the South, Middle and Far West, the prohibitionists were still unable to stop the sale of whiskey in the larger cities of the East. The saloon continued to flourish there. It became apparent to the leaders they must focus their sights on Congress. Between 1913 and 1920 the Anti-Saloon League was to initiate, support and pressure politicians into enacting legislation that would bring about national Prohibition. When it became obvious that the cities were not likely to be dried by state legislation or local option, prohibition forces turned to federal legislation. Their first victory was the Webb-Kenyon Act, which prohibited the shipment of intoxicating liquors into state territory, or districts where they were intended to be used in violation of the local law. This Act was passed over the veto of President Taft in 1913; its constitutionality was upheld (1917) by the Supreme Court. In December of 1913, the prohibition forces presented their first resolution in Congress providing for national prohibition by constitutional amendment. It was not until 1917, however, that such a resolution passed both Houses as the Eighteenth Amendment and was sent to the states for ratification. The political power and influence of the Anti-Saloon League and the organized dry forces was sometimes indeed astounding. "From the passage of the Webb-Kenyon Act in 1913 to the passage of the Eighteenth Amendment, the Drys constituted one of the most effective pressure groups in the history of American politics."[99]

171

The Anti-Saloon League concentrated its efforts on the Congressional elections of 1914. The conducting of this campaign was a revelation to Capitol politicians and created considerable anxiety among the Wets. Wayne B. Wheeler, general counsel of the Anti-Saloon League and one of the great driving forces of the dry movement described the situation:

> Congressional elections were to be held in November 1914, and the consensus of opinion was that we should concentrate our fire nationally on them and on the preceding primaries at which the candidates were to be nominated . . . Back of the drive were virtually all the Protestant denominations which composed and controlled the League; and through the churches of the country the Washington headquarters was in close touch with every section of the United States.
> . . . We started out to let Congress hear from the people back home. Word went out from Washington and state headquarters to the field to send letters, telegrams, and petitions to Congressmen and Senators in Washington. They rolled in by tens of thousands, burying Congress like an avalanche . . . Until the final vote of submission the country kept up a drumfire on Washington . . . We went into every Congressional district where there was a chance to elect a dry and waged as strong a fight as candidates have ever seen . . . While we were fighting back in the districts, we were also bombing the House and Senate at Washington. Our Washington headquarters opened correspondence with every possible friend in Congress. We also went to see them personally . . . The information obtained in our correspondence with members of Congress at Washington was sent back to the state. We kept the field workers advised of the attitude of every individual member of Congress and suggested ways to the local workers of winning converts. . .
> We also knew, often in advance, just what their plans were for influencing this, that, or the other member of Congress. Whenever they opened up on a member of Congress we would wire back to that member's state or district and tell the local drys to start a counterattack. They would do the rest. Within twenty-four hours a storm of telegrams would break over the member's head and he would realize that a revolution had broken loose back home. We confirmed it at Washington.[100]

In December 1914, the supporters of prohibition achieved a significant victory in the Congress of the United States. This was the first time that a full debate on prohibition had taken place in the House of Representatives. The floor leaders of both parties and the President were arrayed against the resolution for constitutional prohibition. Although the Drys had no hope of passing the resolution, they put up a vigorous fight. The

House remained in continuous session from 10:30 A.M. to 11:00 P.M., and 150 speeches were made. The time was evenly divided between the proponents and the opponents of the proposed resolution. When the vote was finally taken, constitutional prohibition received a majority of seven; the vote was 197 to 190. Since it failed to receive the necessary two-thirds, it was defeated.[101] Although they came close to victory, the dry forces did not attempt to secure the introduction and enactment of constitutional prohibition legislation until 1917.

In the 1916 campaign, the Anti-Saloon League increased their efforts and pressure to elect Congressmen who would support their causes. Wayne Wheeler said, "We laid down such a barrage of candidates for Congress as had never been seen before . . . We knew late election night that we had won . . . We knew that the prohibition would be submitted to the states by the Congress just elected . . ."[102]

World War I gave the prohibitionists their golden opportunity to save the nation from the evils of drink. President Woodrow Wilson called the Sixty-fifth Congress into special session to declare a state of war with Germany, on April 6, 1917. Even though a large number of the members of Congress (elected in 1916) were strongly committed to constitutional prohibition, Congress had to act upon a war program which came ahead of dry legislation. In drawing up a program it became obvious that if Americans had to conserve food to win the war, the use of grains for the manufacture of alcoholic beverages would be a drag on the war effort that could not be tolerated by patriotic citizens. After considerable debate and compromise between the opponents and supporters of prohibition it was included in the President's Food Control Bill. In 1917, both the House and Senate approved the Eighteenth Amendment to the Constitution which forbade the manufacture, sale or transportation of alcoholic beverages. By January 1919, 36 state legislatures had acted favorably, and the Eighteenth Amendment went into effect a year later—1920. The Volstead Act, providing the machinery for the enforcement of national Prohibition was adopted by Congress over President Woodrow Wilson's veto in October 1919, and the United States entered the dry decade.[103] There has been considerable discussion and speculation relative to the reason Wilson vetoed the Eighteenth Amendment. It

173

would seem likely that his veto was overruled by the Congress because of the overwhelming victory of candidates supported by the Anti-Saloon League. The fight for national Prohibition was won at the elections of 1916. In every contest prohibition was the principal issue . . . what happened after November 1916 was really a mopping-up operation, the consolidation of a triumph already won. From all indications the American people wanted prohibition and they were determined to secure it. For more than 100 years they had been indoctrinated with the idea that the destruction of the liquor traffic was the will of God and would provide the answer to most, if not all, of mankind's problems.[104]

PROHIBITION

With the passage of the Prohibition Amendment by Congress, the Anti-Saloon League had demonstrated its great influence and power in politics. In the elections of 1920 and 1922, the members revealed even greater power by defeating a number of Congressional incumbents who had dared to oppose dry legislation.[105] The Prohibition decade witnessed Ku Klux Klan attacks against Negroes, Jews, and Catholics. This was also the period when the Negro began to make his way back from the political oblivion into which the southern constitutions had assigned him until the Supreme Court decision in the Grandfather Clause cases reversed the trend. To block his comeback and at the same time to circumvent any brush with federal law, the whites in the one-party South began to systematically exclude Negroes from the Democratic primaries. This was as effective a means of disfranchisement as could possibly be found. Until Negroes could break through this wall, they would have no voice in the political councils of the South. In the North, Middle, and Far West, the Negro enjoyed the franchise and was not considered a political issue. Racial fears still remained a dead hand on the throttle of politics in the South, in spite of the solid achievements of the new disfranchising techniques and the white primaries.[106] Between 1915 and 1920, there was a mass migration of Negroes to the North and West. While they encountered segregation, job discrimination, residential restrictions, and sometimes violence, they met very few obstacles in participating in the political activities of these regions. This augmented the Negro's political strength and made the race an increasingly important factor in local, state, and national elections.[107] It was during this period of the Negro's migration to the North and Midwest that Prohibition became the law of the land.

The enforcement of the National Prohibition Act, better known as the Volstead Act, was largely a political football. Responsibility for the enforcement of the Act was lodged by Congress in the Bureau of Internal Revenue, a subdivision of the Treasury Department. John F. Kramer, an ardent prohibitionist was the first Prohibition Commissioner. With the advice and assistance of the Anti-Saloon League, he formed the Prohibition Unit, the name was changed in 1927 to the Prohibition Bureau.[108]

Less than three years after the beginning of Prohibition, the political domination of the Prohibition Bureau, and the corruption for which is was mainly responsible had become notorious. Although it was impossible to determine precisely how well or how badly, the law was observed and enforced. "But, obviously, the Eighteenth Amendment was the most widely disobeyed part of the Constitution—unless maybe the Fifteenth Amendment, which forbade racial discrimination in the right to vote, received more violations."[109]

When Prohibition was four years old, the political parties held conventions to nominate candidates for national offices. The Republican party platform of 1924 differed little in essentials from that of 1920. The Democrats gathered for their convention in New York City, a divided party. They were split by Prohibition and Ku Klux Klan issues. The South was militantly dry and the northern wing of the party was overwhelmingly wet. The Klan had been revived after World War I as an anti-Negro, anti-foreign, anti-Semitic, and anti-Catholic organization. Such nativist doctrines held a strong appeal for many southerners and for many small town people in the Middle West and other parts of the country. The postwar membership of the Klan reached well into the millions and the Klan had to be reckoned with. Many of the Democrat's northern leaders and rank and file members were drawn from the groups attacked by the Klan as un-American. The party's harmony was destroyed at this convention. The Democratic Convention, in 1924, was the bitterest and bloodiest in the history of the party.[110]

175

In the early days of the Volstead Act, gangsters were merely the "fronts" of ordinary businessmen who owned breweries and distilleries. They provided protection and insured delivery of liquor, while the businessmen had the necessary political influence to prevent interference. During the mid-1920's, in Chicago, gangsters openly intimidated voters at the polls. The politicians would prevent the police force from taking action against gamblers, bootleg kings, and racketeers in turn for large campaign contributions and blocks of voters on election day.[111] No large city escaped the influence of alcohol on politics, but nowhere else did the gangsters attain such power as in Chicago. All of the evils of alcohol in politics came to a head in the Illinois metropolis. In 1925, a committee of interested citizens requested Vice-President Charles G. Dawes to present a petition to the Senate. The petition accused criminals and bootleggers of working in collusion with the police and other public officials. An example was cited of five breweries being operated by a ring of politicians and police officers.[112] From January 1, 1927 to October 1, 1928, *The New York Times* carried stories of cases of corruption which involved government officials and politicians of city, county, and state administrations.[113]

In 1928, the Republican party nominated Herbert Hoover as its candidate for president of the United States, and the Democrats selected Alfred E. Smith. Although Prohibition was a burning political issue, neither party included it in its platform for fear of losing the support of the dry forces. The real disaffection of Negroes in the party of Lincoln began in 1928 when Republicans attempted to resurrect a strong party in the South with leadership. The Republican party was willing to alienate the Negro vote in an effort to build up a following that could crack the southern Democratic stronghold. By 1928, Negroes had learned to vote in considerable numbers for candidates who were not Republicans. At this time, Alfred Smith and his advisers decided to wage the first open and aggressive campaign to win the support of the Negro vote for the Democratic party.[114] The campaign marked the revival of the Negro as a burning issue in southern politics. Smith was depicted as a friend of the Negro and in the South this attack proved to be the most damaging.[115] A new and complicated issue was added by his being a Roman Catholic; the first to be nominated for president by a major political party. The members of the Ku Klux Klan and similar organizations openly attacked Smith on religious grounds. In fact, religion was dubbed the silent issue of the campaign; "it was neither polite nor politically astute to discuss it at least audibly."[116] The flames of religious bigotry were fed by charges that the Catholics had organized Negroes without regard for regional mores. There can be no doubt that the enforcement by statute, of the ban on alcoholic beverages, was an issue of great importance; probably no specific social issue in the campaign was more important. Each party was pledged to uphold the Amendment.[117]

Hoover overwhelmed the Democratic candidate. The Drys immediately hailed the election as a great triumph for Prohibition. It is quite likely that Hoover would have beaten Smith on the dry issue alone for the wet sentiment in the country, though growing rapidly, was not yet strong enough for modification. A combination of factors, so interlaced as to defy complete separation, could be used to explain the defections of half the South from the Democratic candidate. For the country as a whole, prosperity was the key issue. The religious factor was of particular importance both for 1928 and for the future course of American history. "The concomitant social issues of great importance included prohibition, the race question, immigration, snobbery, and a determination that the highest office in the land must not be held by someone thought to be alien to the American tradition."[118] Although Al Smith lost the election, he totaled the largest number of Democratic votes ever cast. In his defeat, he pulled the Northern cities into the Democratic party where they have largely remained.

In the 1928 election, Democrats made deeper inroads on the Republicanism of Negro voters than in any previous election. This election also resulted in the return of a Negro to Congress. The last Negro to serve in Congress had been George White, whose term ended in 1901. Oscar De Priest was the first northern Negro to be elected to United States Congress and serve as a member of the House of Representatives. This election gave Negroes new hope concerning their political activities in American life. The white South was alarmed that a Negro had achieved such distinction in American political life.[119] In 1945, there were two Negroes in the House of Representatives

177

of Congress. Both were Democrats and they were elected from New York and Illinois.

More and more Negroes were using their votes to register their protests and achieve improvements in many areas for their people. This was especially so outside of the South. The Negroes became politically effective in 1930 when they defeated President Herbert Hoover's nomination of Judge John Parker for a seat on the Supreme Court. Judge Parker was reported to have said that "the participation of the Negro in politics is a source of evil to both races."[120] The American Federation of Labor, National Association for the Advancement of Colored People, and other organizations protested the nomination of Judge Parker. "The Negro protest was at first ignored as insignificant by Judge Parker, President Hoover, and the country at large."[121] After a tense and hard-fought six weeks battle, the NAACP and their supporters attempted to defeat those senators who voted for the confirmation of the Judge. By the end of 1934, all of the senators who voted for Parker and who could be reached by colored voters had been defeated. There were other elements in the defeat of Judge Parker. It was the Negro influence which curiously enough in the end solidified the opposition.[122]

Prohibition was a major political issue in the 1932 national elections. At their convention, the Democrats adopted a plank for the outright repeal of the Eighteenth Amendment. "The Democrats had come into the open as the party of the wets. By default, the Republicans were the party of the drys."[123] The Republican plank asked for resubmission of the Eighteenth Amendment to the states which was outbidded by the Democratic plank, which demanded outright repeal. During the campaign of 1932, Hoover stated that he refused to "return to the old saloon with its political and social corruption or to endure the bootlegger and the speakeasy with their abuses and crime."[124] Either was intolerable. Resubmission to the states was the answer. American statesmanship, as exemplified by him, was capable of working out such a solution and making it effective. Prohibition was no longer a moral issue and Roosevelt won the election with a landslide victory. The change in the tone of political life brought about by the great Depression killed the Eighteenth Amendment.[125] Almost immediately after convening in 1933, Congress took up the issue of Prohibition. On February 16, 1933, the Senate voted by 62 to 63 to submit the Twenty-first Amendment, which provided for the outright repeal of the Eighteenth Amendment to state conventions for ratification. The House debate on the measure on February 20 followed the pattern of the Senate. After considerable debate, the House voted on the legislation; it gave the Wets a victory by 289 votes to 121. It was the heavy defection of the South to the Wets, in both the Senate and House, that tipped the scales. "The South had stopped whoring after the false gods of clerical politicians, and had returned to the fold of the Democratic party. As long as the Democratic president was a Protestant and gentleman, the Solid South would follow his lead on prohibition and on economics."[126] The Democratic party was the party of the South, right or wrong, but always the party of the South.

THE DEPRESSION

Prior to the Depression, Negroes in the large cities voted Republican. The Negroes who voted at this time were found largely in the northern and western sections of the country. It was not easy for the Negroes to desert the Republican party in 1932. Many of them remained true to tradition and voted for the GOP. Negroes were afraid that a Democratic victory would promote or advance southern politicians in Washington to bring about degradation of the Negro as had happened during the administration of Wilson. In some northern states the Negro vote became so important as to be almost a balance of power between the two parties. The growth of Negro power within the Democratic party served to further complicate that party's intricate relationship between the North and South.[127] The extent of the shift of the Negro's allegiance was demonstrated in 1934. In 1930, Arthur W. Mitchell of Illinois ran for Congress as a Republican and was defeated. He was elected to Congress on the Democratic ticket to replace Republican Oscar De Priest in 1934. Mitchell was the first Negro Democrat ever to sit in the Congress. It was a source of considerable embarassment to his southern colleagues to have him as a member of their majority.[128] During this period, Negroes all over the country were changing from the party of Lincoln to the party of Roosevelt and they were becoming more active in politics. A majority of the Negro

179

votes went to Roosevelt and the Democratic party in the 1936 election. The Republicans, however, were not without their ardent supporters. They made a desperate bid for Negro support and received it in some quarters. The Democrats' New Deal permitted the Negro, if he did not live below the Mason-Dixon Line, to share equally with his fellow white citizens in most of the government's social and economic programs. The New Deal's political impact on the Negro was to successfully shift the bulk of the Negro vote from the Republicans to the Democrats. By 1940, some opposition to Roosevelt and the Democratic party had developed, and there was a substantial decline in Negro support. Negroes accused the Administration of discriminating in some of the relief agencies and of being excluded from preliminary defense preparations that were being made. In the years that followed the Negro vote came to be more evenly divided, with the groups in the great urban centers of the North still showing an inclination toward the New Deal. The Negroes wielded sufficient influence in the pivotal states—Illinois, Ohio, Pennsylvania, and New York—to cause anxiety in both Democratic and Republican circles.

POLITICAL GROWTH OF THE NEGRO

Prohibition as a political issue began to decline in importance after 1932, and at the same time the influence of the Negro in politics began its ascendancy. Because of the Depression, the American people were more interested in the economic benefits which repeal would bring. Once the Depression had become too blatant to be ignored, the morality of prohibition seemed ridiculous. Hunger was more of a temperance teacher than any advocator of prohibition.[129] The illicit manufacture and sale of alcohol continued throughout the 1930's. This situation existed because of unemployment and the existing facilities to make whiskey. After 1932, bootlegging operated on a much smaller scale than before repeal of the Eighteenth Amendment.

When the United States entered World War II in December 1941, the people were too busy to be concerned about alcohol. During the war, alcohol, along with some meats, sugar, tires, butter and other goods, was rationed in some states. Although America was at war, the Negro continued to influence the political life of this country. The demand for better treatment of

Negroes in the armed forces and increased employment in the war effort, was made by Negro leaders. The change and growth of the Negro's political strength was recognized by the President of the United States and others occupying positions of influence and power in governmental and business circles. The Negro's political strength was dramatically projected upon the national consciousness in the spring of 1941, when A. Phillip Randolph, president of the Brotherhood of Sleeping Car porters threatened to mobilize 50,000 Negroes for a march on Washington. The purpose of the march was to demand jobs for Negroes in the expanding defense industries, many of which, faced with serious labor shortages, refused to employ or upgrade Negro workers. "The White House regarded the political implications of such a demonstration as grave, not only on the domestic front, but also in international relations."[130] As a result of this threat and subsequent conferences with Randolph, President Franklin D. Roosevelt issued Executive Order # 8802, in June 1941. The Order was regarded by many as a sort of second emancipation proclamation. The President reaffirmed the policy of the United States that "there shall be no discrimination in the employment of workers in defense industries or government because of race, creed, color, or national origin."[131] The government also established a Fair Employment Practices Committee to carry out the provisions of the Order. This Committee attempted to guarantee Negroes as well as other minority groups equality of economic opportunity. Northern Negroes repaid the New Deal with their votes.[132] In 1944, President Roosevelt died, and Vice-President Harry S. Truman ascended to the Presidency. Following 1945, in the postwar era, the American people were not too much concerned with prohibition, but the Negro as a political issue refused to fade away. Negroes began deserting the Democratic party and the New Deal by 1946. They had become wary of the domination of Congress by southern leaders who had blocked anti-lynching and fair employment legislation. Like many other Americans, the Negro voter had come to feel that a change was necessary and healthy; and he joined his fellowmen in bringing about that change.

In the thirties and forties, the political strength of Negroes was manifested in the consideration which both major parties gave to them in national elections and their successes in state and local elections. An increasing number of Negroes secured seats in state legislatures in both the Republican and Democratic parties. In 1946, approximately 30 Negroes secured seats in the legislatures of ten states. Eighteen were Republicans while 12 were Democrats. In every section of the United States, on all levels, the Negroes appeared to be making progress in politics. By 1947, a political regeneration had taken place among Negroes that made it possible for them to demand a great deal of consideration from both major parties.[133] Along with this, many persons joined in the assault upon the southern way of treating the Negro. The leadership of this assault was taken by the Truman Administration, which inherited from Franklin D. Roosevelt, the conviction that the duty of the Democratic party was to advance the rights of the lowly Negro. The issue was met October 29, 1947, by the publication of the report of President Truman's Committee on Civil Rights. This document forthrightly urged the immediate abolition of all governmental and some private sanctions of race discrimination or segregation. Among its recommendations was a federal anti-poll tax law, if the states refused to repeal their poll-tax requirement for voting, and a federal statute protecting the rights of all qualified persons to participate in so-called federal primaries and elections without interference by public officers or private persons.[134]

Nineteen hundred and forty-eight was a momentous year in the political history of the United States. It was during this year that the issue between the South and those who would reform its social practices reached a climax. The Negro citizen also was possessed of the greatest ballot potential in his history. The Negro's political influence was derived from strategic balance of power in marginal states whose electoral vote were generally considered vital to the winning candidate and not from numerical strength. Both major political parties recognized the Negro's growing political potential and intensified their efforts to win his support in 1948.[135] The Democratic party convened in Philadelphia, Pennsylvania in 1948, and nominated Harry S. Truman as their candidate for the presidency. The Republicans nominated Thomas E. Dewey for their standard-bearer. The Democratic party adopted a civil rights plank in their platform and immediately the Mississippi delegation and one-half of the Alabama delegates stalked out of the convention.[136]   The defecting Democrats ran Governor Strom Thurmond of South Carolina for president, and Governor Fielding Wright of Mississippi for vice-president as States' Rights or Dixicrat candidates.[137]   Truman won the election because "he received overwhelming backing from labor—Negroes and most white minority groups."[138]   The Negro continued to be a political issue and the race problem festered away spreading infection into every part of American life.   With a mandate from the American people to press his program, Truman, in 1949, put his civil rights program before Congress.   This time he was defeated.   Because of the race issue, Senators Claude Pepper of Florida and Frank P. Graham of North Carolina were defeated. Both had supported social legislation and expressed sentiments in favor of civil rights.

In the election year of 1952, Negroes demanded greater social equality and broader political rights.   Between 1948 and 1952 rallies were held in numerous cities to increase the number of Negroes on voting lists.   The results were disappointing. Stricter registration laws were enacted and voting lists purged. In rural counties the economy of the Negro was so tied up with that of the white man that he was afraid to try to vote.   In cities where Negroes had little difficulty in registering, they did not find much to get politically excited about.   Candidates for municipal and state offices, almost always white men, supported white supremacy with various degrees of intensity.[139]   The Presidential campaign was a different matter.   Among Negroes there was considerable activity and enthusiasm.   Both parties had adopted platforms with civil rights planks.   The Republican party's platform stated:

We condemn bigots who inject class, racial, and religious prejudice into public matters. . . . The Republican party will not mislead, exploit, or attempt to confuse minority groups for political purposes.   All American citizens are entitled to full impartial enforcement of Federal laws, relating to their civil rights. . . . We believe that it is the primary responsibility of each state to order and control its own domestic institutions, and this power reserved to the states is essential to the maintenance of our Federal Republic.   However, we believe that the Federal Government should take supplemental action within its constitutional jurisdiction to oppose discrimination against race, religion or national origin.[140]

The platform of the Democrats also contained a strong civil rights plank. It stated that:

The Democratic party is committed to support and advance individual rights and liberties of American citizens. Our country is founded on the proposition that all men are equal before the law and should enjoy equal political rights. We will continue our efforts to eradicate discrimination based on race, religion or national origin.[141]

The Democrats were also in favor of federal legislation to secure civil rights for everyone. This included the "right to full and equal participation in the nation's political life free from arbitrary restraints."[142]

The Democrats entered the campaign of 1952 with Adlai E. Stevenson as their Presidential candidate and with five straight Presidential victories over their Republican rivals, who had selected General Dwight D. Eisenhower as their candidate. This election found the defenders of the southern position in politics as strong as they had been in 1948 about civil rights. The parties were divided into two hostile camps over the question of equality for the Negro. Each side claimed that the unreasonableness of the other made an equitable settlement of the dispute impossible. The problem was insoluble, and the Truman Administration was in some measure responsible. The Republicans overwhelmingly won the election. The difficulties confronting the Democratic party in 1952 were compounded by its split over civil rights. The President's demands for greater equality for the Negro served only to alienate the majority of the southern white population without adding to the party's voting strength in the North and West. The South and the northern city machines had provided the Democratic party with the bulk of its votes since Reconstruction, but by 1952, the South was ready for political rebellion. Southern senators and governors vied with one another in announcing their hostility to the Democratic regime in Washington. In 1948, southern die-hards had fought the Democrats with a third party, but in 1952, many of the section's voters were prepared to support any Republican candidate who was not outspokenly in favor of equality for Negroes.[143] In this election the Republicans were able to split the solid South for the first time since 1928. They carried four states—Texas, Virginia, Florida, and Tennessee.[144] Although both major political parties were committed to advancing civil rights in 1952, the

Eisenhower Administration entered office with no clear-cut program on civil rights. As a military leader, Eisenhower had given some support to integration in the army; but as a Republican candidate who had won the votes of many white southerners, he was presumably under considerable pressure not to alienate a group whose members generally opposed any break in the color line. The Administration's efforts on behalf of the Negro were overshadowed by a series of historic Supreme Court decisions. On May 17, 1954, in a unanimous decision, the Supreme Court ruled that racial segregation in public schools was unconstitutional in that it denied citizens equal protection under the law as guaranteed by the Fourteenth Amendment. In May 1955, the Supreme Court ordered the states to make a prompt and reasonable start toward complying with the 1954 decision. Local authorities were ordered and directed to establish non-segregated school systems with all deliberate speed. In November 1955, the Court struck still another blow at segregation; it ruled against segregation in public parks and playgrounds and on public beaches and golf courses. The Court's decisions had political repercussions all over the nation, but especially in the South. Many southerners, particularly in the Deep South, were determined to resist integration at all costs. They formed white citizens councils to propagandize for white supremacy and terrify the Negroes, while in some areas the Ku Klux Klan was reactivated.[145] As the Eisenhower Administration began to reach its end in 1956, the country was divided over the status of Negroes. Many southerners were determined to secure revenge at the ballot box.

The 1956 election was similar to that of 1952 in many respects. Both major parties nominated the same candidates for president and adopted platforms with civil rights planks. Because of the Supreme Court decisions on segregation, the Negro became a major political issue in the campaign. The results were a foregone conclusion for Eisenhower's victory which was even more decisive than in 1952. Again he was able to split the South and increase the number of states he won from four to five.[146] Thousands of southerners who voted for Eisenhower in 1952 and 1956 still thought of themselves as Democrats. Most southerners continued to elect Democrats for state and local offices, while Republican national candidates received unprecedentedly large votes.[147]   These developments were ironic, because the issue that had kept the region's whites faithfully Democratic for almost a century, was its actions on Negro rights.

For over two decades the great national battle for Negro rights was in the courts.   The Supreme Court did more than any other branch of the government to destroy the barriers erected by racial prejudice.   The decisions by the Court created controversies and made the Negro a political issue.   They did not improve or advance the Negro's right to vote, which would have provided him with more political power.   Congress contributed to greater equality for minority groups.   In 1957, for the first time in 82 years Congress enacted a bill designed to protect the voting rights of the Negro.   The Civil Rights Bill of 1957 created a bipartisan Commission on Civil Rights.   It was an important act in beginning to redress voting inequities.   The Act authorized the federal government to bring civil suits in its own name to obtain injunctive relief when any person was denied the ballot or when his right to vote was threatened.   The Act also required that the United States government provide attorneys and pay the expenses of all lawsuits involving the violation of voting rights of Negroes.   In addition, the Act gave federal district courts jurisdiction over such lawsuits, without requiring that all state remedies be exhausted.   For the first time, the Justice Department itself could sue in cases involving the denial of voting rights, and the suit could go before the federal courts sooner than had formerly been possible.[148] Although the provisions of this law fell far below the demands of the northern liberals, the Civil Rights Act represented a major defeat for those southerners who had repeatedly refused to compromise their demands for white supremacy and the disfranchisement of the Negro.

Southern concern over the Negro continued to be one of the most deeply rooted sources of political contention in American history.   As the Negro's demand increased for civil rights, the southerner felt that his way of life was being threatened. Despite much oratory to the contrary, the basis of the fear was the Negro.[149]   In the fall of 1960, most southern Negroes of voting age in the 11 former Confederate states (1,500,000, slightly more than one-fourth) were registered to vote.[150]   As the 1960 election approached, both major political parties increased their soliciting for Negro votes, especially in the large cities of the North, Middle and Far West. The 1960 election was one of the closest in the history of the United States with John F. Kennedy, Senator from Massachusetts, eking out a narrow victory over Richard M. Nixon, vice-president of the Eisenhower Administration. The margin of victory was so close that in some states there was some doubt about its certainty for several days.

The election was significant because of the part played by the Negro both as a political issue and participant. In their appeal to the Negro voter, both major political parties adopted the most comprehensive and far-reaching civil rights planks in the history of the country. The increasing number of Negro voters influenced both major political parties in making their platforms. The Democrats made a bid for the Negro vote by stating in their platform:

> The time has come to assure equal access for all Americans to all areas of community life, including voting booths, schoolrooms, jobs, housing, public facilities.

Not only did they take a strong stand on the Civil Rights plank in their platform, the way it was to be done was outlined:

> To accomplish these goals will require executive orders, legal action brought by the Attorney-General, legislation, and improved Congressional procedures to safe-guard majority rule. It will require the strong, active, persuasive, and inventive leadership of the President of the United States.[151]

The Republicans not to be outbidded by the Democrats pledged the following: "a guarantee of the right to vote to all citizens in all areas of the country; desegregation of public schools; equal employment opportunities; prohibition of discrimination from public facilities and services." Along with this, they would use the full power, resources and leadership of federal government to eliminate discrimination based on race, color, religion or national origin.[152]

The Negro voter exerted considerable influence on the 1960 presidential, congressional, gubernatorial, and local elections all over the country. Many believe that the Negro vote decided the outcome of the presidential election. As the campaign was drawing to an end, Senator John F. Kennedy was persuaded to telephone Mrs. Martin Luther King, Jr. Dr. King, a leader in the Civil Rights Movement, had been arrested and jailed in Georgia. The publicity about the call from presidential candidate Kennedy to Mrs. King expressing concern over her husband gained crucial Negro votes. Former President Dwight D. Eisenhower thought that this telephone call won the election for him.[153] From all indications, Negroes held the balance of power and their support of the national Democratic candidates was responsible for their victories in this election.

Between 1960 and 1964, the Negro continued to protest the treatment accorded him in all areas. In the field of politics, the Negro demanded the unrestricted exercise of those political rights guaranteed to every American by the Constitution; the right to participate freely in the selection of local, state, and federal officials; the right to be elected to any office for which the candidate may obtain the necessary votes; and the right to hold appointive office in accordance with individual merit. Negroes were aware that in the majority of the southern states, the right to vote had been restricted by the poll tax, the white primary, complicated registration and educational requirements, and by intimidation and fear of physical injury. The right to hold responsible office had been limited by custom and the practices of the politicians. As a result of the denial of political rights a second-class citizenship status was imposed on the Negro. The Negroes of the country were no longer willing to endure and accept these conditions. They demanded the immediate elimination of discriminatory restrictions in all areas of American life and activity. To support their demands and achieve first-class citizenship, the Negroes engaged in massive street demonstrations. As a result of these demonstrations an observation was made that "Negroes have created more of a stir in American politics with less overall participation than any other comparable groups. Yet, in the surging Negro revolution of the 1960's, political action is surely a major weapon the Negro must acquire."[154]

During the first two years of the Kennedy Administration, Negroes intensified their demands for the enactment of comprehensive civil rights legislation by Congress. To achieve this goal, civil rights leaders and organizations sponsored street demonstrations, freedom rides, and sit-ins. They also undertook a massive registration and voting drive over the country. Special attention was given the South in increasing registration and voting. It was hoped that more voting power by Negroes would change the political complexion of this region.

After numerous conferences with special advisors and civil rights leaders, President Kennedy decided to take some action on civil rights. In June 1963, he sent a special message to Congress, wth the draft of a new Civil Rights Act. The Bill was designed to assure that Negro citizens would not be deprived of every American's right to vote, to go to school, to get a job, and to be served in a public place without arbitrary discrimination. The Bill aroused the bitter opposition of southern Democrats and conservative Republicans. Because of the opposition of key southern Congressmen, the Bill did not even reach the floor for a vote in 1963. After the assassination of President Kennedy, the new Chief Executive, Lyndon B. Johnson, made an eloquent appeal to Congress to pass the measure. But action was postponed until 1964. On August 29, 1963, over 200,000 Negroes and their supporters marched on Washington, D. C.[155] The purpose of this march was to point out the need for Congress to pass Civil Rights legislation.

On Thursday, July 2, 1964, in a dramatic White House ceremony telecast to the nation, President Johnson signed the Civil Rights Act of 1964 into law. This was done only five hours after Congress had completed action on it. The law was the climax to more than a year of debate, discussion and political maneuvering.[156] The political consequences of the act were immediate and profound. The law and its repercussions in race relations were scheduled to play a major part in the 1964 political campaign and outcome.

In one respect, at least, the Democratic Convention of 1964 was much like the Republican. Both were apparently dominated by a single strong personality. Lyndon B. Johnson imposed his will on cheering Atlantic City Hall as forcefully as Barry Goldwater had persuaded the Cow Palace in San Francisco to accept his mandate. With the nomination of Goldwater as candidate for president by the Republicans, the Negro again became a major campaign issue. Barry Goldwater's vote against the Civil Rights Act made him the favorite of the former states of the

Confederacy. The southerners tied all their hopes to Goldwater; an undercurrent of feeling about the Civil Rights legislation ran through those hopes. "But the over-riding considerations were his fiscal conservatism, his emphasis on states' rights; his tough line on communism and what the southerners described as his crusade for individual freedom."[157] James Reston writing in *The New York Times,* October 30, 1964 stated: "A great party, which emanicpated Negroes 100 years ago, has nominated for the Presidency a man backed by every racist gang in the country and lent its name to an attack upon the whole trend of foreign, economic and social policy of the last generation."

Civil rights was by no means the only issue in the South, but it was generally agreed to be the most important one: From the standpoint of many Democratic whites, the position of Senator Goldwater on this issue was far more acceptable than that of President Johnson. The statements of President Johnson on civil rights did not vary, according to the sections in which they were made. He supported and promised to enhance the Civil Rights Act in the Deep South, as well as the other sections of the nation. A few days prior to the election, Goldwater from the steps of the capital of South Carolina, made an appeal to the southern states to vote for him for President. The forces of Goldwater were optimistic about his chances of winning a number of the states of the North, Middle and Far West. They believed that the civil rights demonstrations in the large urban centers of these regions would help him to win the election. Many of the demonstrations resulted in riots, bloodshed, physical injury, and death. This situation projected the great, but hard-to-measure issue of the white backlash. The question was whether whites in large numbers might vote against Johnson because of his backing of the new federal civil rights laws, and because of resentment against Negro demonstrations. Johnson took the stand that for every Democratic voter who turned against him on the civil rights issue, three Republicans would turn against Goldwater because of fear of what he might do with nuclear weapons.[158] Earlier in the year, Governor George Wallace of Alabama ran strongly in the presidential primaries in Indiana, Wisconsin, and Maryland. His campaign was largely focused on the issue of states' rights and he received a surprisingly large number of votes in all of these states. The showing by Wallace encouraged the Goldwater forces that their candidate could win these states.

The 1964 campaign was among the bitterest and dirtiest in the history of this country, especially the Presidential campaign. An editorial in *The New York Times*, November 1, 1964 stated:

> The nation will be breathing a vast collective sigh of relief this weekend in the happy thought that at last, the long, weary, debilitating—and at times degrading—Presidential campaign is virtually over.
>
> Rarely in modern times and never in recent years has there been a campaign in which the issues facing the nation have been so inadequately discussed by the two leading candidates . . .
>
> Our differences with Senator Goldwater on domestic policy are legion; but in no area do we think his election would be more disastrous than in the broad field of civil rights. This is not because we think he does not appreciate the necessity—nor in fact does he have the desire or intention of exercising the continued strong pressure from the very peak of government essential to insure that equality before the law which is guaranteed to every American.

On November 4, 1964, the American people went to the polls and voted overwhelmingly for the Democratic candidates for president and vice-president. The phenomenal Democratic success was reflected in the election returns throughout the country. The Democrats gained at nearly all political levels from courthouse to Congress. Goldwater carried six states in the election. He won his homestate of Arizona and five in the Deep South—Alabama, Mississippi, Louisiana, Georgia, and South Carolina. Not only was the Negro a major political issue in the presidential race, but his vote was important in determining the winners of Congressional, state, county and local elections. The critical importance of the Negro's vote to the Democratic party was pointed out by John Herbers: "In a number of congressional and local races, Democratic candidates were put in office by a margin provided by Negro ballots." He believed that this was due to two factors: "The increase in Negro voter registrations and the fact that for the first time the Negro vote was not split"[159]

North Carolina might have been lost to the Republicans had it not been for the Negro vote. In only one of the 11 southern states, Texas, would the Democrats have won a clear majority without it.[160] From all indications, the Negro became

191

of age in politics and a force to be reckoned with in the future. The number of Negroes elected to the House of Representatives increased from five to six—all Democrats. Edward W. Brooks, a Republican, was re-elected as Attorney-General of Massachusetts. In Georgia, Horace Ward was elected to the state senate where he joined Leroy Johnson, who had been elected to the senate in 1962. Johnson was successful in his 1964 bid to return there. For the first time since Reconstruction, a Negro was elected to the Tennessee general assembly—A. W. Willis, Jr.[161] The Negroes elected to state legislatures of Tennessee and Georgia ran as Democrats. The decisive defeat of Goldwater; the increase in the voting strength of Negroes; and the number running and getting elected to office have led many of the experts to study more carefully and critically the future role of the Negro in American politics. There are many who are of the opinion that racism or the Negroes are dead as political issues. There are few, if any, doubts after the 1964 elections that a candidate can run and be elected to office in very few places in the country, through appealing to racism.

A FEW MORE WORDS ON ALCOHOL

Between 1960 and 1964, while the Negro was intensifying his demands for civil rights, alcohol continued to be a political issue. Although national Prohibition was repealed in 1933, large areas of the United States are still legally dry. This situation exists because in local option elections, the foes of alcohol are still able to secure enough people to vote for its prohibition. A considerable number of the dry counties and cities are located in the rural areas of the South and the Midwest, but larger urban areas of the East continue to be plagued with problems related to the sale of alcohol. An example of the influence and fear of political reprisals from supporters of prohibition was revealed in a newspaper story. When radio station WQXR notified advertising agencies that it was willing to broadcast commercials for whiskey and other hard liquors after 10:30 at night, the executive vice-president and general manager of the station said that "the step had been taken over the protests of the Distilled Spirits Institute and that the Institute had appealed to what is called 'the tiffany of radio' not to set an example that might have nationwide repercussions."[162] Since repeal of the Eighteenth Amendment in 1933, the liquor industry has frowned on radio advertising because whiskey commercials might reach young listeners and might arouse dry groups in various sections. The directors of the Code Authority of the National Association of Broadcasters said that "the Times station was instituting an unwise policy that could give new ammunition to dry forces. These forces were constantly appealing to sympathetic congressmen for stricter control on the advertising of all types of alcoholic beverages."[163] The fear of dry forces reviving alcohol as a political issue continues to haunt the manufacturers and distributors of alcoholic beverages. This fear influences their activities in the sale and advertising of their products.

Between 1619 and 1964, alcohol and the Negro were burning political issues. The debates, over these issues were among the most bitter and controversial in American legislative history, from local to national levels. They were responsible for the rise of political third parties. In the 1800's, the anti-slavery and whiskey supporters joined forces and attempted to use their political strength to eliminate these evils. These groups also influenced the platforms and activities of the major political parties from the 1859's until 1964. The Republican party was formed in the 1850's to stop the extension of slavery into newly acquired territories and states applying for admission to the Union. The disagreement between the northern and southern wings of the Democratic party over slavery finally split the party in 1860. The Republican party fought and won the war as the party of the Union and champion of the Negro. After Reconstruction, the fear of the Negro in politics was responsible for the one-party system in the South. In the early 1870's, the Prohibition party ran candidates for president and vice-president. The purpose of this party was to prohibit the use of whiskey. The Presidenial elections of 1884 and 1888 were influenced by prohibition. The Democrats won New York State and the election because of the statement by a Republican who said that the Democratic party was one of "Rum, Romanism, and Rebellion." The Republicans' Presidential candidate barely defeated the Democrats in the 1888 election. He received the larger share of the quarter million prohibition votes. Again, the Prohibition party seemed to hold the balance of power in a national election.

Between 1876 and 1910, the whites of the South completely disfranchised Negroes through state constitutional conventions. Political fear of the Negro influenced every aspect of the lives of the southerners. The second force which drove the southerners toward prohibition was the Negro in politics. Traditionally, Negroes voted Republican and the whites Democratic. If the Negro ballot could be eliminated at the polls, the white Democrats would be in control. The Anti-Saloon League was founded in 1896; it was formed as a political organization and nothing else. Between 1910 and 1917, the League became so powerful politically that it was able to elect or defeat local, state, congressional, and national candidates for office on its stand on alcohol. The League was responsible for the passage of the Eighteenth Amendment and Volstead Act.

In the 1924 and 1928 Presidential campaigns, religion, alcohol, and the Negro were major political issues. Because of his religion and his stand on alcohol, Alfred E. Smith was defeated for the presidential nomination by the Democratic party in 1924. Although he was nominated as the Democratic candidate in 1928, he was overwhelming defeated on the issues of religion, race, and alcohol. This was the first time since Reconstruction that the Republicans had been able to crack the solid South.

Alcohol was a political issue in the 1932 campaign. The Democrats supported direct repeal and won a larger margin over the Republicans who endorsed a moist plank platform.

After 1932, temperance receded as an issue of paramount political significance in American life. On the other hand, the Negro increased as a major issue. At the 1948 Democratic convention, delegates from some of the southern states walked out because of the civil rights platform adopted by the party. With the support of the Negro vote and the large urban centers of the North and Far West, Harry S. Truman won a surprising victory for the Democrats. The issue of race and civil rights continued to plague the Democrats in 1952. Because of this issue, a large number of Democrats voted for Republican candidates for national office. They were able to win four southern states.

In 1960, the issues of religion and race were foremost in the national campaign. The Democrats won a close national victory over the Republicans. During the Kennedy Administration, civil rights became an issue of such political magnitude and depth that the strongest Civil Rights Bill, since Reconstruction, was presented to Congress by the President. The Bill was enacted in 1964 and immediately became a political issue.

Civil rights and the Negro influenced both political conventions and their platforms in 1964. The Presidential campaign witnessed the most bitter and vicious appeals to racism since the turn of the century. The Presidential candidates of the Republican party, which was founded to free Negroes and prevent the spread of slavery, campaigned against the constitutionality of the Civil Rights Act. The Democrats won the election by a landslide. The Negro was an issue in this campaign, but his vote also determined the winners in many of the local, state, and congressional races. Many individuals hope that this will end the Negro as an issue in politics. The increase in the voting strength and participation of Negroes in politics offers great promise for their future acceptance as first-class citizens.

---

1 Henry Lee, *How Dry We Were* (Englewood Cliffs, New Jersey: Prentice-Hall, 1963), p. 210.
2 Gunnar Myrdal, *An American Dilemma* (New York: Harper & Row, 1944), pp. 430-431.
3 Herbert Asbury, *The Great Illusion* (New York: Doubleday & Co., 1950), p. 8.
4 John Hope Franklin, *From Slavery to Freedom* (New York: Alfred A. Knopf, 1947), p. 71.
5 Ernest Cherrington, *The Evolution of Prohibition in the United States of America* (Westerville, Ohio: The American Press, 1920), p. 24.
6 John Allen Krout, *The Origins of Prohibition* (New York: Alfred A. Knopf, 1925), pp. 8, 10, 15.
7 Leroy H. Woodson, *American Negro Slavery in the Works of Friedrich Strubberg, Friedrich Gertacker, and Otto Ruppius* (Washington, D. C.: The Catholic University of America Press, 1949), p. 2.
8 *Ibid.*, p. 3.
9 Staughton Lynd, "A Constitution Divided", *Columbia University Forum*, 8 (Spring 1965), pp. 18-19.
10 Woodson, *op. cit.*, p. 5.
11 *Ibid.*
12 Lynd, *op. cit.*, p. 18.
13 *Ibid.*, p. 21.
14 *Ibid.*, pp. 20-21.
15 Francis Butler Simkins, *A History of the South* (New York: Alfred A. Knopf, 1963), p. 92.
16 *Freedom to the Free; 1863 Century of Emancipation 1963*, A Report of the President of the United States Civil Rights Commission (Washington, D. C.: United States Government Printing Office, February, 1963), p. 15.
17 *Ibid.*, pp. 15-16.

18 Simkins, *op. cit.*, p. 98.

19 *Ibid.*, p. 98

20 Louis Filler, *The Crusade Against Slavery: 1830-1860* (New York: Harper & Row, 1960), p. 82.

21 Myrdal, *op. cit.*, *p.* 429.

22 Henry Lee Moon, *Balance of Power: The Negro Vote* (New York: Doubleday & Co., 1948), p. 55.

23 John Hope Franklin, *The Free Negro in North Carolina* (Chapel Hlll: The University of North Carolina Press, 1943), p. 106.

24 William B. Hesseltine, *The Rise and Fall of Third Parties* (Washington, D. C.: Public Affairs Press, 1948), pp. 12-13.

25 Peter H. Odegard, *Pressure Politics: The Story of the Anti-Saloon League* (New York: Columbia University Press, 1928), pp. 36-37.

26 Asbury, *op. cit.*, pp. 45, 55.

27 *Ibid.*, pp. 57-58.

28 Norman A. Graebner, ed., *Politics and the Crisis of 1860* (Urbana: The University of Illinois Press, 1961), p. 10.

29 Simkins, *op. cit.*, p. 11.

30 *Ibid.*, and Graebner, *op. cit.*, p. 10.

31 Kirk H. Porter and Donald Bruce Johnson, *National Party Platforms* Urbana: The University of Illinois Press, 1961), p. 13.

32 Robert W. Johannsen, "Douglas at Charleston," *Politics and the Crisis of 1860* (Urbana: The University of Illinois Press, 1961), p. 62.

33 Franklin, *From Slavery to Freedom*, pp. 261-262.

34 Graebner, *op. cit.*, pp. 14-15.

35 Franklin, *From Slavery to Freedom*, p. 263.

36 Hesseltine, *op. cit.*, p. 15.

37 *Ibid.*, and Harold Underwood Faulkner, *American Political and Social History* (7th ed.; Appelton-Century-Crofts, 1957), pp. 399-400.

38 Porter and Johnson, *op. cit.*, p. 27.

39 Don E. Fehrenbacher, "The Republican Decision at Chicago", *Politics and the Crisis of 1860* (Urbana: The University of Illinois Press, 1961), p. 43.

40 *Ibid.*, p. 43; *Freedom to the Free, op. cit.*, pp. 20-21; and Graebner, *op. cit.*, p. 18.

41 Faulkner, *op. cit.*, p. 398 and Fehrenbacher, *op. cit.*, p. 45.

42 *Freedom to the Free, op. cit.*, p. 22.

43 Johannsen, *op. cit.*, p. 61.

44 Faulkner, *op. cit.*, p. 404.

45 Graebner, *op. cit.*, p. 30.

46 Fehrenbacher, *op. cit.*, p. 31.

47 William E. Baringer, "The Republican Triumph," *Politics and the Crisis of 1860* (Urbana: The University of Illinois Press, 1961), pp. 91-92.

48 *Freedom to the Free, op. cit.*, p. 23.

49 Asbury, *op. cit.*, pp. 134-140.

50 Cherrington, *op. cit.*, pp. 134-140.

51 Andrew Sinclair, *Prohibition: The Era of Excess* (Boston: Little, Brown, & Co., 1962), p. 93.

52 Paul Lewison, *Race, Class, and Party* (New York: Oxford University Press, 1932), p. 18.

53 E. Merton Coulter, *The South During Reconstruction, 1865-1877* (Baton Rouge: Louisiana State University Press, 1947), p. 38.

54 Moon, *op. cit.*, p. 56

55 Coulter, *The South During Reconstruction*, p. 39.

56 *Ibid.*, p. 42.

57 *Freedom to the Free, op. cit.*, p. 45.

58 Franklin, *From Slavery to Freedom*, p. 302.

59 Simkins, *op. cit.*, pp. 271-272.

60 Lewinson, *op. cit.*, pp. 50-51.

61 John Hope Franklin, *Reconstruction: After the Civil War* (Chicago: University of Chicago Press, 1961), p. 165.
62 *Ibid.*, pp. 166-168, and *Freedom to the Free*, *op. cit.*, pp. 46-48.
63 Lewinson, *op. cit.*, pp. 44-45.
64 *Ibid.*, pp. 44-45.
65 Franklin, *From Slavery to Freedom*, p. 313.
66 *Ibid.*, pp. 314-315.
67 Negroes ran and were elected on the Republican ticket.
68 Samuel Denny Smith, *The Negro in Congress, 1870-1901* (Chapel Hill: The University of North Carolina Press, 1940), p. 1.
69 *Ibid.*, p. 25.
70 *Ibid.*, p. 25.
71 *Ibid.*, pp. 42-45.
72 Asbury, *op. cit.*, p. 64.
73 Sinclair, *op. cit.*, p. 84.
74 Cherrington, *op. cit.*, p. 168.
75 Raymond G. McCarthy and Edgar M. Douglass, *Alcohol and Social Responsibility* (New York: Thomas Y. Crowell Co., 1945), p. 25.
76 Porter and Johnson, *op. cit.*, p. 46.
77 The period from their admission as "reconstructed" states to the time of the Democratic Conservative victories may be regarded as the maximum extent of the so-called Radical control of the former Confederate states. These periods varied from state to state, they were less than a decade except in Florida, South Carolina and Louisiana.
78 Simkins, *op. cit.*, p. 311-313.
79 Moon, *op. cit.*, *p.* 64
80 *The Charlotte Observer* (Charlotte, N. C.: July 14, 1964), Editorial.
81 Lewinson, *op. cit.*, p. 61.
82 Moon, *op. cit.*, p. 69.
83 Harry J. Carman, Harold C. Syrett, and Bernard W. Wishy, *A History of the American People Since 1862* (New York: Alfred A. Knopf, 1961), Vol. 2, p. 240.
84 Edmund A. Moore, *A Catholic Runs For President* (New York: The Ronald Press, 1956), pp. 12-13.
85 Sinclair, *op. cit.*, pp. 84-85.
86 Hesseltine, *op. cit.*, p. 17.
87 Franklin, *From Slavery to Freedom*, p. 332.
88 Asbury, *op. cit.*, p. 32.
89 McCarthy and Douglass, *op cit.*, pp. 3, 32.
90 Asbury, *op. cit.*, p. 101
91 Helen G. Edmonds, *The Negro and Fusion Politics in North Carolina, 1894-1901* (Chapel Hill: The Universty of North Carolina Press, 1951), p. 37.
92 Franklin, *From Slavery to Freedom*, p. 333.
93 Langston Hughes and Milton Meltzer, *A Pictorial History of the Negro in America* (rev. ed.; New York: Crown Publishers, 1963), pp. 230-231.
94 Odegard, *op. cit.*, p. 38.
95 *Ibid.*, p. 47.
96 James H. Timberlake, *Prohibition and the Progressive Movement, 1900-1920* (Cambridge: Harvard University Press, 1963), pp. 112-113.
97 Carman, Syrett, and Wishy, *op. cit.*, p. 412.
98 Asbury, *op. cit.*, p. 121.
99 Joseph R. Gusfield, *Symbolic Crusade* (Urbana: The University of Illinois Press, 1963), p. 120.
100 *The New York Times*, (March 29, 1926).
101 Odegard, *op. cit.*, p. 156.
102 Asbury, *op. cit.*, pp. 128-129.
103 Carman, Syrett, and Wishy, *op. cit.*, pp. 413-414.
104 Asbury, *op. cit.*, p. 136.
105 Gusfield, *op. cit.*, p. 120.

106 Lewinson, *op. cit.*, p. 187.
107 Moon, *op. cit.*, p. 103.
108 Asbury, *op. cit.*, p. 134.
109 David A. Shannon, *Twentieth Century America: The United States Since the 1890's* (Chicago: Rand McNally & Co., 1963), p. 283.
110 Carman, Syrett, and Wishy, *op. cit.*, p. 542.
111 Sinclair, *op. cit.*, p. 269.
112 Kenneth Allsop, *The Bootleggers and Their Era* (New York: Doubleday & Co., 1961), pp. 100-101.
113 Asbury, *op. cit.*, p. 187.
114 Walter White, *A Man Called White* (New York: The Viking Press, 1948), p. 99.
115 Moon, *op. cit.*, p. 106.
116 Moore, *op. cit.*, p. 23.
117 *Ibid.*, pp. 27, 117-118.
118 Moore, *op. cit.*, p. 196.
119 Moon, *op. cit.*, p. 106.
120 Quoted from Franklin, *From Slavery to Freedom,* p. 515.
121 Moon, *op. cit.*, p. 111.
122 *Ibid., p.* 110.
123 Sinclair, *op. cit.*, p. 375.
124 *Ibid.*, p. 110.
125 Gusfield, *op. cit.*, p. 127.
126 Sinclair, *op. cit.*, p. 391.
127 Shannon, *op. cit.*, p. 347.
128 Franklin, *From Slavery to Freedom,* p. 517.
129 Sinclair, *op. cit.*, p. 389.
130 Moon, *op. cit.*, pp. 135-136.
131 *Ibid.*, p. 136.
132 Carman, Syrett, and Wishy, *op. cit.*, pp. 639-640.
133 Franklin, *From Slavery to Freedom,* pp. 518-519.
134 Simkins, *op. cit.*, p. 603.
135 Moon, *op. cit.*, pp. 198-199.
136 Simkins, *op. cit.*, p. 604.
137 Alexander Heard, *A Two-Party South* (Chapel Hill: The University of North Carolina Press, 1952), p. 21.
138 Eric F. Goldman, *The Crucial Decade* (New York: Alfred A. Knopf, 1956), p. 89.
139 Simkins, *op. cit.*, p. 630.
140 Porter and Johnson, *op. cit.*, p. 504.
141 *Ibid.*, p. 487.
142 *Ibid.*, p. 487.
143 Carman, Syrett, and Wishy, *op. cit.*, pp. 749, 751-756.
144 *The New York Times* (August 10, 1964).
145 Carman, Syrett, and Wishy, *op. cit.*, pp. 768-769.
146 *The New York Times* (August 10, 1964).
147 Simkins, *op. cit.*, p. 613.
148 Harry Golden, *Mr. Kennedy and the Negroes* (New York: The World Publishing Co., 1964), pp. 136-137.
149 Heard, *op. cit.*, p. 27.
150 Shannon, *op. cit.*, p. 594.
151 Porter and Johnson, *op. cit.*, pp. 599-600.
152 *Ibid.*, p. 20.
153 Anthony Lewis, "Shriver Moves Into the Front Rank", *The New York Times Magazine* (March 15, 1964).
154 William Brink and Louis Harris, *The Negro Revolution in America* (New York: Simon & Schuster, 1964), p. 79.
155 *The New York Times* (August 29, 1963).
156 *The New York Times* (July 5, 1964).
157 *The Charlotte Observer* (Charlotte, N. C.: July 14, 1964).

158 J. W. Davis, "Strange Bitter Campaign Nears End" *News and Observer,*
     (Raleigh, N. C.: November 1, 1964).
159 *The New York Times* (November 22, 1964).
160 *Ibid.,* November 22, 1964.
161 *Afro-American* (Baltimore, Maryland); and *Journal & Guide,* (Norfolk,
     Virginia: ed., for the weeks of November 7, 14, & 21, 1964).
162 *The New York Times* (March 18, 1964).
163 *Ibid.,* March 18, 1964.

BOOTSIE

By OLLIE HARRINGTON

Courtesy The Pittsburgh Courier

"... Then this fool, Bootsie, hollers, 'Give everybody in the joint a drink on old Bootsie,' an' after I served 'em all, he commenced to gigglin' and says, 'April Fool!'"

200

CHAPTER FIVE

The Social Control of Alcohol

THE SOCIAL CONTROL OF ALCOHOL

A LTHOUGH the use of alcoholic beverages by man dates from prehistoric times, the human race, strangely enough, has never been able to reach a final decision concerning the social control of alcohol. "There have been millions of people who have enjoyed and defended it, and millions who have loathed and condemned it. . . . Practically all societies that use or have used alcoholic beverages have recognized, sooner or later, that widespead use by the population produces a definite social problem."[1] The numerous voluntary and legal methods that have been employed to control the manufacture, sale, and consumption of alcoholic beverages attest to the problems created by their use. Since the early settlement of this country efforts to prohibit or control the use of liquor have taken a number of forms, ranging from moral persuasion to total prohibition. Public concern over the use of alcohol has been expressed through laws, local and statewide, license systems, and national Prohibition.

In a country with such a heterogeneous population as the United States the social control of alcohol has posed serious problems. Because of variations of race, religion, and culture not all people have been accorded the same treatment in the use of alcoholic beverages. This has been especially true of Indians and Negroes.

THE COLONIAL PERIOD

During the Colonial period alcohol was considered a prime necessity. "It was a common article of diet, in many places almost as much so as bread, while even physicians looked upon it as a preventive of all diseases and specific for many. Everybody drank—both sexes and nearly all ages."[2] During the period of colonization, there was no particular condemnation excepting by the founders of Georgia. "In the other colonies, the settlers agreed that the use of alcoholic beverages was not only beneficial, but also necessary. They were quick, however, to rebuke individual excesses. . . . The liquor problem, they felt, embraced little beyond the occasional lapse of individuals from judicious self-control."[3] All of the early laws relating to alcoholic beverages, with the exception of Georgia's prohibition statute, were directed not against the use of liquor, but against the misuse. The first feeble outcries of laymen and the clergy were concerned with excessive drinking.

By 1619, it was necessary for the Virginia Assembly to enact laws to "strictly regulate drinking."[4] This was the same year that the first Africans or Negroes were landed at Jamestown, Virginia. "As early as 1630, John Winthrop, Governor of Massachusetts Bay Colony, who arrived that year with 700 Puritan settlers, recorded in his journal his views and protests about the use of alcohol."[5] When the colonists decided to restrain the incorrigibles who insisted on flaunting the evidence of their over-indulgence on the faces of their more abstemious fellows, they turned to the regulatory ideas of the mother country. The English had developed reasonably effective control over the liquor traffic through the device of licensing. The colonists, in a few instances, re-enacted statutes of the mother country, but such legislation was a temporary expedient until more satisfactory measures could be formulated. The regulative measures of the Colonial period were not designed to reform social customs. They were largely for the purpose of outlawing drunkenness.[6]

The authorities in the colonies were persuaded to interfere with the natural development of traffic in alcoholic beverages for a variety of reasons, the chief of which was probably the desire to prevent personal excesses and public disorders. Along with the fear of the American Indian under the influence of alcohol being a menace to life and property; there was the necessity of providing adequate accommodations for travellers; the importance of the brewing and distilling industries; and the fact that sorely needed revenues could be easily secured from an assessment against the liquor traffic. All played their part in determining the character and course of regulation. Each was responsible for specific statutes in every one of the colonies.[7]

Some interesting laws relative to the consumption of alcoholic beverages were passed by some of the colonies and towns in 1658. Plymouth, Massachusetts, enacted a law disfranchising drunkards. Maryland prohibited drunkenness under a penalty of confinement in stocks for six hours or a fine of 100 pounds of tobacco; the second offense provided for public whipping or a fine of 300 pounds of tobacco; and for the third offense the law violator was adjudged as infamous and disfranchised for three years. For those convicted of drunkenness three times, Virginia created a law labeling them common drunkards. Those considered as such were incapable of being witnesses or of holding public office.

The desire of each colony to have public houses operating within its borders to meet the increasing demands of commercial activity had a far-reaching influence upon the license system. Whenever the number of inns was insufficient, the legislatures were to provide relief. This was to be done through a statute that would produce accommodations for travellers where private initiative had failed. In order to encourage the establishment of inns, some of the colonies granted a special license, conferring on the licensee a monopoly to sell liquor in his district. "In all parts of the colonies operators of important ferries and toll-bridges were compelled to furnish all the conveniences of a tavern under the terms of a special license. The spirit controlling the regulation of the liquor traffic manifested no tendency toward prohibition. The legislators appreciated the vast social importance of the trade and desired to utilize its manifold possibilities for the best interests of the community."[8] In the machinery of regulation, the device of licensing was of primary importance. The authority to license was early assumed by the legislatures, which delegated the power as they saw fit, usually vesting the right of selection in one of three agents: the Governor, the Proprietor, or the County Court of the town board of selectmen. These agents were virtually free to make whatever choice they pleased; however, the law assumed that they would license only persons of good standing in the community. The restrictions placed upon innkeepers by legislatures and local governments involved: (1) age limitations; (2) limitations on the amount of whiskey that could be sold to a person at a given time; (3) the character of amusement that might be offered; (4) the hours for closing, and (5) beer-making was regulated to insure a wholesome product. These conditions prevailed throughout the colonies.

In the middle of the seventeenth century, the Puritans of New England adopted stricter regulations for the use of alcohol. The New England laws forbade the sale of liquor on the Sabbath, and/or closed the bars of public houses during the hours of worship.[9]

During the Colonial period there was a practice of restricting the sale and use of liquor to certain classes. The early laws universally forbade the sale or gift of wine or distilled spirits to Indians, but beer and malt liquors generally escaped the ban. Total prohibition was undesirable for those interested in the development of commerce. Economic considerations, more powerful than any fear of drunken Indians, wrought a gradual withdrawal of governmental restrictions. Of all the conditions imposed upon the liquor traffic, none was more important from the social standpoint than the prohibition of the sale of intoxicants to Negroes, servants, and apprentices.[10]

The increasing Negro population and the fears of uprisings and insurrections resulted in the colonists enacting a body of laws to control the activities of Negroes—North and South. The slave code of Virginia was established in the second decade of the seventeenth century. In the 1660's Maryland also enacted stringent laws designed to keep order among the Negroes. These statutes forbade slaves to deal in stolen goods and liquor. The slave code enacted by the South Carolina Colony became a model for the other colonies in severity scope. In 1686, the South Carolina legislature passed laws to insure the complete domination of slaves by their masters. Negroes were forbidden to engage in any type of trade and the use of alcoholic beverages was prohibited under penalty. An act of 1773 forbade keepers of ordinances to sell liquor to slaves against the will of their masters.[11]

The colony of Georgia was founded in 1733 and prohibited free land titles, alcoholic beverages, and Negroes. Nine years after its founding, the trustees approved the use of alcoholic drinks. By 1750, the hated prohibition against Negroes was repealed. Early in its history, Georgia adopted a slave code. In step with the other colonies, the sale of rum and spirituous liquors to slaves and Indians was prohibited.[12]

The first laws to regulate the slaves and their use of alcohol in the colony of New Netherland, later New York, were local and intended chiefly to protect the property of their owners. The New York City Council on March 1681, prohibited the entertainment of slaves in houses, the selling of liquor to them, and the taking of money or goods from them for any reason. Each offense was punishable by a fine of five pounds, of which one-half went to the informer. By 1702, it was necessary to enact a comprehensive slave law for the colony, which in the main prohibited any trade with slaves. The law was enacted because of the places that would supply slaves with liquor and take stolen goods in return. These conditions became such a problem that in April 1741, Supreme Court Justice Frederick Phillips, in an address to a grand jury stated:

> I cannot omit recommending to your serious and diligent inquiries to find out and present all such persons who sell rum and other strong liquor to Negroes. It must be obvious to everyone that there are too many of them in this city who under pretense of selling what they call a penny dram to a Negro, will sell him as many quarts or gallons of rum as he can steal money or goods to pay for. This notion of its being lawful to sell a penny dram, a penny-worth to a slave without the consent of his master has prevailed; but this I am sure of, that there is not only no such law, but that the doing of it is directly contrary to an act of the Assembly now in force, for the better regulating of slaves.[13]

From 1664-1702, New Jersey was a Proprietary Colony and from 1702-1776, a Crown Province; its laws prohibited the selling of rum or giving of strong liquors to Indians or Negroes, except as a stimulant in relief of physical distress. A violation of this offense carried with it a penalty of five pounds.[14]

The history of the Negro in Pennsylvania and Delaware, down to 1730, was closely interwoven. Long before formal recognition was granted to the institution, slavery existed in both colonies. In the early years of the Pennsylvania Colony, the regulation of the movement of slaves rested primarily in the hands of their masters. Slavery had been in existence in the colony since 1636, but it was not until 1725-1726 that a law was enacted placing restriction on the movement of Negroes. The law prohibited slaves and free Negroes from frequenting "tippling" houses. Ten lashes was the penalty for the violation of this act. The enforcement of the laws controlling Negroes were more theoretical than real and loosely observed. The early laws of Pennsylvania applied to Delaware, but they were not enforced until 1721. It was in this year that Delaware passed its first law and gradually drifted away from the mother colony. Delaware then became more identified with her southern neighbors whose slave codes were more restrictive than those of the Pennsylvania Colony, under which Delaware had earlier operated.[15]

The slave codes began in the New England colonies about 1680 and were in operation in all of the colonies—Massachusetts, Rhode Island, New Hampshire, Maine, Connecticut and Vermont. Some of the slave statutes attempted to deal with running away, drunkenness, theft, destruction of public property, and prevention of riots and insurrections. The laws enacted to keep liquor from the slaves were rather stringent. Massachusetts set the example for the other New England colonies and in 1693, the legislature forbade tavern and innkeepers to allow any apprentice, servant or Negro to drink in their houses, except by permission of their owners. For each violation there was a penalty of ten shillings.[16]

The legislation against the offense of selling liquor to Negroes and Indians was relatively severe in Rhode Island, possibly because this colony had a larger number of Negroes than the others. In 1750, a law was enacted which forbade the sale, barter, or exchange of liquor of any kind with any Indian, mulatto or Negro servant or slave. The sale of cider was also prohibited to this group. For each violation, there was to be a fine of 30 pounds. In Rhode Island, "Slavery was the element which most affected the life and customs of the proprietors, in the middle and third quarter of the eighteenth century."[17]

There were very few Negroes imported into Connecticut, and it was not until 1730 that a statute was passed which "prohibited any licensed inn or tavernkeeper or retailer of strong drink from selling to apprentices, servants or Negroes. Members of these three groups were unable to sit in these houses and have a drink or purchase any alcoholic beverages from them without special orders from their masters."[18]

Between 1619 and the American Revolution, the colonies also enacted laws to discourage the excessive use of alcoholic beverages by whites. Disfranchisement, public whipping, confinement in public stocks, denial of the privilege of holding office, branding the letter "D", were some of the methods of punishment for drunkenness.

COLONIES TO STATES

On the eve of the War of Independence, the colonists were confronted with a number of problems, among which were the use of alcohol and slavery. The Declaration of Independence of 1776, asserted the natural rights of man, but made no mention of slavery. The Constitution subsequently sanctioned and protected the institution of slavery. The adoption of the federal Constitution marked the end of an era in the political history of the United States. The Revolution had brought about some important changes in the geographical distribution of slavery; it would assume a sectional character.

The transition from colony to state did not alter the fundamentals of Colonial legislation as it related to alcohol. Insofar as they were applicable, the liquor laws were enacted by the new state governments, and with minor variations remained in force until the early part of the nineteenth century. Even though there was a noticeable lack of uniformity, certain features were common to all state laws. Intoxicants could be sold legally only by dealers licensed under provisions of the statutes. The sale of liquors was universally associated with the business of keeping a tavern; other dealers might, however, be licensed. The retailer who did not provide entertainment for travellers was seldom permitted by the terms of his license to sell small quantities to be drunk on the premises. His place of business contained no bar, and his patrons were persons who were unable to buy large quantities from importers or manufacturers, but desired to secure a gallon or less for home consumption. The laws usually limited the sale of drinks by draught in the taverns. The manufacturer and importer did not come within the provisions of the license system, but at times special permits were required.[19]

More serious and effective activities against the use of distilled liquors as beverages began with the movement for American independence. The popularity of distilled whiskey was enhanced during the War of Independence because of the scarcity of good rum. Each colony attempted to provide its militia with the best liquor obtainable and frequently only poor or bad whiskey was available. The members of the Continental Army were provided a specified amount of whiskey daily, on the basis of the supply available. The problems created by the soldiers and the need of manpower created concern among some members of the Colonial legislatures. In 1777, Dr. Benjamin Rush, a noted physician of his day, who was also a public-spirited man and one of the principal figures in drafting and signing the Declaration of Independence, prepared a sweeping statement against the use of strong drink. The document was approved and adopted by the War Board of the Continental Congress. It was printed and circulated among all of the troops in the United States Army. "The objective of the document was to urge all soldiers to abstain from the use of distilled liquors, while in the service of their country." This was the first appeal against the use of distilled liquors in any official way by government.[20]

After the war, some of the legislation enacted by the states revealed the serious concerns for and importance they put upon the control of the manufacture, sale and use of alcohol by slaves and free Negroes. A North Carolina Act of 1783 specifically forbade the sale of spirituous liquors or wines to any slave or free Negro unless prescribed by a doctor.[21]

South Carolina, in 1831, enacted a law prohibiting any free Negro from owning or operating a still. No master was to allow any of his slaves to participate in the manufacture and sale of alcoholic beverages. By 1834, there was legislation prohibiting the sale of liquor to a slave without the consent of the master. Some of the larger cities had ordinances to reinforce the Black Codes of the state. An ordinance of 1850 prohibited any owner of a saloon to allow a slave or free Negro to loiter or sit in his place.[22]

During a visit to the Slave States, in the 1850's a traveller stopped at a hotel in Virginia and was advised by the lady of the house that all of the servants believed that "they have at least one day for frolic at Christmas. On their return the next day, they would be drunk."[23] Olmsted observed in Virginia, in 1852, that "from Christmas to New Year's Day most slaves, except house servants, enjoy a freedom from their labors. The night before Christmas, the young ones begin firing crackers . . . and the older getting drunk and making business for the police."[24] One plantation owner informed Olmsted that, "the poor white people (who bring nothing to market but their labor) corrupted the Negroes and encouraged them to steal, or work for them at nights and on Sundays, and pay them with liquor, and constantly associate licentiously with them. They seem more than any

209

other portion of the community to hate and despise the Negroes."[25]

Many of the slaves were able to secure whiskey because they were able to earn money. This made the control of the use of whiskey difficult or even impossible for the masters. "When the slave had money in his pocket, he was a potential buyer, and slave money was as good as the master's money. As soon as the free Negro had more than enough to supply his immediate wants, he invested in a keg of whiskey or a jug of brandy and traded it to slaves for stolen goods."[26]

In Virginia, some of the plantation owners would give their slaves their food allowances on Wednesdays instead of Fridays or Saturdays to prevent them from extravagantly using their allowances for whiskey on Sundays.[27] Some of the slaves saved as much as five bushels of their meal ration a week which they sent to town to be sold and had it exchanged for whiskey. "This whiskey was exchanged with some 'rascally' white people in the neighborhood and kept concealed. The slaves were very fond of whiskey and sometimes injured themselves very much with it."[28]

The Black Codes prohibiting the manufacture, sale, and use of alcoholic beverages by Negroes in Mississippi, Alabama, and Louisiana, were repressive and strict and as all three of these states were carved from the Mississippi Territory, their control of the behavior of Negroes was similar. The manufacture, sale, and purchase of liquor by slaves or free Negroes was prohibited. In Mississippi, slaves could not hire themselves out or in any other way conduct themselves as free men. Their relationships with whites and free Negroes were to be kept at a minimum, and they were unable to visit the homes of either nor could they buy or sell any goods.

The plantation owners in Louisiana were confronted by the problem of slaves stealing and selling their ill-gotten goods for whiskey. "A great nuisance in this state was petty traders dealing with the Negroes and encouraging them to pilfer. The traders generally came at night by boats, which they moved on the shore adjoining the Negro quarters. They would float away, after they had obtained any 'booty'."[29] There was small chance of detecting them. The operator of a sugar-works in Louisiana believed that "a large brass cock and some pipe had been stolen by his Negroes.

These materials were sold on one of these boats for 75¢, and the money immediately spent for whiskey in the same boat."[30]

Control of the use of alcoholic beverages by Negroes—free and slave—was not confined to the South. New York, New Jersey, Rhode Island, Maryland, and Pennsylvania, all prohibited the manufacture, sale, and use of alcoholic beverages. There were variations from state to state, but the general objective was the same. In the North, the Negro faced a long period of political disfranchisement, economic discrimination, and "social obstracism."

TEMPERANCE FORCES

As previously discussed, the organized movement for temperance began in 1826. Prior to this, numerous local societies and one or two state organizations had played their part in the progress of the temperance movement. The organization of the American Temperance Society in Boston, Massachusetts electrified the people throughout the country. Immediately, state and local auxiliaries by the hundreds sprang up all over the United States. They were bound together by a common purpose and program—prohibition of the use of alcoholic beverages. When the first national convention was held in Philadelphia in 1826, there were state organizations in all but five states. By 1835, there were approximately 5,000 local temperance societies with an estimated total membership of nearly two million members. In the decade between 1840 and 1850, there were more temperance organizations of a general national character founded than in any other similar period in the history of this country.[31]

The first great wave of prohibition swept the country in the 1850. As mentioned in the chapter on politics, the state of Maine was the pioneer under Neal Dow, with a statewide prohibition law enacted in 1851.[32] Twelve states followed Maine into prohibition—New Hampshire, Vermont, Delaware, Michigan, Indiana, Iowa, Minnesota, Nebraska, Connecticut, Rhode Island, Massachusetts, and New York. This early wave of prohibition receded and by 1863, the 13 prohibition states had been reduced to five. Prohibition began as a temperance movement concerned with the winning of converts by persuasion rather than law.

211

THE PROHIBITION OF THE SALE OF ALCOHOL TO
NEGROES WITHOUT CONSENT OF THEIR MASTERS*

(IN THE SOUTH)

STATE	YEAR
Alabama	1809
Arkansas	1806(1)
Florida	1828
Georgia	1755
Kentucky	1834
Louisiana	1806
Maryland	1832
Mississippi	1839
North Carolina	1789
South Carolina	1740
Tennessee	1813
Texas	1840
Virginia	1848
West Virginia	1848(2)

*Source: Leonard Stott Blakey, *The Sale of Liquor in the South* (New York: Columbia University Press, 1912), p. 40.

(1) The Louisiana law was adopted here.
(2) The Virginia law was used in this state.

The 1870's witnessed the beginning of a second temperance and general reform wave, due largely to the fact that the evil saloons had multiplied. Both the Prohibition party founded in 1869 and the Woman's Christian Temperance Union, in 1874, were instrumental in the temperance movement again going forward. In 1880, Kansas wrote prohibition into its constitution; something no state had ever done before. But again the temperance movement declined.

Other methods were employed to regulate or control the use and traffic of alcoholic beverages. South Carolina tried a dispensary system borrowed from Europe; Pennsylvania, Missouri, and Illinois experimented with high license fees. Massachusetts tried prohibition, then a license system and then prohibition of everything except malt liquors. Some of the other states experimented with licenses, exemption of wine and beer from prohibition laws, and with local option legislation under which counties and towns or villages could outlaw the saloon.[33]

From out of these experiments, the third great wave of prohibition arose. Georgia led the way in 1907 by enacting prohibition legislation, and was followed by Oklahoma, Mississippi, North Carolina, Tennessee, and West Virginia. All of these states were south of the Ohio and Potomac rivers and were predominantly agricultural. They had not been too greatly influenced by the industrial revolution which had so thoroughly changed the interest and point of view of many northern states in the half century from the first wave of prohibition. By 1913, a third prohibition wave swept the country, which was to develop into national Prohibition.[34]

Several incidents between 1840 and 1850 gave evidence of hidden feelings over the questions of abolition and temperance. At the first session of the World's Temperance Convention, which met in London in August 1846, a minister from the United States remarked that many slaveholders were good men. This aroused the anger of those with abolitionist views. At the closing of the conference, bitter feeling was again aroused by Frederick Douglas, a Negro. He attacked the temperance movement in the United States for "its failure both to make provisions for the Negro in its ranks and to concern itself with bondage or slavery."[35]

During the Civil War, it was impossible to control the use of alcohol and the activities of Negroes, both free and slave. "In the minds of many people, whiskey was almost as necessary as salt, if not for satisfying thirst, then for medicinal uses in hospitals."[36] The excessive use of alcoholic beverages and drunkenness were prevalent in the Union and Confederate armies. This type of behavior was probably more common among the soldiers of the Union than the Confederacy. This does not mean that the southerners were naturally more abstemious than their northern counterparts, but drinking was largely a matter of opportunity, and intoxicants were more abundant in the North than in the Confederacy. The Union soldiers had more money than the Confederates and whiskey was more often an item of government issue in the Union armies and the federals had a better supply.[37]

Prohibition of the manufacture of whiskey became a burning issue in the Confederacy. It was mandatory to enforce prohibition as a war conservation measure. Although, it was never a high moral issue, the Confederate Congress, on two occasions, had to pass acts to discourage drunkenness in the army. "Prohibition

213

arose from the two-fold necessity of conserving the grain supplies in order to feed the armed forces and of conserving the inbound tonnage of the blockade runners to increase the importation of war supplies. The policies of the several state governments concerning the manufacture of liquor often clashed with those of the general government."[38]

Although the Confederacy had passed laws prohibiting the manufacture and use of alcohol, whiskey flowed in almost every town and hamlet. The excessive use of whiskey was blamed for nearly all of the ills from which the army suffered. Heavy drinking was not confined to the soldiers; many of the officers drank excessively, and it was frequently charged that battles were lost because of drunken officers. In 1862, it was necessary for the Confederate Congress to pass a law, which provided for a trial and dishonorable dismissal from the army of any officer found drunk on or off duty. By the end of 1864, 151 officers had been charged with drunkenness and 80 had been found guilty.[39]

The excessive use of alcohol in the Union armies produced the same problems confronted by the Confederates. One soldier attributed the death of his commanding officer to an overdose of whiskey. Another soldier said about his officers, "they get all the glory and most of the pay and don't earn ten cents apiece on the average, the drunken rascals."[40] Among the enlisted men, fighting and brawling, inspired by liquor, were common offenses. Drinking, when not on duty and when held to moderation, was usually not regarded as a breach of discipline. The Union army made corporal punishment mandatory for drunkenness on guard, and habitual intemperance sometimes led to dishonorable discharge. Numerous and varied efforts were made to combat the tide of drinking which beset Union camps. Sutlers and peddlers caught selling liquor in camps forfeited their trading privileges, and some were punished.

The use of whiskey by Union and Confederate soldiers was considered important to their ability to fight. When disparagers of southern bravery were confronted by a dashing performance which contradicted their generalizations, they usually had a ready answer, "The rebels were crazy drunk on whiskey and gunpowder. This claim . . . was also used by rebels to explain yankee gallantry."[41]

214

With the South at war, efforts were made to prevent the use of alcohol by Negroes. The fear of insurrection and rebellion was always present. "Whiskey was scarce on account of the laws against the distillation of grain. The penalties for letting slaves use it without the master's order were heavy. The slaves contrived to get it surreptitiously on occasions. The practice of the masters' giving the slaves a dram for medicinal purposes was curtailed during the war."[42]

Following the war, in 1865 and 1866, the legislatures of the southern states enacted a series of laws, varying in harshness, to define the status and rights of Negroes. These laws, in general, recognized the rights of Negroes to hold property, to sue and be sued, to contract legal marriages and have legitimate offspring. There were some important qualifications in these laws. Negroes were competent witnesses only in cases where one or both parties were Negroes. Negroes with no visible means of support were considered as vagrants and were to be taken up, fined, and turned over to individuals who would pay their fines. Negroes were to possess no firearms or alcoholic beverages. In some states, Negroes were not permitted within the town limits without special permission. In some states, Negroes had to be off city streets by a given hour. "The majority of the laws employed such terms as 'master and servant' and strongly resembled those previously regulating the relationship of master and slave. . . . The effect of the Black Codes was to consign the Negro to a position of legal inferiority. This position was reinforced by the fact that he could vote."[43] At the beginning of the Reconstruction era, fear of violence by drunken and armed Negroes ran deep among the southern whites, especially former slave owners.

During the war, the legal and social control of the use of alcoholic beverages had broken down in the South, and had not been too rigidly enforced in the North. As a result, there was an excessive use of alcohol throughout the country. Army life had acquainted many young soldiers with drinking, and they found little incentive to stop when the war ended. Grogshops grew up in many country settlements and crossroads and peppered the big cities after the war.[44]

RECONSTRUCTION

There continued to be variations on the interpretations of the behavior of Negroes by historians and students of the Reconstruction period. Some writers and newspapers pictured the Negro as a sub-human, who drank excessively, refused to work, and was extremely dangerous while drinking. At the other end were those who did not believe the Negro could do any wrong. The actual behavior of Negroes during the Reconstruction era was probably somewhere between the two poles. There was general belief that the greatest difficulty for the South in handling its liquor problem related to the control of drinking by Negroes. Since they had been denied whiskey in slavery, they gave full reign to their appetites in freedom. "With little experience in self-control, they would spend their last piece of money for a drink of whiskey, and they would break in and steal this article before all else. Many of the Negroes spent half of their earnings for liquor."[45]

A former slave owner in Mississippi made this observation: "The Negroes were crazed and drunken with this new sense of power, which was carefully impressed upon them. Simple, credulous, ignorant, and more or less vicious by reason of the inflammatory teachings of their self-constituted masters, they acted like mad men from the first. In Woodville, Mississippi, it was not unusual to see 1,000 Negroes on foot and horseback, marching around the public square and yelling like mad men. A large number of the Negroes would be drunk from some vile imitation of whiskey."[46]

In Mississippi, in this period of newly found freedom, many of the rural Negroes would go to the nearest town or village. Frequently, they sought diversion where it could be found and with little wisdom. This resulted in public drunkenness, disorderly conduct, fighting, and the use of profane language. Activities of this type led to the mayor's courts and from there to the city jail. The Negro was more likely to be arrested for minor offenses, which included drunkenness, than the white man. After arrest, only a small number of them were able to avoid a jail sentence by paying the fine.[47]

The treatment accorded the Negro in South Carolina, during Reconstruction was as harsh, cruel, and restrictive as anywhere in the United States. As early as 1864-1865, the general assembly enacted laws to regulate and control the behavior of Negroes. "The laws prohibited a person of color to own partly or entirely a distillery where spirituous liquors of any kind were to be

216

made. The same law included any establishment where whiskey was to be sold at retail. The punishment for the violation of these laws was left to the discretion of the district judge or magistrate. A fine, corporal punishment, and hard labor were usually the punishment given out."[48] As late as 1878, after the Negro had been disfranchised in South Carolina, there were some individuals who did not believe there was excessive drinking among Negroes. A prosecuting officer in the southern part of the state near the islands, expressed the opinion that "drinking was much less a cause for crime among the blacks than whites. Drunkenness is not a very prevalent crime among Negroes."[49]

It is possible that whites influenced Negroes in the use of liquor as they did in other things. The drinking of hard liquors in South Carolina seemed to have been part of the everyday way of life. The use of liquor let loose the slumbering emotions of lawlessness inherited in a people recently removed from the frontier. People were also driven to drink because of their misfortunes. Along with these conditions, the wider distribution of ready cash, and the growth of the country store and the commercial village greatly stimulated drinking. The country stores were disguised whiskey shops, and the numerous saloons of the villages sustained a large number of drunkards. On Saturdays, bedlam broke out on the otherwise quiet streets of the villages. The money of many of the farmers was spent as readily for drink as for family necessities. Men, who were law-abiding at other times, became profane and noisy and fell in ditches in a helpless stupor. Those of bad character drew pistols and knives and sometimes committed crimes.[50] The conditions in South Carolina, during this era were conducive to excessive drinking by the whites and Negroes.

There was a great deal of disorder all over Georgia in the Reconstruction period, especially in Atlanta, Savannah, and other cities. A large amount of the crime and lawlessness in Savannah was due to the number of Negro refugees who crowded the city from Florida and South Carolina and the surrounding Georgia districts. Frequently, there would be drunkenness and disorder which resulted in injury and death among white and black. "A Freedman's Bureau official pointed out that the prevalence of intemperance among the Negroes was due to the whiskey wagons that travelled through the country and the unrestrained sale of liquors in towns. Negroes received money for their wages and were able to buy liquor as they pleased.[51]

In Alabama, the problem of the control of alcohol was not created by Negroes or civilians, but was the result of the behavior of the Union soldiers—white and black. Officers waiting to be released from service devoted their time largely to drinking, women, and gambling. The enlisted soldiers followed their example. The traffic in whiskey was enormous, and the majority of the sales were to white and Negro soldiers of the lowest class. The streets of some of the towns and cities were often crowded with drunken and violent soldiers.[52]

The Negro was also the central figure in Alabama during Reconstruction. In the social control of whiskey, the "deadfall" was considered one of the worst evils in the black belt. A "deadfall" was a low shop or store where a white thief encouraged black people to steal all kinds of farm produce and exchange it with him for bad whiskey. This type of activity was to be found all over the state where there were Negroes. Many of the whites and industrious blacks lost hogs, poultry, cattle, corn, and cotton in the fields and in the gin. "The business of the 'deadfall' was usually done at night. The thirsty Negro would go into a cotton field and pick a sack of cotton worth a dollar, or take a bushel of corn from the nearest field and exchange it at a 'deadfall' for a glass of whiskey, a plug of tobacco, or a dime."[53]

During the early part of Reconstruction, the governor of Tennessee, became alarmed about the crime existing in his state, and sent a communication to the legislature concerning these situations. He pointed out that "the reputation being acquired by Nashville is humiliating to every friend of law and order. No man is safe, day or night, within a circuit around Nashville, whose radius is eight or ten miles. Most of these outrages grow out of the abundant use of intoxicant spirits connected with gambling halls to be found in full blast on every street in the city. The same may be said to a considerable extent of all the larger cities of the state."[54] These conditions were prevalent among the total population, but they were excessive among Negroes.

A Negro minister, in 1872, painted a dismal picture of vice and crime in Memphis. He stated that "a cesspool existed that sent forth a stream of death, and there were 200 licensed dram shops, selling by the glass over the counter, and a countless number of grocery stores dealing in liquor."[55]

It was true that an element of the Negro population of Tennessee did commit crimes and their behavior was unruly. The records of the public press, the courts, and the penal institutions corroborated this fact. The majority of the Negroes, however, were law-abiding and temperate citizens. The passage of the 1875 federal Civil Rights Act brought about speculation among the whites of Tennessee relative to the effect it would have on Negroes. They did not have long to wait. Immediately, the Negroes began to demand "the privilege of riding in cars, and asking for liquor at bars, and seats in the theatres, claiming the same rights and privileges of the white man under the Civil Rights Bill."[56]

During Reconstruction in Louisiana the number of Negroes slightly exceeded that of the whites in the total population. The large number of Negroes in Louisiana created fear and the former slave owners inflicted punishment on the newly free Negroes which the laws no longer regarded as excusable. "The town of Opelousas (and there were others) passed an ordinance that no Negro or freedman should be allowed to rent or keep a house in the town, and that none should reside in the town who was not in the regular service of some white person or former owner; nor could any freedman barter, sell, or exchange within the town without a permit." There was also an attempt to control the behavior and activities of Negroes through legal means and custom. The whites attempted to prohibit and prevent their use of alcohol because of fear of riots. "They saw their former slaves avoiding them, being insolent, acquiring habits of vagrancy, and manisfesting little fear, and over-indulging in drink."[57]

In North Carolina after the war, the Negro could buy liquor as readily as the white man if he had the money. There were many whites who believed that Negroes took advantage of this new-found freedom to an excess, and public drunkennes was not uncommon. "Liquor gave to the Negro a feeling of being equal or superior to the white man, an attitude intolerable in the South. It made him unreliable as a laborer, quarrelsome in his disposition, and susceptible to petty crimes and violent outrages. The presence of the freedmen aided prohibition reform."[58] People who before the war would have regarded prohibitary legislation as invading the field of their private rights now lent hearty cooperation for prohibition to keep liquor away from the Negro.

During Reconstruction, Negroes and whites were served at the same taverns and bars in the South. In 1875, Tennessee adopted the first *Jim Crow* law, and the rest of the South rapidly followed suit. Negroes and whites were separated on trains, in depots and on wharves. This segregation was extended to other facilities. The United States Supreme Court, in 1883, outlawed the Civil Rights Act of 1875 and the Negro was banned from white hotels, barber shops, restaurants and theatres. When the twentieth century arrived, it was clear that the Negro would be effectively disfranchised throughout the South. He would also be firmly relegated to the lower rungs of the social and economic ladder, and neither equality nor aspirations for equality in any area of life were for him. The public symbols and constant reminders of his inferior position were the segregation statutes or *Jim Crow* laws. These segregation codes lent the sanction of law to racial ostracism that extended to churches, school, housing, jobs, and places of eating and drinking.[59]

The treatment of the Negro in the North was not much better than that of the South. In the North, the Negro was denied service in practically all of the hotels, restaurants, bars, and taverns. It was necessary to pass an anti-discrimination act in New York, as early as 1881, but this law did not cover places of public accommodation.[60]

After the Civil War, a plethora of organizations and movements to eliminate the use of alcoholic beverages were created.

As previously mentioned the National Temperance Society was founded in 1865 and rapidly grew into a position of strength and influence. Its major focus and emphasis was the distributing of anti-liquor literature. In 1869, the Prohibition party was founded which nominated a ticket of candidates for office. And in 1874, the Women's Christian Temperance Union was organized.

The second great statewide anti-whiskey wave swept the country between 1880 and 1890. During this period, not as many states adopted prohibition as in the first statewide movement in the 1850's but there were more states actively involved and more legislative bodies called upon to vote directly on the prohibition question than in earlier periods. The largest number of state legislatures submitted the prohibition issue in the form of constitutional amendments than at any other time in the history of the country. People were given an opportunity to vote directly upon this question in more states than in any similar periods; prohibition was a prominent issue in the legislative sessions of three-fourths of the states and territories of 1880-1890.[61]

The most potent organization in the prohibition movement and instrumental in the third great wave of prohibition was founded in 1895; the Anti-Saloon League was to dry up the United States in steps—first the towns and the villages, then the counties, then the states, and finally the nation.[62] "The singleness of purpose represented in the idea of the League and the sense of opposition suggested by the anti-character of its name were dominant features of the Temperance movement in the period between 1900 and the passage of the Prohibition Amendment in 1920."[63] The League shifted the temperance issue from the drinker to the saloon. Its major object was to abolish the saloon and in this way achieve prohibition.

THE TWENTIETH CENTURY

MORE TEMPERANCE

At the beginning of the twentieth century, five of the 45 states had statewide laws prohibiting the manufacture and sale of intoxicating beverages: Maine, Kansas, North Dakota, New Hampshire, and Vermont. Four states—Pennsylvania, Tennessee, Idaho, and Nevada—relied heavily upon high license fees to regulate the traffic of liquor. The remaining 36 states and the District of Columbia often resorted to high license rates, and they also allowed some form of local option. By 1900, 18 million of the nation's approximately 75 million people were living in saloonless territory, and about 17 percent of these were in the five prohibition states.[64]

After 1900, the temperance cause was revived and soon was reflected in the stricter enforcement of liquor regulations, the enactment of more effective local option laws, and in an increasing tendency to use local option to drive out the saloon. The local option laws were similar, in that they applied only to the sale of liquor. The League favored local option because it kept attention focused on the saloon problem. It enabled the League to win support of many people who drank, but who objected to public bars near their homes or places of business. It opened the way for national Prohibition because it permitted the League to attack the liquor traffic first at points of least resistance—rural crossroads, townships, villages, and counties. The Leagues' other main weapon was to direct its efforts against the liquor traffic rather than the drinker.[65]

In 1906, a new wave of prohibition campaigns broke out. By that time about 35 million people were living in dry territory, mostly under local option. This number together with the people living in the remaining prohibition states meant that roughly 40 percent of the nation's population was living in territory without saloons. The greatest strides in prohibition were made in the South. Over two-thirds of the counties in the 11 states of the old Confederacy had voted out the saloon by the beginning of 1907. It was also in the South that dry sentiment first developed to the extent that it could carry the reform from the local to the state level. Georgia was the first state to outlaw the manufacture and sale of liquor by statute in 1907. In the same year, Oklahoma entered the Union with prohibition written into her constitution, and Alabama abolished liquor traffic by law. North Carolina and Mississippi enacted statutory prohibition in 1908, and Tennessee in 1909. None of these were bone-dry laws, all allowed liquor to be made and drunk at home and all permitted a person to import liquor from another state for his personal consumption. But commercial liquor traffic was destroyed within the boundaries of the states.[66]

By 1913, the League had been at work for 20 years, and it was battle-scarred with information. It had raised the number of prohibition states from three to nine and added to these states many no-license counties. This was the year of the enactment of the Webb-Kenyon Bill, a measure intended to prevent the shipment of liquor from wet states into states with prohibition laws. President Taft vetoed the Bill, but the prohibitionists mustered enough votes to override the president's veto. The Anti-Saloon League shielded its state law programs, and demanded a constitutional amendment. The other prohibitionists joined the League in making national Prohibition their next goal.[67]

Prior to the war, a number of states had adopted prohibition laws, but only 13 had passed bone-dry laws. Local option was the established principle in most of the populous states. In some of the other states, theoretically dry, the adoption of prohibition had not been intended to prohibit absolutely the purchase or use of intoxicating liquors, but rather to abolish the saloon and place the traffic under rigid supervision. Some of the states permitted importation of limited amounts and some permitted importation in limited percentages of alcoholic content. There were some states which permitted the manufacture of alcoholic beverages in certain forms at home. Some made a distinction between men and women in the purchasing of liquor. In the social control of alcoholic beverages, the methods and penalties of prohibition varied according to local customs, standards, and taste.

From 1900 to 1917, the United States had been moving toward national Prohibition. There were a number of social, economic, and political forces responsible for this trend. Numerous individuals, groups, organizations, and events were responsible for the conditions that existed relative to the control of alcoholic beverages. Among the groups exerting considerable influence on the prohibition movement were the middle-class whites and Negroes. "Prohibition did not command universal support, however, for its appeal lay largely with the old-stock, middle-class section of the American community. . . . The old-stock middle-class constituted the backbone of the movement and wielded disproportionate political power; it was able to overcome the opposition of the urban masses and to impose its own standard of sobriety on the nation by law."[68] The middle classes were the sources of temperance support and emulation. "The class least touched by the evil thus far is that which here, as elsewhere in the land, forms its bone and sinew—the self-respecting and self-supporting class whose chief pleasures in life center in and about the home."[69]

There has not been as much unanimity of opinion about the influence of Negroes on the prohibition movement as the middle-class whites. The only scientific study of the Negro as a factor in the movement concluded: "The Negro has been a inconsiderable factor in the prohibitary movement in the South, because the saloon has been abolished and retained in the communities of the South without apparent reference to the presence of the Negro."[70]

The Negro did have some influence upon the prohibition movement in the South; the extent of which is debatable. One writer made this observation: "Some writers have interpreted the rise of prohibition campaigns in the South after 1906 as an effort to control the Negro. Our interpretation is quite different. After 1900 whatever political power the Negro had was broken by effective legal disfranchisement. As long as the Negro had been anti-prohibitionist and had voting influence, there was fear among southern politicians that prohibition questions were likely to bring about appeals by the Wets for Negro votes. It was the disfranchisement of the Negro which made the political movement for prohibition feasible in the South."[71]

PROHIBITION

On January 17, 1920, at 12:01 A.M., Constitutional Prohibition went into effect everywhere in the United States. "The American people began the joyous march into the never-never land of the Eighteenth Amendment and the Volstead Act. Everything was ready for the great transformation. More than fifteen hundred enforcement agents, badges shined, guns oiled, and fingers trembling upon the trigger, were on their toes, ready to pounce upon the rum demon wherever he showed his ugly mug."[72] The next 13 years would witness "the longest, saddest, wettest, craziest, funniest and bloodiest period of reform in American history."[73]

The passage of the Eighteenth Amendment did not produce a drastic decline in anti-temperance sentiment. If the victory of the temperance movement meant a change in the cultural legitimacy of drinking, there is little evidence that this occurred. Neither is there much evidence that the sale of liquor disappeared. The bootlegging and systematic evasion of the Volstead Act, especially in the urban areas, was evident to the most rabid anti-alcohol supporter.[74] The Eighteenth Amendment was violated from the time it was put into effect until its repeal. Less than a month after the Amendment, two agents of the

224

Internal Revenue Department engaged in Prohibition work were arrested in Baltimore on charges of corruption.[75] Three months later, in New York City, a deputy collector of Internal Revenue, engaged in prohibition was arrested on charges of corruption.[76] A special train of the Massachusetts delegation to the Republican National Convention was raided by prohibition agents who seized its stock of liquor.[77]

The Prohibition experiment introduced an era of lawlessness, such as this country has never known. It was marked by wholesale murder and open warfare between rival bootleg gangs and there was complete cynicism and disregard for law and order by a segment of the public. "The illegal liquor traffic broke down the prohibition, the tariff, and revenue laws; in accomplishing this, it had to break down officers of law by bribery. The whole fabric of lawlessness was based on the fact that respectable society had driven outside the boundaries of its own law and order the merchant of liquor whom it continued to patronize."[78] The Prohibition era turned a large part of America into a kind of sub-culture, a huge group living like outlaws. They distilled liquor by moonlight; tucked booze into their hip pockets; sneaked into speakeasies, and conspired against their government. Prohibition did more to give respectability to the organized criminal than any other single force in our national history.[79]

The robberies, murders , and other violations of the law grew progressively worse as Prohibition staggered toward its destined end. The people of this country had become disgusted with the lawlessness, and breaking down of law and order related to Prohibition. By the end of 1928, 19 referendums on some phase of Prohibition had been held under the auspices of various states. Nine of these referendums were on questions relative to modifying the Volstead Act. This was to be done through some state device or an appeal to Congress to repeal the Eighteenth Amendment outright. Two of the referendums were won by those in favor of Prohibition, and the other seven by those against it.[80]

Between 1920 and 1930, several hundred persons were killed as a result of the liquor traffic. The majority were killed in gang wars or fights, but some were innocent victims and others were attempting to enforce the laws. These murders and gang killings reached a bloody climax on St. Valentine's Day, February 14, 1929, in Chicago. Several men were lured to their death by a promise of highjacked liquor. They were lined up against the wall of a garage and machine gunned. Six of them were killed instantly and one left dying. The American people were stunned and shocked and aroused public opinion demanded justice.[81]

Following the St. Valentine's Day shooting, there was a change in sentiment throughout the country about the gangsters and bootleggers; a grave wave of resentment was sweeping the country. The Chicago Crime Commission and the Chicago Association of Commerce Subcommittee for the Prevention and Punishment of Crime had fought Al Capone and his fellow gangsters for years without visible success until the Crime Commission hit upon a publicity idea which captivated the entire nation. This was the famous list of public enemies headed by Al Capone as Public Enemy No. I. This list was sent to authorities with a recommendation that the gangsters be hounded and harassed in every possible way. This barrage of publicity against the gangsters stirred up the country and brought good results. Within four years 15 men who had been branded as public enemies had been convicted of various crimes; nine had died, and the cases of nine were pending in the courts.[82]

THE DEPRESSION

As the country headed into the 1930's, following the Stock Market Crash of October 1929, the United States was a different place than in the preceding decade. It was the Depression which finally accelerated the repeal of Prohibition.

As in other aspects or areas of American life, the Negro was discriminated against in the enforcing of Prohibition laws. All over the country, Negroes were arrested, convicted, and sentenced to prison much more often than whites, especially in the South. In the large industrial cities of the North and West, they were not permitted to enter speakeasies or nightclubs as guests. Through intimidation, violence, and custom, they were kept in a subordinate position, even in the violation of the laws. During the early years of the 1930's, the people were busy attempting to extricate themselves from the most devastating Depression in the history of the country. The impact of the most severe and longest

226

Depression upon daily life could be observed everywhere. Quite possibly the social conditions were responsible for the relaxation of attempts to control the Negro. After 1933, the people turned to the federal government to lead them out of the Depression.

When the Twenty-first Amendment was adopted in 1933, the control of alcoholic beverages was returned to the states. A large number of individuals were in substantial agreement that the evils of the pre-Prohibition era were not to be allowed to return. The bootlegging, lawlessness, and violence of the 1920's must be eliminated. The return of the saloon was undesirable because it had been intertwined and associated with evil. The state officials responsible for the framing of new alcohol legislation were expected to be guided by policies which should encourage temperate habits among the people in the use of alcoholic beverages.[83]

REPEAL TO THE PRESENT

Between 1933 and 1960, there were relatively minor changes in the legislation to control the sale and use of alcoholic beverages in the United States. At the present time, there are two major plans used: the monopoly and license systems. The monopoly system where the states engage in the buying and selling of alcoholic beverages are Alabama, Idaho, Iowa, Maine, Michigan, Montana, New Hampshire, North Carolina, Ohio, Oregon, Pennsylvania, Uath, Vermont, Virginia, Washington, West Virginia, and Wyoming.

The states where the alcoholic beverage business operates as private enterprise under state regulation and control through a license system are Alaska, Arizona, Arkansas, California, Colorado, Connecticut, Delaware, Florida, Georgia, Hawaii, Illinois, Indiana, Kansas, Kentucky, Louisiana, Maryland, Massachusetts, Minnesota, Missouri, Nebraska, Nevada, New Jersey, New Mexico, New York, North Dakota, Oklahoma, Rhode Island, South Carolina, South Dakota, Tennessee, Texas, Wisconsin, and the District of Columbia. Mississippi is the only state still operating under statewide prohibition law.[84]

Both systems of control have their adherents and opponents. The endorsers of the monopoly or state authority system believe that it provides the opportunity for reducing the competition of sales and the motivating force of private profit. This plan can be extremely flexible and adjusted to meet the specific needs of a state or an area within the state. It is supposed to automatically eliminate the possibilities of tie-ups between manufacturers and retail outlets financed by produce. Under the license system, the control boards attempt to limit the socially harmful competition by regulating prices and locations of retail outlets. Those individuals who violate the terms of their licenses are denied the privilege of continuing in business. In some states high license fees are used as a means of excluding undesirable persons from opening a tavern or package retail store.[85] From all indications, neither system of control can be considered overwhelmingly successful in the social control of alcoholic beverages.

Several months ago, a writer in a feature newspaper article wrote:

> It has been 30 years since booze came back from the basement, and bathtub gin became mostly a matter of history. Prohibition died, but left behind a complex and restrictive legacy of state and local laws. Some of the vestiges are paradoxical. Maine won't let a tippler sit when he drinks in a tavern, or stand when he drinks anywhere. Illinois permits drinking places, but won't let them call themselves "bars" or "saloons." Florida, while it doesn't regulate the names, bans swing doors on such establishments. North Dakota forbids food where drinks are sold. New York forbids drinks unless food is available. Nevada lets you take your drink right to the gambling table so you won't have to miss the pass of dice . . .
> The state which produces 75% of the nation's bourbon, Kentucky, contains four times more dry counties than wet. A Kentucky barmaid may serve drinks to a customer only if a male has opened the bottle. Utah charges her drinkers a dollar a year for a permit. Michigan forbids liquor advertisers to use Santa Claus, Merry Christmas or Noel, or public figures such as George Washington or Abraham Lincoln or even Ben Franklin.
> A Georgia host has to do some traveling. He can buy only two bottles at any one whiskey store.[86]

The crazy quilt pattern of the sale or control of alcoholic beverages leaves much to be desired. When the experience of the various states, the nation as a whole, and other nations with systems of liquor control are studied and considered, it appears wise not to depend upon any single system as a cure-all.

Since the early history of this country until the present time, there has been and continues to be a need for some type of system to control the use of alcohol. "More than half the total number of all arrests in this country," said James V. Bennett, Director of the Bureau of Federal Prisons, "can be traced to alcohol and drunkenness. Increasing numbers of persons committed to our institutions are compulsive alcoholics rather than cool calculating criminals."[87] "Today, there are about 70,000,000 Americans who drink liquor from time to time; for most of them alcohol is not a serious problem, but one person in 13, some 5,000,000 in all, drinks compulsively and is unable to stop even though his health may be eroded, and his personal relationships destroyed. This alcoholism is a progressive disease which today stands fourth among the major health problems of the country, after mental illness, heart disease, and cancer. If alcoholism is not treated or at least arrested, it can drive its victims to insanity and to death."[88] The staggering and sobering statistics relative to the extent of the use of alcoholic beverages, and the corrosive impact upon the individual, group, and society may shock the American public out of its complacency concerning this problem.

We have attempted to achieve social control of alcoholic beverages largely through moral persuasion and law. After the religious fervor of the eighteenth, nineteenth, and early twentieth centuries passed away, the people were not in the mood for reform. The history of legislation to control the use of liquor has taught us that all too often we have imposed on law a task which by itself it has been unable to accomplish. "Law has been resorted to in an attempt to overcome the failures of other agencies of social control. We have frequently fallen into the fallacy of believing that we could change by means of law and police force, tendencies which in their nature are not easily modified by command or coercion. We have labored under the illusion that words on a statute book, could as if they contained magical power, alter the tastes, preferences, habits, and customs of men.[89] Finally, it is possible that all attempts at social control have failed and will continue to fail, because we have not applied the "spirit or the letter of the law" with equality to all people. There have been variations in the treatment of people who violate the alcoholic beverage laws based on social class, race, wealth, and employment or occupation. When this situation has been corrected or eliminated, it is possible that the people will accept legislation that will control the use of alcoholic beverages.

1 Clarence H. Patrick, *Alcohol, Culture, and Society* (Durham: Duke University Press, 1952), p. 120.
2 Herbert Asbury, *The Great Illusion* (New York: Doubleday & Co., 1950), p. 4.
3 John A. Krout, *The Origins of Prohibition* (New York: Alfred A. Knopf, 1925).
4 Foster Rhea Dulles, *America Learns to Play* (New York: Appelton-Century Co., 1940), p. 5.
5 Asbury, *op. cit.*, p. 5.
6 Krout, *op. cit.*, p. 2.
7 *Ibid.*, p. 3.
8 *Ibid.*, p. 7.
9 *Ibid.*, pp. 7-13, and Ernest Cherrington, *The Evolution of Prohibition in the United States of America* (Westerville, Ohio: The American Press, 1920), p. 13.
10 Krout, *op. cit.*, pp. 3-4, 17.
11 John Spencer Bassett, *Slavery and Servitude in the Colony of North Carolina* (Baltimore: The Johns Hopkins Press, 1896), pp. 40-41.
12 Ralph Betts Flanders, *Plantation Slavery in Georgia* (Chapel Hill: The University of North Carolina Press, 1933), pp. 6-11.
13 Samuel McKee, Jr., *Labor in Colonial New York, 1664-1776* (New York: Columbia University Press, 1935), pp. 145-147.
14 Henry Scofield Cooley, *A Study of Slavery in New Jersey* (Baltimore: The Johns Hopkins Press, 1896), p. 36.
15 Edward Raymond Turner, *The Negro in Pennsylvania: 1639-1861* (Washington, D. C.: The American Historical Association, 1911), pp. 32, 113-114.
16 Lorenzo Johnston Greene, *The Negro in Colonial New England* (New York: Columbia University Press, 1942), pp. 128, 135-136.
17 *Ibid.*, pp. 135-136, and William B. Weeden, *Early Rhode Island: A Social History of the People* (New York: The Grafton Press, 1910), p. 305.
18 Bernard C. Steiner, *History of Slavery in Connecticut* (Baltimore: The Johns Hopkins Press, 1893), pp. 12-13.
19 Krout, *op. cit.*, p. 24.
20 Cherrington, *op. cit.*, pp. 39-40.
21 Guion Griffis Johnson, *Ante-Bellum North Carolina* (Chapel Hill: The University of North Carolina Press, 1937), pp. 498-499.
22 H. M. Henry, *The Police Control of the Slave in South Carolina* (Emory, Virginia: Emory and Henry College, 1914), pp. 44-48 and 91-95.
23 Frederick Olmsted, *The Slave States Before the Civil War* (New York: G. P. Putnam's Sons, 1959), p. 64.
24 *Ibid.*, p. 84.
25 *Ibid.*, p. 71.
26 Johnson, *op. cit.*, pp. 531-533.
27 Olmsted, *op. cit.*, p. 84.
28 *Ibid.*, p. 90.
29 *Ibid.*, p. 117.
30 *Ibid.*, p. 117.
31 Cherrington, *op. cit.*, p. 93.
32 Daniel Jay Whitener, *Prohibition in North Carolina, 1715-1945* (Chapel Hill: The University of North Carolina Press, 1945), p. 34.
33 Charles Merz, *The Dry Decade* (New York: Doubleday & Co., 1931), pp. 3-5.
34 *Ibid.*, pp. 2-5.
35 Krout, *op. cit.*, p. 217.
36 E. Merton Coulter, *The Confederate States of America, 1861-1865* (Baton Rouge: Louisiana State University Press, 1950), Vol. 7, p. 248.
37 Bell Irvin Wiley, *The Life of Billy Yank* (New York: The Bobbs-Merrill Co., 1952), p. 253.
38 William M. Robinson, "Prohibition in the Confederacy," *The American Historical Review*, 37 (1931-32), pp. 50-58.

39 Coulter, *The Confederate States of America, 1861-1865*, p. 459.
40 Wiley, *The Life of Billy Yank*, pp. 186, 199.
41 *Ibid.*, pp. 118, 251, 349.
42 Bell Irvin Wiley, *Southern Negroes 1861-1865* (New Haven: Yale University Press, 1938), p. 42.
43:*Freedom to the Free: 1863 Century of Emancipation 1963*, A Report to the President of the United States Civil Rights Commission (Washington, D. C.: United States Government Printing Office, February, 1963), pp. 32-33.
44 E. Merton Coulter, *The South During Reconstruction, 1865-1877* (Baton Rouge: Louisiana State University Press, 1947), Vol. 8, p. 335.
45 *Ibid.*, p. 336.
46 James P. Shenton, *The Reconstruction: A Documentary History of the South After the War: 1865-1877* (New York: G. P. Putnam's Sons, 1963), pp. 123-124.
47 Vernon Lane Wharton, *The Negro in Mississippi, 1865-1890* (Chapel Hill: The Universty of North Carolina Press, 1947), p. 235.
48 Alrutheus Ambush Taylor, *The Negro in South Carolina During Reconstruction* (Washington, D. C.: The Association for the Study of Negro Life & History, 1924), p. 45.
49 Francis Butler Simkins and Robert Hilliard Woodward, *South Carolina During Reconstruction* (Chapel Hill: The University of North Carolina Press, 1932), p. 362.
50 Simkins and Woodward, *op. cit.*, pp. 321-332, 362.
51 Clara Mildred Thompson, *Reconstruction in Georgia: Economic, Social, Political, 1865-1872* (New York: Columbia University Press, 1915), pp. 279-382.
52 Walter L. Fleming, *Civil War and Reconstruction in Alabama* (New York: Columbia University Press, 1905), p. 263.
53 *Ibid.*, pp. 761, 769-770.
54 Alrutheus Ambush Taylor, *The Negro in Tennessee, 1865-1880* (Washington, D. C.: The Associated Publishers, 1941), p. 40.
55 *Ibid.*, p. 40.
56 Taylor, *The Negro in Tennessee, 1865-1880*, p. 40, 41, 226.
57 Ella Lonn, *Reconstruction in Louisiana* (New York: G. P. Putnam's Sons, 1918), p. 12; and John Rose Ficklen *History of Reconstruction in Louisiana* (Baltimore: The Johns Hopkins Press, 1910), p. 135.
58 Whitener, *op. cit.*, p. 57.
59 C. Vann Woodward, *The Strange Career of Jim Crow* (New York: Oxford University Press, 1955), pp. 7-8.
60 Harry S. Ashmore, *The Other Side of Jordan* (New York: W. W. Norton Co., 1960), p. 126.
61 Cherrington, *op. cit.*, p. 176.
62 Asbury, *op. cit.*, p. 101.
63 Joseph R. Gusfield, *Symbolic Crusade* (Urbana: The University of Illinois Press, 1963), pp. 99-100.
64 James H. Timberlake, *Prohibition and the Progressive Movement, 1900-1920* (Cambridge: Harvard University Press, 1963), p. 149.
65 *Ibid.*, pp. 146-147.
66 Timberlake, *op. cit.*, p. 150., and Wayne B. Walker, *Federal and State Laws Relating to Intoxicating Liquor* (2d ed.; Westerville, Ohio: The American Issue Press, 1918), pp. 157-158.
67 Merz, *op. cit.*, p. 15, and David A. Shannon, *Twentieth Century America: The United States Since the 1890's* (Chicago: Rand McNally & Co., 1963), p. 107.
68 Timberlake, *op. cit.*, pp. 2-3.
69 Richard Hofstader, *The Age of Reform* (New York: Alfred A. Knopf, 1955), chap. 4.
70 Leonard S. Blakey, *The Sale of Liquor in the South* (New York: Columbia University Press, 1912), pp. 27-28.

71 Gusfield, *op. cit.*, p. 105.
72 Asbury, *op. cit.*, p. 141.
73 Henry Lee, *How Dry We Were* (Englewood Cliffs, New Jersey: Prentice-Hall, 1963), p. 1.
74 Gusfield, *op. cit.*, p. 118.
75 Associated Press Dispatch, Baltimore, February 19, 1920.
76 *The New York Times* (May 19, 1920).
77 *The New York Times* (June 7, 1920).
78 Gus Tyler, *Organized Crime in America* (Ann Arbor: University of Michigan Press, 1962), p. 60.
79 *Ibid.*, p. 151.
80 Merz, *op. cit.*, p. 221.
81 Kenneth Allsop, *The Bootleggers and Their Era* (New York: Doubleday & Co., 1961), pp. 142-143 and Asbury, *op. cit.*, p. 308.
82 Asbury, *op. cit.*, pp. 310-311.
83 Raymond C. McCarthy and Edgar M. Douglass, *Alcohol and Social Responsibility* (New York: Thomas Y. Crowell Co., 1949), pp. 132-133.
84 This information supplied by Mrs. Olga C. Palotai, Librarian, Institute of Government, University of North Carolina, September 25, 1963.
85 McCarthy and Douglass, *op. cit.*, p. 133.
86 Charles L. West, "Prohibition Left Sloppy Maze of Confusion," *The Raleigh Times* (Tuesday, November 12, 1963).
87 *The News and Observer* (Raleigh, N. C.: Saturday, October 26, 1963). 1963).
88 Gertrude Samuels, "In Search Of A Cure for the Alcoholic," *The New York Times Magazine* (October 27, 1963), p. 61.
89 Patrick, *op. cit.*, p. 135.

Patterns of Consumption
of Alcohol

BOOTSIE

By OLLIE HARRINGTON

Courtesy The Pittsburgh Courier

*"Whoooee, jes' look at him! Brother Bartender, give me some
of the same thing he just had!"*

234

CHAPTER SIX

PATTERNS OF CONSUMPTION OF ALCOHOL

THERE have been many theories concerning the reasons people drink alcohol. The use of alcohol varies from country to country and among people living in the same country. The nature and extent and the prevalence and forms of alcoholic indulgence are influenced by the society in which they are used. "The use of alcoholic beverages in a group or society is primarily a cultural phenomenon and it is in the light of the culture of the group or society that the uses of such beverages are to be understood."[1] Culture determines the function or functions which alcoholic beverages may perform in a particular society. It is also culture that determines those within a given society who may use alcoholic beverages. "Social tradition and social pressure are among the extremely important factors involved in the use of alcoholic beverages, irrespective of the degree to which they may be used."[2]

The drinking customs of Europe were brought to the American colonies by the first settlers and the use of alcoholic beverages was universally accepted and approved by the colonists. From an early period in the history of the country, Indians, Negroes, and servants were prohibited from drinking alcohol. Fear of violence was responsible for the attempted control of their use of alcohol. After Negroes were enslaved, they were considered as property and too valuable to be permitted to use alcohol. That indentured servants might injure themselves and not be able to work was among the reasons that they were not permitted to drink. But all of the precautions taken by the colonists did not prevent Negroes, Indians, and servants from securing and drinking alcoholic beverages. Free Negroes were permitted to use alcohol from the Colonial period until the early part of the nineteenth century, in the South. After the colonies became states, slaves were prohibited the use of alcohol without the permission of their masters. In most of the South, there were two times in the year when masters permitted their slaves to drink and relax—after the summer crops had been harvested and at Christmas. During both of these periods, the slaves were

235

permitted to engage in singing, dancing, and drinking. The fear that free Negroes would encourage and assist slaves to revolt or rebel against their masters resulted in their being prohibited the use of alcohol in the nineteenth century. By the middle of the century, the status of free Negroes had deteriorated to the extent that the distinction between them and slaves was hardly discernible. In the ante-bellum period, the Negro was considered childish, irresponsible, shiftless, lazy and addicted to the excessive use of liquor. "The poor slave imbibes until he becomes intoxicated when he is ready for a general fight or any species of rascality."[3] Southern whites were convinced that Negroes were too irresponsible to be trusted with alcohol. They believed that Negroes would get out of hand and become ungovernable.

The beliefs concerning the Negro's irresponsibility and love of alcohol continued after the Civil War. General Robert E. Lee stated that "Negroes as a race were spendthrifts and gullible, though some were amenable to the advice to save their money. They were easily influenced by peddlers and store-keepers . . . They also had a great liking for tobacco and whiskey."[4] Having been denied whiskey while in slavery, they gave full reign to their appetites in freedom. With little experience in self-control, they would spend their last piece of money for a drink of whiskey.[5] Although there was considerable or excessive use of alcohol among some of the newly freed slaves, a large number were steady in work habits and temperate in their use of whiskey.

At the beginning of the twentieth century, there was increasing concern over the excessive use of alcohol by the total population. And there had been little or no change in the beliefs of the whites about the Negro's use of alcohol. Even some of the Negro leaders expressed concern over their drinking. At a meeting of religious and educational leaders, a Negro minister stated, "Drink has hurt us socially. If there is one thing to which we may attribute our present social status, it is to the drink habit."[6] Another minister observed that, "The Negro had been taught that strong drink would import strength to him and he would be able to satisfy his employer. This idea was false in its conception and practice. We find by observation that it still obtains among our people today to a great extent."[7] Another interesting and pertinent idea was projected by a speaker at the same meeting:

I am here today to say to you with shame and confusion of face that we ourselves are about to mar our magnificent record of the past and turn back into a more awful slavery than that from which we have just emerged, because of our love for strong drink. There can be no longer a hiding of the fact that the Negro is addicted to strong drink. It will not help the case to say that the Anglo-Saxon is also addicted to strong drink.[8]

On the basis of his findings, a pioneer in the study of Negro life advanced the following theories:

Drunkenness is considered one of the chief causes of direct aggressive criminal acts and may almost be said to be a special tendency of the negro [sic] of the present generation. Among the chief circumstances which are believed to lead directly to the criminality of the Negro are idleness and the use of intoxicating drinks and general ignorance.[9]

Prior to and during World War I, there was a mass migration of Negroes from rural to urban areas in the South. At the same time, there was a steady stream of Negroes from the South to the North and the Midwest. On their arrival in the cities, they were able to escape from the system of conformity required of them in the rural South. This resulted in more personal freedom. Many of these Negroes used this new freedom to indulge in the excessive use of alcohol. Because they were ignorant of the rules which govern living in large cities, an increasing number of colored people were arrested for drunkenness, in the 1920's. The tendency toward drunkenness was not surprising in view of the fact that a large number of the migrants were young men without family ties in the North. They were often forced into the streets and saloons by the housing situation.[10] In a New England city, reports of the press and courts revealed an exceptional amount of conflict and violence in Negro families. "To judge from the details of these accounts two causes predominated, alcohol and sex jealousy."[11]

One theory attributed the excessive use of alcohol by Negroes to the fact that citizenship with its many privileges was thrust upon the race and hence they were not prepared by educational tradition for social confidence to handle these privileges. According to one psychiatrist:

Instinctively, the negro [sic] turned to ways of the whites under whose tutelage he had been and made an effort to compensate for his psychic inferiority by imitating the superior race . . . Efforts to imitate his white neighbors in speech, dress, and social customs, are often overwrought and ludicrous. The insidious addition of white blood to the negro [sic] race has produced significant effects upon the latter. Healthy negro [sic] children are bright, cunning, full of life and intelligent, but about puberty there begins a slowing up of mental development and a loss of interest in education as sexual matters and a good time begin to dominate the life and have first place in the thoughts of the negro [sic] ... From this period, promiscuous sex relations, gambling, petty thievery, drinking, loafing and a care-free life, full to the brim with excitement, interspersed with the smallest amount of work, consume his time.[12]

An outstanding sociologist and authority on Negro life has offered a theory that "excessive drinking and sex seem to provide a means of narcotizing the middle-class Negro against a frustrating existence. A social function is hardly considered a success unless a goodly number of the participants 'pass out'."[13] Among the lower classes, there are strong needs for compensatory activities and these activities are made less traumatic through alcohol and drugs. In these activities, the males predominate. Narcotics have a wide use among Negroes; but their high cost makes alcohol much more available.[14]

In the middle of the twentieth century, there continued to be concern among Negroes about the amount of alcohol consumed by the members of their group. One of the most influential weekly newspapers editorialized:

Among the most serious problems afflicting Negro communities is the disproportionate number in the grip of alcoholism.
Negro communities are the greatest consumers of alcoholic beverages, and this is proved not simply by *sales statistics,* but by the great number of broken homes, dependent children, juvenile delinquency, crime and hospitalization.
Alcoholism is a disease which is the direct or contributing cause of numerous other ailments, including social maladjustments, which lead to prison, hospitals, mental institutions and early *death.*[15]

The editor of a publication aimed at the national Negro beverage market voiced concern:

No greater charge has been made against him (Negro) since the days of Reconstruction, than an alleged over-abundant indulgence of alcoholic beverages. His social service agencies and civic groups have wailed loud and long against the almost unnatural concentration of taverns in his residential neighborhoods.[16]

Some of the racial theories concerning the excessive use of alcohol continue to persist. These theories are usually based on the number of Negroes arrested and those receiving assistance from social welfare agencies. There is no doubt that Negroes are arrested more frequently than whites in the South and border states. The theory that "the Negro crime pattern is directed toward violence primarily, and also sex, liquor and drug offenses"[17] may be open to question. The same writer attempts to inject race in the use of alcohol by members of broken families receiving aid from a social welfare agency.

Often the problem is not that the family is broken, but that it never existed. In such cases, the females (Negroes) are often sexual delinquents since puberty or before . . . They spend their relief checks on 'liquor' and men, letting their children prowl the streets, sleep in cars and grow up to be delinquents, thieves and muggers.[18]

The theories concerning the excessive use of alcohol by Negroes are many but there has been a paucity of scientific research on the subject. Students of Negro life—social and psychological—are aware that the numerous and complex factors of their history in America makes any simple theory inadequate. On the basis of available research data, the position of the Negro in America has been such as to make him ready to engage in the excessive use of alcohol. There have been and continue to be all the conditions fostering frustration and the desire to escape. There is the oppression of the rural and landless black farm population and the super exploitation of the urban proletariat. There is economic and social discrimination in every phase of American life. There was, until the Civil Rights Act of 1964, a vast, vicious, and crushing system of *Jim Crow* sanctified by law and hallowed by custom. There is a denial of equal opportunities for work, for education, for health, and for the release of the race's creative abilities. The treatment accorded the Negro has, at times, been cruel and harsh. This has created fertile fields for excessive drinking. The theories concerning the use of alcohol by Negroes are interesting and revealing, but more important, are the reasons men drink.

People give many reasons for using alcohol: it makes them feel good; like the taste; practically everybody in their group drinks; a small drink before meals gives a better appetite; when tired and worn out it relaxes; it helps to make them forget worries and unpleasant experiences; it enables them to make better conversation. These reasons comprise a part of the interpretation of what individuals feel they receive or expect to receive from drinking.[19] "Alcohol is utilized as an escape from the responsibility and burden of mature emotional life and its decisions,"[20] are the reasons given by one writer. Others believe that "relief of discomfort and a feeling of well-being wherein the worries of today and the anxieties of tomorrow are cast aside with the substitution of calm indifference and plausible relaxation."[21] The use of alcohol to escape from day to day living seems to be a common reason given by students of the problem. "Alcohol offers an escape to the blissful state of infantile omnipotence."[22] "Drinks in some cases seem a definite substitute for sexual satisfaction because of the diminished libido which results."[23] "A desire for liberation of that part of the personality which is kept in check by convention."[24] Some individuals drink: "To be a 'he-man'; to find a way of rebelling and allowing relief of destructive impulses; and to obtain pleasure."[25]

Alcohol is also used "to promote the social instincts and alleviate and narcotize the many mental conflicts to which we must all, to some extent, be victims."[26] In general:

Men drink in celebration as well as for relief. They drink to lend ceremony, color, and fellowship to life, just as surely as to banish anxiety, dread and frustration. They drink out of recklessness and abandon which is not at all necessarily a compensation for an inherent caution and fatigue of spirit. They drink, too, because the inhibitions of life seem at times ridiculous and alcohol represents not an 'escape,' but a 'revolt' against the overstressed perhaps necessary caution, decorum, and orderliness of existence.[27]

The reasons for using alcohol may be largely divided into four categories which provide the general motives for drinking:

1. Alcoholic beverages may be used as condiments or thirst-quenching drinks or simply to add color at meals and social gatherings.
2. Alcoholic beverages may be used because of the feeling of exaltation which they induce. In such a case the desire may be to heighten fun and enthusiasm, release inhibitions, socialize or celebrate.
3. Alcoholic beverages may be used because of the narcotic, or depressant effect which they produce. Here

the desire may be for an escape from something, to banish anxieties and frustrations, to relieve tensions, or to get relief from physical pain.

4. Alcoholic beverages may be used because people desire to conform or feel they should conform to the social custom of using such drinks.[28]

The preceding statements are highly significant in that they furnish some insight into the values and meanings which alcoholic beverages have acquired in the history of the groups of societies which use them. "These reasons are not the underlying forces, the basic etiological factors, which have to do with the origin of the use of alcoholic beverages in a particular society. They are important to an understanding of the problem in that they can give the general attitudes toward alcoholic drinks as objects to be desired or avoided."[29] There may be other reasons why some racial and religious groups abstain from or use alcoholic beverages.

The American Negro may use alcohol to protest against the treatment accorded him and his position in the social, economic, and political structure. During the ante-bellum period, what was taken as the slaves' irresponsibility and intractability in the use of alcohol, could have been a way of protest. During the early part of the twentieth century, Negroes drank liquor because "it gave them a feeling of being equal or superior to the white man in the South."[30] The cartoons of Ollie Harrington appearing in *The Pittsburgh Courier* (several of which are reproduced here) reveal the Negro's protest of social, economic, and political conditions that exist in this country. Through Mr. Bootsie, the major character, satire is used to call attention to these conditions. Bars are often the scene of Harrington's cartoons. The characters engage in considerable drinking, fighting, and ridiculing of racial conditions in every area of American life.

An internationally-known poet and writer has also created Negro characters to protest and point out racial injustices. Langston B. Hughes uses the activities of Mr. Jesse B. Semple, better known as Simple, to ridicule and protest race relations and the Negro's plight in America. Simple drinks excessively and uses the racial situation to justify his actions:

"A bar is something to lean on," said Simple.
"You lean on bars very often," I remarked.

241

"I do," said Simple.

"Why?"

"Because everything else I lean on falls down," said Simple, "including my peoples, my wife, my boss, and me" . . . .

"And you have been leaning on bars?"

"What do you think I do all day long?" Simple objected. "From eight in the morning to five at night, I do not lean on no bar. I work" . . . "Gimme another beer, Tony! I can lean on this bar, but I ain't got another thing in the U. S. A. on which to lean."[31]

When Simple's niece arrived in Harlem (New York), from the South, he advised her on conditions there.

"Down South they say Harlem is heaven," says Minnie! "Yet, you have nowhere for me to rest my head?"

"You know that old song," said I, " 'Rest Beyond The River?' In Harlem, we 'all' got one more river to cross before we can rest. Set down and I will tell you about Harlem, Minnie, so you will be clear in mind. In fact, I will tell you about the North. Down South, you're swimming in a river that's running to the sea where you might drown, but at least you're swimming with the current. Up North, we are swimming the other way, against the current trying to reach dry land."

"Ain't you got just a drop of something that ain't water in the house?" asked Minnie, "to help me swim better?"

"Come on girl, put on your coat," I said, "and I will take you to a bar before my wife comes. I reckon we both need a drink to help us swim better."[32]

An attempt has been made to present some of the theories and reasons why alcohol is used by the American people, and especially Negroes. It has been pointed out that the determining factor involved in the use of alcoholic beverages is culture. This does not mean that other factors—physical, biological, and phychological—are not involved. To some extent, they all enter into the total situation.

Culture exerts a far-reaching influence upon the habits, customs, and practices of the people in any society. Some individuals continue to have racist theories relative to the drinking of alcoholic beverages. They believe race is an important factor in the use of alcohol. These beliefs and myths are being dispersed and eliminated through scientific social research.

Drinking behavior is not determined by such qualities as race. We have heavy drinkers and light drinkers; we have fighting drinkers and passive, and peaceful drinkers, within every race . . . The same people racially and genetically may be divided into different groups with different cultures, thus, behave very differently in similar situations . . . Drinking habits are rather a question of the social conditions which are reflected through the individual and his behavior.[33]

242

"The Negroes have developed social and economic class lines of their own within their own hierarchies."[34] The drinking habits of Negroes follow class lines as those of white.

A study of Negro life in a community of the South reveals that there are two distinct styles of life—the respectable and non-respectable. Behavior and attitudes in this with respect to whiskey, sex, family, the law, and the use of leisure time define repectability and non-respectability. One characteristic of the non-respectable person is a reputation for excessive drinking or public drunkenness. The respectable person does not drink in public or frequent taverns. There is a basic distinction between the social classes—respectable and non-respectable, in this community and it is based largely upon the drinking of alcoholic beverages. The respectable persons are concerned with reputation and status. They choose their drinking companions and tend to confine their drinking to their homes. The non-respectable drink publicly and with anyone. They are likely to have an arrest record for public drunkenness, and are proud to make fools of themselves. Public release and indulgence in the use of alcoholic beverages is frowned upon by the respectables.[35]

The authors of a study of Negro life in a metropolis of the Midwest, also discovered a class system. The Negro class structure is stratified or divided into upper, middle, and lower. The standard behavior of the upper class approximates that of the white middle class. One of the characteristics of this class is a restrained good time.[36] They seldom drink excessively and usually not in public. The pattern of behavior of the middle class is largely concerned with putting up a front of respectability, and a drive for getting ahead. All of this is reflected in their standard of living and public behavior. As a result, they are careful in their use of alcoholic beverages. The middle-class Negro sees nothing wrong in enjoying life and drinking, during his leisure time.[37] The lower class is characterized by less restraint and without the symbols of higher social prestige. The patterns of their use of alcoholic beverages vary from those of the upper and middle classes. The members of the lower class drink excessively; they are habitual drinkers of illicit liquor, and they drink whiskey publicly out of a bottle. In their public behavior, they are boisterous. Both men and women appear on the street

243

drunk. Education and money are important in defining the status and social class of Negroes in this city. Rowdy or indecorous behavior in public seemed to be the trait that emerged most consistently as an index to lower-class status.[38]

Americans are ceremoniously egalitarian in their more conspicious behavior patterns, they reflect sometimes wittingly and often unwittingly, their class status by the nuances of their demeanor, speech, taste, drinking, and dining patterns and favored pastimes.[39] In the United States, the neighborhood tavern and cocktail lounge are two types of retail business which are numerous. The lounge is located in a commercial area. Primarily mixed drinks will be served. A tavern is located in a residential section of the city. The principal drinks are beer, served on draught, and whiskey. Leisure activity in taverns and lounges vary by social class. The lounge is most used by the upper middle class, and its use declines rapidly in the lower middle and still further for the upper lower classes. The upper middle class patronizes lounges and lower middle class taverns. Patrons of the neighborhood tavern are commonly of a similar religious, ethnic, and social class. In the selection of a tavern, indivdiuals seem to depend on contacts with others in the neighborhood who are of a similar ethnic background. Social changes in neighborhoods are reflected and observed in the taverns. Usually white neighborhood taverns attempt to resist potential Negro patrons.[40] Because of the paucity of available data, it is not possible to determine to what extent Negroes frequent lounges and neighborhood taverns throughout the country. Taverns located in large urban centers not only cater to a specific social class, but often to a special group within that class.[41]

Although, Negroes drink alcoholic beverages along social class lines, there are some characteristics which are largely indigenous to them. Usually special groups have a national or special drink—English, Poles, Italians, French and even American hillbillies—but the American Negro does not. Whether it be in New York or Los Angeles, Philadelphia or Oregon, New Orleans, or Boston, Atlanta or Pittsburgh, the Negro is predominantly a weekend drinker. Many employers of Negroes pay them on Monday instead of Friday or Saturday to prevent or reduce the high rate of absenteeism on Monday. The scheme does not work too effectively, because whatever day they are paid, they stay away from the job the following day. This situation is improving throughout the country. In the purchase of whiskey, Negroes have coined a new word—"spike." When two or more Negroes buy a bottle of whiskey, they divide the cost equally among the group. This is a "spike." Negroes also purchase expensive or high-priced alcoholic beverages, especially middle-class Negroes, largely as a status symbol. Over the years, Negroes have been denied access to many places of recreation and restricted in the use of hotels, bars, and clubs offering entertainment. This has forced them to do a considerable amount of their entertaining at home. In order to show their affluence, the middle and upper classes serve costly foods and alcoholic beverages. An increasing number of members of these classes are moving to suburbia and neighborhoods in which Negroes have not been permitted to live before. In order to compensate for their restricted social activities, they entertain lavishly at home.

In this chapter, data have been presented on the theories of the use of alcohol by Negroes; why mankind uses alcohol; and the patterns of consumption of alcoholic beverages, especially, as they relate to Negroes. An attempt has been made to present fairly and accurately various theories which have been advanced concerning drinking by Negroes. An endeavor has also been made to show the inadequacy of these theories. On the basis of available data, the conclusions of the author are that Negroes use alcohol for the same reasons as the rest of the total population. There are not any racial factors related to drinking. The determining factor involved in the use of alcoholic beverages is culture. The members of any group or society ordinarily use alcoholic beverages only because such beverages have been set up by social definition and social sanction as a means by which certain needs and desires may be met.[42] The patterns of use of alcoholic beverages are influenced by social class. In fact, some researchers believe that it is the most important and transcends all others. The evidence indicates that this is the situation for the total population and Negroes do not deviate from this pattern. It must be remembered that like others in the population they started out with ambitions and hopes and the willingness to go on and on in their pursuit of success. Like others they faced frustrations, defeats, and reprisals. More than most others, their way of life is roughened and obstructed from birth to death by the factor of race. Race may not dominate but at least it throws a shadow across every phase of the Negro's life in the North and envelops every aspect of it in the South. From birth to death, the Negro is not only confronted by an outer environment of social and economic problems and adjustments, but also an inner environment of being a Negro. In the United States, this is interpreted to mean inferior, impoverished, and inconvenienced. Both of these environments are real, effective and inescapable. They not only determine the status of Negroes, but they also create the Negro personality. This personality has had to develop in whatever way and to whatever extent it could within the ring of race prejudice. The Negro has developed protective devices for survival and has been shaped by the environments that nurtured him. Very possibly these conditions have and will continue to exert some influence upon the drinking habits of Negroes. This is an area that should be explored by students of race relations and human behavior.

---

1 Clarence H. Patrick, *Alcohol, Culture and Society* (Durham: Duke University Press, 1952), p. 5.

2 *Ibid.,* pp. 59-61.

3 Guion Griffis Johnson, *Ante-Bellum North Carolina* (Chapel Hill: The University of North Carolina Press, 1937), p. 58.

4 E. Merton Coulter, *The South During Reconstruction, 1865-1877* (Baton Rouge: Louisiana State University Press, 1949), Vol. 8, p. 49.

5 *Ibid.,* p. 336.

6 I. Garland and J. W. E. Bowen, (eds.), *The United Negro: His Problems and Progress* (Atlanta, Georgia: D. E. Luther Publishing Co., 1902), p. 266

7 *Ibid.,* p. 245.

8 *Ibid.,* p. 249.

9 Howard W. Odum, *Social and Mental Traits of the Negro* (New York: Columbia University Press, 1910), pp. 187-189.

10 Louise Venable Kennedy, *The Negro Peasant Turns Cityward* (New York: Columbia University Press, 1930), p. 188.

11 Robert Austin Warren, *The Negro in New Haven* (New Haven: Yale University Press, 1925), p. 221.

12 W. M. Bevis, "Psychological Traits of the Southern Negro With Observations As to Some of His Psychoses," *American Journal of Psychiatry,* 78 (1921-22), pp. 69-78.

13 E. Franklin Frazier, *Black Bourgeoisie* (Glencoe, Illinois: The Free Press, 1957), pp. 231-232.

14. Abram Kardiner and Lionel Ovesey, *The Mark of Oppression* (New York: W. W. Norton Co., 1951), pp. 313-314.

15 *The Pittsburgh Courier* (December 14, 1957).

16 *The National Leader* (Philadelphia, Pa.: October, 1963).

17 Nathaniel Weyl, *The Negro in American Civilization* (Washington,

D. C.: Public Affairs Press, 1960), pp. 225-226.
18 *Ibid.*, p. 233.
19 Patrick, *op. cit.*, pp. 44-45.
20 Edward A. Strecker and Francis T. Chambers, *Alcohol — One Man's Meat* (New York: The Macmillan Co., 1938) p. 12.
21 J. A. Waddell and H. B. Haag, *Alcoholism in Moderation and Excess*, (3d rev. ed.; Richmond, Virginia: William Byrd Press, 1940), p. 119.
22 James H. Wall, "A Study of Alcoholism in Man," *American Journal of Psychiatry*, XCII (May 1936), 1389-1401.
23 H. H. Hart, "Personality Factors in Alcoholism," *Archives of Neurology and Psychiatry*, *XXIV* (July 1930), 116-134.
24 R. T. Morris, "Alcohol and Narcotics," *Interstate Medical Journal*, XXII (1916), 450-454.
25 J. L. Henderson, "Alcoholism: It's Psychiatric Treatment," *California and Western Medicine*, LII (January 1940), 11-15.
26 C. S. Read, "The Psycho-pathology of Alcoholism and Some So-Called Alcoholic Psychoses," *Journal of Mental Science*, IXVI (July 1920), 233-244.
27 Abraham Myerson, "Alcohol: A Study of Social Ambivalence," *Quarterly Journal of Studies on Alcohol* (June 1940), pp. 13-20.
28 Patrick, *op. cit.*, pp. 44-48.
29 *Ibid.*, p. 48.
30 Daniel Jay Whitener, *Prohibition in North Carolina 1715-1945* (Chapel Hill: The University of North Carolina Press, 1945), p. 57.
31 Langston Hughes, *Simple Speaks His Mind* (New York: Simon & Schuster, 1950), pp. 176-178.
32 Langston Hughes, *Simple Stakes A Claim* (New York: Rinehart & Co., 1957), p. 50.
33 Donald Horton, "The Function of Alcohol in Primitive Societies," *Quarterly Journal of Studies of Alcohol* (September 1945), pp. 170-171.
34 Max Lerner, *America As A Civilization* (New York: Simon & Schuster, 1957), p. 524.
35 Hylan Lewis, *Black Ways of Kent* (Chapel Hill: The University of North Carolina Press, 1955), pp. 4, 63, 66, and 208.
36 St. Clair Drake and Horace Cayton, *Black Metropolis* (New York: Harcourt, Brace & Co., 1945), p. 531.
37 *Ibid.*, p. 714.
38 *Ibid.*, pp. 561-562
39 Vance Packard, *The Status Seekers* (New York: David McKay Co., 1959), p. 139.
40 David Gottlieb, "The Neighborhood Tavern and the Cocktail Lounge — A Study in Class Differences," *American Journal of Sociology* (May 1957), pp. 559-562.
41 Packard, *op. cit.*, p. 144.
42 Patrick, *op. cit.*, p. 78.

ACKNOWLEDGMENTS

The writing of a book inevitably piles up a wide variety of debts. In the case of this volume, they are so numerous that the author will not attempt to describe most of them. He received encouragement, guidance, support, and assistance from many individuals; to all of them he is grateful.

It would make the acknowledgments cumbersome, if an attempt were made to recognize the indebtedness to all who have contributed in various ways to this work. There are a number of individuals who merit special attention. The writer is obligated to Dr. Lillian Parker Wallace, formerly of the History Department, Meredith College, for counsel and encouragement in the early stages of this book. She read and offered valuable suggestions on Chapter One. Dr. John Hope Franklin, Professor of American History, University of Chicago, was consulted for his views and knowledge. He provided ideas and recommended readings that have been of considerable benefit. Dr. Vivian M. Henderson, Chairman, Department of Economics and Business Administration, Fisk University, read Chapter Three, and made constructive criticisms. To Dr. Clarence H. Patrick, Chairman, Department of Sociology, Wake Forest College, the author is deeply indebted for creating his interest in this study, and the reading of Chapter Five. Dr. W. A. Gaines, Chairman, Department of Sociology, Saint Augustine's College, also made some suggestions about Chapter Five.

The author is deeply indebted to Dr. Elmer C. Schwertman, History Department, Saint Augustine's College, for a detailed reading of the entire manuscript. His suggestions were responsible for the revising of several sections. Along with this, he gave guidance and assistance at a critical juncture in the writing of this book.

Mrs. Mollie H. Lee, Head Librarian, Richard B. Harrison Library, Raleigh, N. C., assisted the author in the search for needed materials. Miss Annie Lee Yates, Reference Librarian, and members of the staff of the State Library rendered inestimable service in securing books and materials from other libraries and verifying references. Because of their cooperation, the author was spared considerable time and difficulty in securing many needed books.

249

The author owes a special debt to Miss Bessie M. McKnight for the careful and efficient typing of the entire manuscript. She worked under considerable handicap and was confronted by many obstacles. Without her able assistance, it would have been considerably more difficult to have completed the manuscript.

Mrs. Norma Cartwright Scofield, Chapel Hill, rendered yeoman service in editing, reorganizing, and arranging the final format of the manuscript. Her able assistance and suggestions have been responsible for considerable improvement in the manuscript.

No author can recall everyone from whom he has borrowed unfootnoted facts. An honest attempt has been made to acknowledge the ideas the writer may have unconsciously incorporated into his own. Due acknowledgment has been made in the footnotes to authors and publishing companies for the use of their materials in this publication.

Although the author has received help from many individuals and sources, he alone is responsible for the findings and conclusions reached in this book.

Finally, the author would like to thank the following publishers for permission to use materials from books they have published:

Alfred A. Knopf Company, *From Slavery to Freedom* (1947), by John Hope Franklin; *A History of the South* (1963), by Francis Butler Simkins; *The Crucial Decade* (1956), by Eric F. Goldman; *A History of The American People Since 1862* (1961), by Harry J. Carman, Harold C. Syrett, and Bernard W. Wishy; *The Peculiar Institution* (1956), by Kenneth M. Stampp.

Appelton-Century-Crofts, *American Political and Social History* (7th ed., 1957), by Harold Underwood Faulkner.

Dodd, Mead, and Company, *The Social History of Bourbon* (1963), by Gerald Carson.

Harcourt, Brace and Company, *Black Metropolis* (1945), by St. Clair Drake, and Horace R. Cayton

Harold Ober Associates, *Simple Stakes a Claim* (1957), by Langston Hughes.

Harper and Row Publishers, *An American Dilemma* (1944), by Gunnar Myrdal.

Little, Brown, and Company, *Prohibition: The Era of Excess* (1962), by Andrew Sinclair.

The Pittsburgh Courier, Cartoons of *Mr. Bootsie*, by Ollie Harrington.

Prentice-Hall, *How Dry We Were* (1963), by Henry Lee.

Rand McNally and Company, *Twentieth Century America: United States Since The 1890's* (1963), by David Shannon.

Simon and Schuster Publishers, *Simple Speaks His Mind* (1950), by Langston Hughes.